Abraham Kuenen

The Religion of Israel to the Fall of the Jewish State

Vol. 2

Abraham Kuenen

The Religion of Israel to the Fall of the Jewish State
Vol. 2

ISBN/EAN: 9783744727280

Printed in Europe, USA, Canada, Australia, Japan

Cover: Foto ©ninafisch / pixelio.de

More available books at **www.hansebooks.com**

THEOLOGICAL
TRANSLATION FUND LIBRARY.

VOL. IV.

THE
RELIGION OF ISRAEL.

By DR. A. KUENEN.

VOL. II.

THE
RELIGION OF ISRAEL

TO

THE FALL OF THE JEWISH STATE.

BY

DR. A. KUENEN,

PROFESSOR OF THEOLOGY AT THE UNIVERSITY OF LEYDEN.

Translated from the Dutch

BY

ALFRED HEATH MAY.

VOL. II.

WILLIAMS AND NORGATE,
14, HENRIETTA STREET, COVENT GARDEN, LONDON;
AND 20, SOUTH FREDERICK STREET, EDINBURGH.
1875.

TRANSLATOR'S PREFACE TO VOL. II.

In rendering this volume into English, the translator has to acknowledge the assistance of the author, who has continued to read the proofs, and of Mr. Milroy, who has read the translation in manuscript.

The valuable table of contents given in the original will be published at the end of the third volume.

CONTENTS OF VOL. II.

	PAGE
CHAPTER VI.	
The Religion of Israel to the Fall of Jerusalem in 586 B.C.	1
Notes on Chapter VI.	77
CHAPTER VII.	
The Israelitish Exiles in Babylonia	98
Notes on Chapter VII.	174
CHAPTER VIII.	
The Establishment of the Hierarchy and the Introduction of the Law .	202
Notes on Chapter VIII.	286

THE RELIGION OF ISRAEL.

CHAPTER VI.

The Religion of Israel to the Fall of Jerusalem in 586 b.c.

Towards the end of the 8th century before our era, Hezekiah had attempted to effect a complete revolution in the religious practices of his subjects. From the very brief account by the author of 2 Kings*—which is enlarged and embellished, but not really supplemented, by the Chronicler†—we should scarcely infer that his measures had so wide an aim. Yet we do not go too far when we say "a complete revolution." We already know that the "high places" which Hezekiah abolished had existed for centuries all over the kingdom, and that the use of pillars, *asheras* and images of Jahveh, according to Isaiah and Micah,‡ was general. It is very improbable, therefore, that the king met with no opposition of any sort and gained his end entirely and at once. The historian, it is true, makes no mention of the obstacles which were put in his way, but this fact could possess value as evidence only if he had shown himself to be accurately informed and had entered into details. Nevertheless the possibility remains, that Hezekiah was powerful enough to deter his subjects from any attempt at resistance, or to nip their opposition in the bud. But no one can well think it likely that he altogether changed the *persuasions* and *ideas* of his people during his reign of thirty years. The means which he employed—the "removing," "cutting down," and "breaking to pieces"—however suitable they may have been for altering the outward appearance of things in a short time, did not reach the root of the evil. In a word, but little pene-

---

* 2 Kings xviii. 4, comp. 22. † 2 Chr. xxix.—xxxi. ‡ Vol. I. pp. 79, sqq.

tration was required to foresee that these violent measures would necessarily be followed by an equally violent reaction. And this is what actually occurred.

In the year 696 B.C. Hezekiah died. His son Manasseh, a boy of twelve, became king in his stead: his reign lasted 55 years, until 641 B.C. Amon his son and successor trod in his father's footsteps until 639 B.C. For 57 years, then, the kingdom was governed in one spirit, in the spirit of the party whose tenderest feelings had been wounded by Hezekiah's reformation.

We should indeed remember that Manasseh and Amon, just as much as their predecessor, represented a conviction. In reading the accounts concerning them,* our first impression is that they were crowned miscreants, and Manasseh especially. The author can find no words strong enough to express the abhorrence with which Manasseh's deeds inspire him. He twice compares him to Ahab.† One of his atrocities, the placing of the Ashera-pillar in the temple, is a desecration of that building, and is diametrically opposed to Jahveh's promises and commands to David and Solomon.‡ It is with evident approbation that the author mentions the prediction of Manasseh's contemporaries among the prophets, that, on account of his transgressions and of the readiness of the people to take part in them, Jerusalem shall be laid waste and its inhabitants scattered among the nations.§ Over and above all this, he accuses him of having "shed very much innocent blood, till he had filled Jerusalem with it from one end to the other."‖ The painful impression made by these accusations would certainly be considerably lessened, if we might assume, with the Chronicler,¶ that Manasseh subsequently repented of his sins and, after his return from a temporary captivity in Assyria, hastened to repair as much as possible the evil he had done. But for various reasons this account is unworthy of credit. So

---

* 2 Kings xxi.; 2 Chr. xxxiii. † 2 Kings xxi. 3, 13. ‡ 2 Kings xxi. 7, 8.
§ 2 Kings xxi. 10-15. ‖ 2 Kings xxi. 16. ¶ 2 Chr. xxxiii. 11, seq.

long, therefore, as we continue to occupy the standpoint of the Israelitish historians, we shall judge most unfavourably of Manasseh—and of Amon. But it is precisely this standpoint which we must attack. It is that of Manasseh's antagonists, who afterwards regained and kept the upper hand. They judge him by the standard of their own ideas, which he, however, did not embrace, or, rather, would have condemned as revolutionary and dangerous.

Of course, this makes it none the less necessary to give the verdict of the Israelitish historian its share of our attention, if we wish to form a true idea of Manasseh's character and designs. This we do the more readily, now it appears that it is the echo of the warnings uttered by the king's contemporaries respecting the punishment which was to come.* We remember too that Jeremiah† also attributes the fall of the kingdom to that which Manasseh the son of Hezekiah did at Jerusalem. What, then, had he done?

In the first place, Manasseh restored the worship of Jahveh as it had been before Hezekiah's reformation. He built up again—we are told‡—that is: he allowed to be built up again, the high places which his father had destroyed. He also worshipped other gods besides Jahveh, and he placed in the temple at Jerusalem the symbol of Ashera, the tree-stem stripped of its branches, which was frequently erected next to the altars of Jahveh.§ Like his grandfather Ahaz, he encouraged the service of Molech, and following his example, he— we do not know under what circumstances—dedicated one of his sons to this deity by fire.‖ It is told of him further, that he "bowed down to all the host of heaven and served them (the stars)," and built altars in honour of these deified celestial bodies in the two courts of the temple at Jerusalem.¶ Did he adopt this latter worship from abroad, from the Assyrians or

---

* 2 Kings xxi. 10-15.   † Jer. xv. 4.   ‡ 2 Kings xxi. 3.
§ 2 Kings xxi. 3, 7; comp. Deut. xvi. 21.   ‖ 2 Kings xxi. 6; comp. xvi. 3.
¶ 2 Kings xxi. 3, 5; comp. xxiii. 4, 5; Zeph. i. 5.

the Babylonians? He saw nothing reprehensible in the service of their gods, no more than in the time-honoured worship of the Canaanitish deities. But we are not surprised that this imitation of the foreigner was a new and inexcusable grievance to those who served Jahveh alone. Manasseh's conduct was the more abominable in their estimation, in that he established the worship of false gods—both that known of old, and that introduced by him—in the place that was the very centre of the service of Jahveh. It is true that, even under his rule, the temple of Solomon did not cease to be a sanctuary of Jahveh; but besides the principal deity, many other gods were also worshipped there, each after its own fashion. This was in harmony with the heathen custom. As we remarked before,* it cannot be considered absolutely antagonistic to the intentions of the founder of the temple. There is no doubt either, that Manasseh was not the first who had done this.† Nay, we must even regard it as improbable, that Hezekiah had succeeded in banishing all traces of the worship of the other gods from the temple.‡ Yet Manasseh went further than any king before him. And—what cannot but have increased the dissatisfaction which he caused—his acts led, either in his reign or subsequently, to the solemnization of still other religious rites, and among them Egyptian rites, in the temple itself, or in its immediate vicinity.§ In short, it was as though he was bent upon thwarting, or was trying to introduce the opposite of, the ideal cherished by the worshippers of Jahveh, the realization of which had seemed to them so near at hand in Hezekiah's reign. Is it to be wondered at, that they abhorred him as an enemy to Jahveh?

The descendants and successors of the prophets of the 8th

---

* Vol. I. pp. 335, seq.

† Comp. what is said of "the kings of Judah" in 2 Kings xxiii. 5, 11, 12.

‡ Had that been the case, in all probability Manasseh alone would have been named in the verses just quoted.

§ Ezek. viii. comp. Note I. at the end of this chapter.

century B. C. must have altogether degenerated, if they could look upon all this in silence. The writer of the books of Kings relates—and we have no hesitation in believing him—that Jahveh raised his voice, "by the mouth of his servants the prophets," against Manasseh's abominations. Here and there their words were echoed. Were there, perchance, some men who, enflamed by these words, offered resistance to the king's measures? The statement that he "shed very much innocent blood in Jerusalem" would lead one to suppose so. Free from all exclusivism, Manasseh cannot well have become a persecutor of his own accord. If he took this part upon him, he was driven to it by the reception accorded to his measures. In judging of his conduct, we must not forget both how intimately religion was linked to politics in Israel, and how the Jahvistic party bore themselves when they were in authority. The connection between religion and politics fully explains why the prophets and their adherents were looked upon as dangerous to the good order of the state. And when we call Hezekiah and Josiah to mind, we lack the heart to castigate Manasseh severely for his persecutions.

At the same time, we should not forget that in order to form a well-grounded judgment of Manasseh and Amon, our information ought to be more precise. It is indeed to be deplored that we cannot throw light from contemporaneous records upon so remarkable a period of nearly half a century. Perhaps a few of the Psalms were composed during that time.* But nothing certain is known of their age. When we assign them to the reign of Manasseh, it is because they express what we suppose to have been the feelings of his pious contemporaries, judging from what we already know. They do not extend our knowledge. We have no alternative but to rest content with this ignorance. Fortunately it does not prevent us from comprehending the period which dawned after Amon's death. In

* Comp. my *H k. O.* iii. 294, seq.

fact, this period lies before us so clearly that it dissipates in some degree the mist which hangs over Manasseh's reign.

Nothing can be more natural than that the upholders of the exclusive worship of Jahveh—for the sake of brevity we can call them the Mosaic party—not only looked forward longingly to better times, but also did their best to prepare the way for them. They neither could nor would submit to their defeat. They could not well do otherwise than exert all their strength to win back the days of Hezekiah. In connection with this, we involuntarily ask, whether Amon's violent death* was not, perchance, their work? They certainly had grounds enough for being exasperated against him; and they reaped substantial benefit from the change. But we believe we may acquit them of this crime. It is expressly said that the conspirators against Amon were "his servants," and that the "people of the land" slew them all, and then made the son of Amon king. Probably the unfortunate prince fell a victim to some court intrigue, and the people came forward for the rightful successor, and also for the race of their beloved David.

But whoever may have caused it, Amon's death was a blessing for the Mosaic party. They had nothing to hope and everything to fear from him. Josiah, his successor, was a boy of eight :† what might not be effected if they could only acquire influence over him, and make him embrace their views! A king's power is absolute in the East, and so it was in the kingdom of Judah. "When there was yet no king in Israel, every man did that which was right in his own eyes;" ‡ afterwards —we can add to the historian's remark—afterwards all or most of them bowed, at all events outwardly, to the will and orders of the prince. No wonder that the Mosaic party first conceived the hope, and then formed the plan, of winning Josiah, and, through him, of carrying out what, in their eyes, was the duty and also the interest of the state.

---

* 2 Kings xxi. 23, 24.   † 2 Kings xxii. 1.   ‡ Judges xvii. 6.

But before they could succeed in this, it was necessary that they should speak out their wishes plainly, and lay them before the king in such a manner that there could remain no doubt as to their meaning and the way in which they were to be realized. It sounds strange, and yet it is a fact, that hitherto they had had no accurately defined programme. They knew very well what they thought needful, but they had failed to commit their demands to writing with the necessary fulness. Probably it was partly to this that the failure of their plans after the temporary triumph under Hezekiah was to be attributed. In any case, a collection of legal precepts was deemed indispensable in order to obtain any permanent result. But to understand this thoroughly, it will be necessary for us again to glance back for a moment.

It need not be repeated here that Moses bequeathed no book of the law to the tribes of Israel.* Certainly nothing more was committed to writing by him or in his time than "the ten words" in their original form. We do not know with certainty where these fundamental laws were kept. Probably, however, it was in the temple;† perhaps even, as subsequent tradition says, in "the ark of Jahveh," which may then have borrowed from this circumstance its later name of "ark of the covenant of Jahveh."‡ In Manasseh's reign "the ten words" were no doubt formulated and enlarged nearly as we now read them in the Pentateuch. But for the end which the Mosaic party were struggling to gain, they were altogether inadequate. In the first place, they were absolutely silent upon many most important points. In the second, they were wanting in what one might call legal validity. Jahveh's temple at Jerusalem, where they had been deposited, was by no means the only sanctuary, merely the first or chief one. That which was ac-

---

* Comp. Vol. I. pp. 272, seq.

† According to the ordinary translation of 2 Kings xi. 12, the "testimony," i.e. the Decalogue, was used at the coronation of Jehoash (878 B.C.). But this rendering is rejected by many, who consider that a royal ornament is referred to.

‡ Comp. Vol. I. pp. 257, seq.

knowledged and proclaimed there as the will of Jahveh was not binding upon the other sanctuaries, on "the high places," and upon those who regularly frequented them.

But surely other written laws existed? Undoubtedly, but they were of a private nature, so to speak. At all events nothing certain is known of their promulgation and introduction by the competent authority, *i.e.* the king. The prophetic historians included them in their narratives concerning the Mosaic time, and no doubt made use of the opportunity to add to and extend them. In so far as these laws did not simply reproduce that which had long been legalized by custom, and was therefore also followed in the administration of justice, they had as much—or as little—effect as the exhortations of the prophets, *i.e.* they were observed by those who saw in them the expression of Jahveh's will, and by no one else. This is evident from the very character of these laws. The oldest collection which we know, the so-called Book of the Covenant,* contains a number of precepts concerning the civil life, of which the majority are obviously taken from existing customs.† But side by side with these we find purely moral commandments and admonitions for which express motives are alleged, *i.e.* which are made dependent upon the assent of the reader.‡ The Book concludes with a thoroughly prophetic discourse, setting forth the blessing attached to the observance of Jahveh's laws and the curse to their neglect.§ Collections such as these were by no means official. In that case surely men would not have dared to alter them, and would have considered themselves bound to accept them in their integrity. The contrary occurred. The author of Exodus xxxiv borrows‖ from the Book of the Covenant and from a few other laws¶ the rules which seem to him to be the most important, and makes of

---

* Exod. xxi-xxiii. Comp. Vol. I. p. 128.
† Exod. xxi. 12-14; 15, 17; 16; 18-21; 22, &c.
‡ Exod. xxii. 21; 22-24; 25-27; xxiii. 9, &c.   § Exod. xxiii. 20-33.
‖ Vers. 10—26.   ¶ Exod. xiii. 1-10, 11-16.

them a whole after his own fashion. We shall see presently how the writer of Deuteronomy treats in exactly the same way the laws written before his time. Such freedom is conclusive proof that the codes of various ages which were extant at the beginning of Josiah's reign, had no validity in law.

But granting even that it was otherwise, still the Mosaic party in Josiah's reign would not have thought themselves released from the duty of committing their demands to writing. If they found much in the more ancient collections with which they could agree with all their hearts, they missed also in them things which were absolutely necessary in their eyes, nay, they met in them with that which by no means harmonized with their opinions. Thus the Book of the Covenant* insisted upon the celebration of the three high festivals, but in such a way that the manner in which this was to be done was left to each man's own discretion or to custom, and the pilgrimages to "the high places" were decidedly not prohibited. Nay, in this very Book of the Covenant—or, at all events, in an old law which now immediately precedes it—express permission is given to sacrifice to Jahveh at more than one place†—a liberty which is also understood in other regulations.‡ We already know enough of the ideas and wishes of the Mosaic party of those days to perceive that they could not rest content with such a code.

What we asserted above, therefore, remains true: a double duty devolved upon the Mosaic party; they had to set forth their views plainly and definitely, and to prevail upon the king to carry them out. They understood their mission, and fully acted up to it. We have their programme in the book of Deuteronomy; Josiah's reformation proved that they had won the king. Let us begin by examining this reformation.

It occurred when Josiah had reached his twenty-sixth year,

---

* Exod. xxiii. 14-17. † Exod. xx. 24.
‡ Exod. xxi. 6, &c., comp. Note II. at the end of this chapter.

and in the 18th year of his reign (621 B.C.).* It is true, the Chronicler tells us that in the 8th year of his reign the king already "began to seek after the God of David his father," and four years afterwards "began to purge Judah and Jerusalem."† But his account is irreconcilable with that of the older historian, and deserves no credit. It is founded on fact to this extent, however, that before the 18th year of his reign, Josiah's policy towards the Mosaic party already differed from that of his predecessors. At all events, we find no trace of persecutions instituted by him. Zephaniah—probably a relation of the king‡—and Jeremiah laboured actively as prophets, from the year 626 B.C.,§ without molestation. Huldah, a prophetess of Jahveh, lived in Jerusalem and enjoyed great distinction.‖ The very cause of the event which we shall presently relate, shows that Josiah gave substantial proof of his interest in the temple.¶ It would not be unimportant now to know the exact political condition of the kingdom in the above-mentioned year of Josiah's reign. Our information respecting this condition is not quite positive.** But it may be accepted as probable that the kingdom not long before had happily escaped from an imminent danger. Scythian hordes had penetrated into Media, and had forced King Cyaxares to raise the siege of Nineveh. They had then turned westwards, and subsequently had taken the road to Egypt. In their course thither they would necessarily touch Palestine, and it seemed far from improbable that they would commit ravages in Judæa also. The prophets Jeremiah and Zephaniah actually announced this. Their opinion of the religious-moral condition of the kingdom was so unfavourable, that a divine chastisement seemed to them to be at hand. They thus took advantage of the ap-

---

* 2 Kings xxii. 3. † 2 Chr. xxxiv. 3.
‡ Zeph. i. 1. Comp. my *Hk. O.* ii. 369, sq. § Jer. i. 2; xxv. 3.
‖ 2 Kings xxii. 14, seq. ¶ 2 Kings xxii. 3, seq.
** Comp. Oort, *Jeremia in de lijst van zijn tijd*, pp. 42, seq., with my *Hk. O.* ii. 177, 371, sq.

proach of the Scythians to exhort the people to repentance.* It is quite possible that then, as so often happens, the fear of a great calamity brought about a certain revival of religious feeling. In the meantime the danger was averted. The Scythians hardly entered Judæa, if at all. They marched to Egypt by the sea-coast; this forced Psammetichus, who was then king of that country, to raise the siege of Gaza; but subsequently they allowed themselves to be persuaded by him to give up their plans and turn back. This occurred, according to the most probable calculation, in or about the year 625 B.C. Four years afterwards the remembrance of those anxious days had not faded, nor the fear that perhaps they would soon return. The Scythians were still roving about in Asia. Did the thought of them add weight, in the estimation of Josiah and his counsellors, to the threats which they heard in the year we have mentioned? This is not impossible. But let us see what took place at this time.

Some repairs were to be made in the temple at Jerusalem. Josiah sends his scribe, Shaphan the son of Azaliah, to Hilkiah the high priest, to order the latter to make up the amount of the voluntary gifts which the doorkeepers had received from the people, and to hand this money to the men charged with the superintendence of the work.† When Shaphan had delivered these injunctions, Hilkiah made an important communication to him: "I have found," he said, "the book of the law in the house of Jahveh." Shaphan immediately read the book, went back to Josiah and hastened to inform him of the discovery and to read it to him. It made the deepest impression upon the king. Did it not contain precepts which had been broken by the fathers and by the generation then living, and also terrible threats of punishment which there was every reason to fear would consequently be fulfilled?‡ Josiah wishes at once to ascertain for certain what he and his

---

* Jer. ii.-vi. Comp. my *Hk. O.* ii. 174, seq.
† 2 Kings xxii. 3-7. ‡ Vers. 8-11.

people have to expect. He sends five men of high rank, among
whom are Hilkiah and Shaphan, to consult Jahveh for him.
They go to the prophetess Huldah and lay before her the king's
wishes.* Her reply does not seem to have been reported by
the historian with literal exactness.† It is not probable, at all
events, that on this occasion she would have represented the
fall of Jerusalem and the ruin of the kingdom as irrevocably
decreed. But the main point was that she recognized "all the
words of the book which Hilkiah had found" as the expression
of Jahveh's will and counsel. Now Josiah could hesitate no
longer as to what he had to do. He called the people—probably represented by their elders and great men—together in
the temple at Jerusalem and read to them "the book of the
covenant." Whether it be that this reading made the same
impression upon all of them as it had previously done upon the
king, or that no one dared oppose the monarch, "the whole
people" solemnly bound themselves "to walk after Jahveh and
to keep his commandments, his testimonies and his statutes,
with all their heart, and to perform the words of the covenant
written in the book" which had been read to them.‡ Not a
moment was lost in carrying out this engagement. At the
king's command, Hilkiah and the rest of the priests remove
out of the temple everything that is connected with the worship
of false gods. The following are specified: the holy vessels
which were used in the service of Baal, Ashera and the host of
heaven;§ the Ashera-symbols themselves, which had been
erected by Manasseh, as we have seen;|| the chapels in (or
adjoining) the temple, in which the priestesses of Ashera sold
themselves to the worshippers of that goddess;¶ the horses
and chariots of the sun, which the kings of Judah had placed
at the entrance of the temple, in the chamber of Nathan-
melech;** and the altars which had been built by the kings of
Judah on the roof of the upper chamber of Ahaz, and by

---

* Vers. 12-14. † Vers. 15-22. ‡ 2 Kings xxiii. 1-3.
§ Ver. 4. || Ver. 6. ¶ Ver. 7. ** Ver. 11.

Manasseh in the two courts.* This return of the things in or adjoining the temple that required reform, can give us some idea of all that there was to be done beyond it, in order fully to carry out the decrees of Hilkiah's book. In the immediate vicinity of Jerusalem, in the valley of Ben-Hinnom, there was the Topheth, the holy place where the worshippers of Molech burned their children in honour of that god; it was defiled.† On the right hand of the "mount of corruption," *i.e.* on the south-western slope of the mount of Olives, there stood the sanctuaries of Ashtoreth, Chemosh and Milcom, founded by Solomon; they were laid waste.‡ The "pillars" and Ashera-symbols were everywhere broken in pieces and hewn down.§ The priests of the false gods, the *chemarim* appointed by the kings of Judah, were prevented from pursuing their calling.‖ From Geba to Beersheba, *i.e.* from the northern to the southern limits of the kingdom, "the high places" (dedicated to Jahveh) were defiled; their (Levitical) priests, thus deprived of their only means of support, were brought to Jerusalem, and "ate" from that time forward "unleavened bread among their brethren," who served in the temple; they were not permitted, however, "to sacrifice upon the altar of Jahveh;" probably they performed other, subordinate functions.¶ Josiah was not content with these measures. He worked zealously in the same spirit, even beyond the borders of his kingdom. At Beth-el and in "the cities of Samaria" in general, the high places were destroyed and their priests slain by his command.** And finally, the work of purification was crowned by the splendid celebration of the passover, in accordance with the regulations of the "book of the covenant." "There was not holden such a passover"—says the historian—"from the days of the judges that judged Israel, nor in all the days of the kings of Israel, nor of the kings of Judah."††

* Ver. 12.   † Ver. 10.   ‡ Ver. 13.   Comp. Vol. I. p. 331.
§ Vers. 14.   ‖ Ver. 5.   ¶ Vers. 8, 9.   ** Ver. 15-20.
†† Vers. 21-23.   Comp. Note III. at the end of this chapter.

So runs the oldest and thoroughly credible account of Josiah's reformation. It will now no longer be asked why we expressed above* some doubt of the complete success of Hezekiah's measures. If he had already worked as vigorously as Josiah did after him, how was it that the latter found so much idolatry and illegal Jahveh-worship to reform at Jerusalem and elsewhere? We can make Manasseh and Amon account for much, it is true, but not for all. That which the historian indicates as the work of the "kings of Judah" or definitely ascribes to Solomon,† was not introduced by Manasseh, but was not abolished by Hezekiah. Our conception of the religious condition of the kingdom of Judah during the centuries which preceded Josiah's reign, must of course adapt itself to the accounts given of what he found in existence. What a difference there was, then, between the prophets' demands and the reality! How lofty was the ideal of the Mosaic party compared with what they saw around them! Their conception of Jahvism differed so much from what their predecessors and the multitude knew by this name, that its introduction may, without the least exaggeration, be called a revolution.

There can hardly be any difference of opinion with regard to Josiah's intention. No other gods but Jahveh; no other Jahveh-worship than in the temple at Jerusalem: these two demands show the drift of his reformation. We have already pointed out more than once‡ that the one is intimately connected with the other; that the centralization of the public worship in the one sanctuary at Jerusalem was deemed necessary, in order to put an end to the serving of false gods and of Jahveh with idolatrous practices. But we cannot possibly remain content with the knowledge of this outline of the tendency which now predominated. We desire to know more of the ideas, the spirit, and the wishes of the party which received Josiah's powerful aid to realize their plans. This desire is legitimate, and need not remain unsatisfied. Josiah's refor-

* P. 1, seq. † 2 Kings xxiii. 5, 11, 12, 13. ‡ Vol. I. pp. 80—82.

mation was the result of the enforcement of the code found by Hilkiah. If we consult this code, we are almost certain to find what we seek.

As we have already said, Hilkiah's book of the law has not been lost; we possess in Deuteronomy the programme of the Mosaic party of that day. It will be necessary for us, however, to explain more fully, and at the same time to prove, this assertion, before we make ourselves acquainted with the contents of the book itself. As every one will at once perceive, it is of such vital importance to Israel's religious history, that it is less than any other assertion to be taken upon trust.

The book of Deuteronomy is now a part of a whole, the Pentateuch. Not merely in the sense that it is reckoned among the "books of Moses," but also because it is interwoven in many respects with the four preceding books, from Genesis to Numbers. To name a few instances: when we have finished reading Numbers, we have not yet arrived at the end of the history of Moses: the narrative of his death—already referred to in Num. xxvii. 12-14—is wanting; we find it in Deut. xxxiv. In the beginning of the book* there occurs a date which fits on to the chronology of Numbers.† The first discourse‡ delivered by Moses is a free recapitulation of what has already been said in the previous books about the Israelites' wanderings through the desert, and especially the events of the fortieth year. Now let it be taken into consideration that part of the narratives and laws which we possess in the first four books of the Pentateuch, are more recent than the seventh century before our era, and therefore cannot have been linked to Deuteronomy before Josiah's reformation. Let it be further remembered that the writing found by Hilkiah is called the "book of the law," and the "book of the covenant,"§ and that it cannot have been of any great length, if we may believe the statement that it was read by Shaphan, and then read before

---

* Deut. i. 3.   † Num. xx. 22-29 (xxxiii. 37-39); xxi. 1, seq.
‡ Deut. i. 6—iv. 40.   § 2 Kings xxii. 8, 11; xxiii. 2, 3, 21, 24, 25.

Josiah, in one day, and was subsequently read out from beginning to end to the people in the temple.* We thus arrive at the supposition that to find Hilkiah's book we must detach Deuteronomy from its present connections, and strip it of its historical accessories, which only belong to it inasmuch as it forms part of the present Pentateuch. We now discover to our astonishment that this can be done without difficulty. In Deut. iv. 44-49, we find a title which is somewhat superfluous after all that precedes it,† but which becomes quite intelligible if we take it as an introduction to the discourse which begins with chapter v. This discourse continues without interruption to the end of Deut. xxvi. The following chapter gives one the impression that it is parenthetical. At all events, Deut. xxviii. appears to be the continuation of chap. xxvi., and—what is especially worthy of attention—concludes with a note which corresponds to chap. iv. 44-49, and intimates that the laws and ordinances there set forth are now ended.‡ The chapters which follow Deut. xxviii., are, indeed, but loosely connected with that which precedes them. This is especially true of Deut. xxxi.-xxxiv., which embrace the conclusion of the history of Moses' life. In short, the analysis of Deuteronomy authorizes us to extract from it chap. iv. 44—xxvi. and xxviii., and to believe in the separate, independent existence of this discourse —for a discourse it remains, in spite of all the laws and precepts which it includes. Now this, at the same time, is the book of the law which was found by Hilkiah.

To those who deny or doubt our right to look for Hilkiah's book of the law in Deuteronomy, this operation will, of course, seem only shocking caprice. But this right is well established. All that we are told of that code, corresponds, point for point, with Deuteronomy, *i.e.* with the chapters which we have just selected. Let us consider the names which Hilkiah's book

---

* 2 Kings xxii. 8, 10 (also 2 Chr. xxxiv. 18); xxiii. 3.   † Deut. i. 1—iv. 40.
‡ Deut. xxix. 1—which verse ought to have been added to chap. xxviii., as is actually the case in the Hebrew text.

bears;* the statements respecting its length;† the severe threats which it is said to contain;‡ the law concerning the feast of the passover, which occurs in it;§ and finally and especially the tendency of its precepts, which comes to light most plainly in the reformation which was founded on them. We shall return shortly to this last point in particular. Here I may confine myself to the remark, that Deuteronomy especially insists upon one sole place of worship;‖ the same spirit of centralization pervades, as we have seen, Josiah's measures also; the similarity is so striking that we can only explain it by the king's dependence upon Deuteronomy.

We continue fearlessly to build, therefore, upon the supposition that Hilkiah's book of the law contained everything that we now read in Deut. iv. 44—xxvi. and xxviii. We must not feign greater certainty, however, than we really possess. Before we go further, therefore, I will admit that the possibility remains that only a portion of this whole was handed by the high priest to Shaphan. In fact, it cannot be denied that the accounts respecting Hilkiah's book, taken by themselves, give us the impression that it was even shorter than the twenty-three chapters we have mentioned. But, in any case, nothing essential of that which we now find in these chapters was omitted from it. It may have been filled in and expanded afterwards, but this enlargement made no change in its spirit and tendency. To become acquainted with these, we consult Deut. v. and the following chapters without the least hesitation.

But the question is not merely whether this portion of Deuteronomy agrees with Hilkiah's book of the law, but also whether we may regard it as the programme of the Mosaic party at that time. At first sight this seems to be open to doubt. On the one hand, *Moses himself* appears as the speaker

---

* See p. 15, note §, and comp. Deut. iv. 44; xxix. 1, &c.   † See p. 16, n. *.
‡ 2 Kings xxii. 13, seq.; comp. Deut. xxviii. and elsewhere.
§ 2 Kings xxii. 21, seq.; Deut. xvi. 1-8.   ‖ See below, p. 25.

in Deuteronomy: we read this not only in the titles,* but also again and again in the addresses themselves.† On the other hand, Hilkiah declares that he "has *found* the book of the law."‡ Does it not follow, that this book came to light, indeed, in Josiah's eighteenth year, but was written long before, nay, by Moses himself, or at least in his time and under his eye? Are we authorized simply to reject the evidence of Deuteronomy as to its origin, and that of Hilkiah as to his discovery?

It may now be accepted as proved, that the discourses and laws of Deuteronomy were put in the mouth of Moses, and that this was done about the time at which we see this book make its appearance. Immediately after Josiah's reformation it is frequently used by the prophet Jeremiah;§ the prophets of the eighth century B.C., on the contrary, are not yet acquainted with it—undoubtedly because it did not yet exist in their time. From the contents of the book also we infer that it is a product of the seventh century B.C. In every respect—by its teaching concerning faith and morals, by its relation to the older laws and narratives, by its very tendency—it shows itself a production of that time. What I wish to say directly as to its contents will confirm this. It is thus certain that an author of the seventh century B.C.—following in the footsteps of others, *e.g.* of the writer of the Book of the Covenant—has made Moses himself proclaim that which, in his opinion, it was expedient in the real interests of the Mosaic party to announce and introduce. At a time when notions about literary property were yet in their infancy, an action of this kind was not regarded as at all unlawful. Men used to perpetrate such fictions as these without

---

* Deut. i. 1, seq.; iv. 44, seq. &c.

† Let it be noticed, among other things, how the passage of the Jordan is throughout represented as yet to come, *e.g.* Deut. vi. 1; vii. 1; xi. 8, 10, 11, 29; xxiii. 20; xxviii. 21, 63. But it is unnecessary to quote more passages which show this: from one end to the other Moses is indicated as the person who speaks.

‡ 2 Kings xxii. 8.

§ The similarity is so great that some have held Jeremiah to be the author of Deuteronomy.

any qualms of conscience.—If we are to judge thus of the Mosaic origin of Deuteronomy, it is certainly still possible in the abstract that the work of the Deuteronomist was by some accident mislaid in the temple, and, by another accident, was found there by Hilkiah. But this is not probable. Deuteronomy was written, not for the mere sake of writing, but to change the whole condition of the kingdom. The author and his party cannot have made the execution of their programme depend upon a lucky accident. If Hilkiah *found* the book in the temple, it was put there by the adherents of the Mosaic tendency. Or else Hilkiah himself was of their number, and in that case he pretended that he had found the book of the law. This provision for the delivery of the programme to the king was of a piece with the composition of the programme itself. It is true, this deception is much more unjustifiable still than the introduction of Moses as speaking. But we must reflect here also, that the ideas of those days were not the same as ours, but considerably less strict. "Now or never" the Mosaic party had to gain their end. If they made no use of Josiah's disposition in their favour and of the awakened interest in religion, when were they to act? Nor must we forget that at all times and in all countries faction and intestine quarrels have stifled delicacy in the choice of means. And finally we must not overlook the fact that the victory of the Mosaic party, although gained by cunning, must not be attributed to the stratagem of which they made use, but to the good cause which they upheld, and to the weapons with which they defended it.

Yea, even to the weapons with which they defended it. For in truth Hilkiah's book of the law rises, both in form and contents, far above mediocrity, and tends to the imperishable honour of those who prepared it and of the party whose convictions it expressed. It will need no apology if I attempt to describe it somewhat more minutely. Scarcely anything can be more welcome to the historian of Israel's religion than such a writing. It is more valuable to him than, *e.g.*, a collection of prophecies or an historical book of the same period. The lawgiver must pay much more attention to the state of affairs which he sees around him than the prophet or the historian. He too expresses his conviction, but he does it with a view to its practical adoption. Thus the reality is reflected in his laws and regulations much more plainly than in the discourse of the prophet and the narrative of the historian. And there is another thing to be considered. The lawgiver occupies a different standpoint from the seer, and by so doing undertakes peculiar duties. While another can allow his individuality tolerably free scope, he must attempt as much as possible to be nothing more than the organ of his party: the whole of his undertaking depends upon the success of this endeavour. He is thus led involuntarily to take count, as it were, of the times in which he lives. How far have we got? in what direction must we proceed? what have we to do at this moment? These are questions which he must always keep before him, if he understands his vocation. What precious contributions to our knowledge of the development of Jahvism, therefore, does a writing such as Hilkiah's book of the law promise us! Let the whole of the sketch which I am about to give be studied from this point of view: I will myself draw special attention to a few particulars which are important above others.

The opinion expressed above in favour of Deuteronomy applies first of all to the plan which the author adopts. It is very happily chosen. In the 40th year of the wanderings in the desert, shortly after the great victories gained over Sihon and Og, whilst the Israelites stand ready to cross the Jordan and take possession of Canaan—Moses speaks to the whole people. The days of the great leader are numbered; his words claim the respect with which one hears and obeys the last directions of a dying man. Not to a chosen few, to priests or elders, but to his whole people does he address himself, with all the earnestness and all the authority with which the venerable Envoy of God could speak to those who knew him and who owed him so much. It is also worthy of notice, that the comparative completeness of the law which Moses delivers is fully justified by the plan which has been selected. The author expressly distinguishes "the covenant which Jahveh commanded Moses to make with Israel *in the land of Moab*," from "the covenant which he had made with them *on Horeb*."* But the latter covenant is founded, according to the author's representation, exclusively upon "the ten words," which are given, superfluously, once more.† It is true, Moses, after the promulgation of these "words," had received from Jahveh other "commandments, statutes and judgments" besides,‡ but as they were only intended to be observed in Canaan, he had waited until the boundary of the land, the Jordan, was about to be crossed, before he announced them to the people. This is how the author represents the case, although he is acquainted with and uses the Book of the Covenant. But, as we have already observed,§ that book had not yet any force as law in Judah about 620 years B.C. It could therefore be regarded as non-existent. And by so doing, the author acquires the right to include in his own legislation the matters which have already been handled there.

We are even more struck by the tone which the Deuteronomist adopts, than by the fitness of the plan. It is true he has been accused, not without reason, of diffuseness and monotony. If, however, as justice demands, we leave out of consideration Deut. i.-iv. and xxix. xxx., which are later additions, even though they be from his own hand, there are but few repetitions left, and those few are decidedly not prejudicial. On the contrary, they testify to the zeal and conscientiousness with which the author writes. It is as if he were afraid of saying too little, and again and again resumes the thread of the exhortation, in order, if possible, still to win some. His exhor-

---

* Deut. xxix. 1 (see above, p. 16, n. ‡). † Deut. v. 6-21.
‡ Deut. v. 31. § Page 8.

tations breathe a spirit of fervour and love which is very affecting. His pathos is the natural expression of a warm heart. We read of Josiah, that upon hearing the threats in Hilkiah's book of the law, he rent his clothes.* And, indeed, when we read Deut. xxviii. we are not surprised that it made so deep an impression upon him. But the tenderness, the unction, with which the Deuteronomist adjures his readers to choose Jahveh's blessing and not his curse, touches *us* more than these expatiations upon God's anger and judgments.

In the meantime, we cannot be edified by the tone which the author adopts, unless we perceive that it is genuine and harmonizes with the conviction which it expresses. What are the ideas which the Deuteronomist both entertains himself and wishes to impress upon others?

He is a servant of Jahveh. Jahveh is "the God of gods and Lord of lords."† To him belong the heaven and the heaven of heavens, the earth and all that is thereon.‡ He is the only God: "Hear, O Israel, Jahveh our God, Jahveh is one!"§ This Jahveh has chosen Israel. He has given the other nations the sun, moon and stars to adore;|| he has reserved Israel to himself. For this privilege the Israelites have to thank, not their numbers—on the contrary, they are one of the least of nations;¶ nor their righteousness—for they are a stiff-necked and stubborn people;** but Jahveh's love†† and the faithfulness with which, in spite of the people's errors, he has kept the promise sworn to their fathers.‡‡ Jahveh has delivered the children of Israel out of Egypt the house of bondage; during the 40 years of the journey in the desert he has provided for all their wants with tender care; if he has with-

---

* 2 Kings xxii. 11.   † Deut. x. 17.   ‡ Deut. x. 14.
§ Deut. vi. 4, comp. iv. 35, 39; xxxii. 39.
|| Deut. iv. 19; xxix.15, comp. xxxii. 8, and also de Goeje in *Theol. Tijdschrift*, ii. 179, seq.   ¶ Deut. vii. 6, 7, comp. vii. 1; ix. 1; xi. 23; iv. 38.
** Deut. ix. 4, seq.   †† Deut. vii. 8, 13; x. 15; xxiii. 6.
‡‡ See Deut. vi. 10, 18, 23, and the other numerous passages where the covenant with the fathers is mentioned.

held aught from them or subjected them to privations, even in this his wisdom and love have been revealed: "As a man chasteneth his son, so Jahveh thy God chasteneth thee."* It speaks for itself, that the Israelite may not and cannot be indifferent to such great love; he must "love Jahveh with all his heart, with all his soul, and with all his might,"† and cleave to him.‡ The observance of Jahveh's commandments is inseparable from this love and adherence, yet it is not coincident with it, but results from it naturally and of itself as it were. All depends upon the state of the heart: the inward, and not the outward, circumcision is the main thing.§ In a word, religion, to the Deuteronomist, is above all *a matter of the heart*.

The author's conviction as to the false gods and their service is the reverse side of these ideas concerning Jahveh and his relation to Israel. We have already remarked that he regards the worship of the heavenly bodies by the heathen as an arrangement of Jahveh himself and therefore is not hard upon them for it, although he more than once lays special stress upon the uselessness of image-worship, the adoration of "wood and stone."‖ So much the more exacting is he in his demand that the Israelite may have no sort of intercourse with idolatry.¶ He founds two series of precepts upon this principle. In the first place, he requires that every Israelite who follows after other gods than Jahveh, shall be stoned.** He considers him or her especially guilty of death, who, in whatever way it may have been, has tempted others into idolatry.†† Even though it be a whole city that has sinned by serving strange gods, it may not be spared. "Thou shalt smite the inhabitants of that city" —he says‡‡—"with the edge of the sword, utterly destroying

---

* Deut. viii. 2-5.
† Deut. vi. 5; x. 12; xi. 1, 13, 22; xiii. 4; xix. 9, comp. xxx. 6, 16, 20.
‡ Deut. x. 20; xi. 22; xiii. 5; comp. iv. 4; xxx. 20.
§ Deut. x. 16, comp. xxx. 6.   ‖ Deut. iv. 28; xxviii. 36, 64; xxix. 17.
¶ Deut. iv. 23, seq., and elsewhere.   ** Deut. xvii. 2-7.
†† Deut. xiii. 1-6, 7-12; xviii. 20-22.   ‡‡ Deut. xiii. 12-18.

it, and all that therein is, and the cattle thereof, with the edge of the sword. All the goods of it shalt thou gather together in the midst of the market-place thereof, and thou shalt burn with fire the city and all the goods thereof as a burnt-offering to Jahveh thy god; and it shall be a sepulchral mound for ever and shall not be built up again." In the second place he insists that the inhabitants of the land of Canaan shall be utterly destroyed (made *cherem*). This inhuman precept, which the Deuteronomist repeats again and again,* has no other motive than the fear of the seductive influence of the Canaanitish worship. He says this himself in so many words: when Israel summons a city in a foreign land and it surrenders, all its citizens shall be made slaves; if it offers resistance and is conquered, then all its male inhabitants must be killed, and the women, children and property fall into the hands of the conqueror; but "of the cities of the people which Jahveh thy god doth give thee for an inheritance, thou shalt save alive nothing that breatheth, for thou shalt surely make them *cherem*, the Hittite, the Amorite, the Canaanite, the Perizzite, the Hivite and the Jebusite, as Jahveh thy God hath commanded thee; that they teach thee not to do after all their abominations, which they have done for their gods, and thou sin against Jahveh thy god."† As if to show that this commandment is not prompted by bloodthirstiness or cruelty, the author immediately adds, that if a foreign city is besieged a long time, the fruit trees are not to be cut down!‡ This is truly a proof that it is only the fear of Israel's pollution by idolatry that leads him to pen such inhuman rules. Let it not be forgotten, moreover, that the Canaanitish tribes had no longer any substantive existence in the 7th century B.C., and that it was no longer possible to exterminate them; in reality, therefore, it is merely by the supposition of the ban to be enforced against them, that the author attempts to deter the Israelites from idolatry.

From the avoidance of idolatry and of all that resembles it,

---

* Deut. vii. 2, 16, and elsewhere. † Deut. xx. 10-18. ‡ Deut. xx. 19, 20.

it naturally follows that nothing which belongs to the service of false gods may be included in the worship of Jahveh. "Ye shall not do so"—after the manner of the Canaanites—"in honour of Jahveh your god:" this prohibition the Deuteronomist places in the foreground,* and he lays down his precepts concerning the service of Jahveh in conformity with it. I will give here a cursory review of his principal rules. I need scarcely say that he does not allow any similitude of Jahveh. The "ten words," as he gives them, expressly forbid the making of a graven image of any form whatever.† If we remember when and for whom he wrote, we are not surprised that he attaches great significance to this prohibition, and does all he can to promote its observance.‡ But still more emphasis is laid upon the limitation of the worship of Jahveh, with sacrifices, feasts, &c., to the temple at Jerusalem, "the place which Jahveh shall choose to cause his name to dwell there." It is the custom of the Canaanites to build altars to their gods everywhere, "upon the high mountains and upon the hills and under every green tree:" this the Israelites are not to do; they are to bring their offerings to that one spot.§ It is also worthy of notice, that the author, in laying down this commandment for the first time, clearly intimates that it is a new one, and, while he seems to be describing the Mosaic times, is really sketching his own. "Ye shall not do after all the things that we do here this day, every man whatsoever is right in his own eyes; for ye are not as yet come to the rest and to the inheritance, which Jahveh your god giveth you."‖ It is unnecessary here to analyze any more of the constantly recurring exhortations to be faithful to the one sanctuary¶—admonitions against "the high places" one might call them: nothing can be more obvious than that in them the Deuteronomist gives

---

* Deut. xii. 4, 30, 31. † Deut. v. 8. ‡ Deut. iv. 12, 15-18, &c.
§ Deut. xii. 2-7. ‖ Deut. xii. 8, 9.
¶ Deut. xii. 5, 8, 11, 14, 18, 21, 26; xiv. 23-25; xv. 20; xvi. 2, 6, 7, 11, 15, 16; xvii. 8, 10; xviii. 6; xxvi. 2, comp. xxxi. 11.

utterance to one of his principal ideas. To the one temple corresponds in his estimation the one tribe of priests. The priests of the tribe of Levi are the only ones whom he recognizes as lawful and as chosen by Jahveh.* Every Levite is not a priest, but he is qualified by birth to become one. If, therefore, he leaves the city where he sojourns as a stranger, and goes to Jerusalem and presents himself at the temple, "he shall minister in the name of Jahveh his god, as all his brethren the Levites do, which stand there before the face of Jahveh."† At first the position of the Levites, who are not connected with the temple, is far from enviable. Their tribe has no inheritance of its own, as have all the rest of the tribes : "Jahveh is its inheritance ;" the Levite lives upon the offerings made to Jahveh. Consequently, the Levites, scattered throughout the cities of Judah, are in very needy circumstances, and receive their share of the tithes in the third year, and of the sacrificial feasts, together with the widows and orphans, or are recommended generally to the charity of the Israelites.‡ The ministering Levitical priests, on the contrary, have their fixed dues, which are probably given by the Deuteronomist as they existed in his time.§ Compared with what was claimed at a later period, after the exile, the Deuteronomist's demands are very moderate : whereas at that time the tithes of fruits and cattle were assigned to the Levites, he speaks of the former as destined for another purpose, and is altogether silent regarding the latter.|| Other discrepancies also occur, upon which we shall fix our attention in a subsequent chapter.¶ Yet in spite of all this, the priests stand very high in his estimation—not only as servants of Jahveh, competent to bless in his name,**

* Deut. x. 8, 9; xviii. 1, seq. † Deut. xviii. 6, 7.
‡ Deut. xii. 19; xiv. 27, 29; xvi. 11, 14; xxvi. 11, et seq. § Deut. xviii. 3, 4.
|| With regard to the tithes of the fruits of the field, see Deut. xii. 6, 17-19 ; xiv. 22-27 ; xv. 19-23 : they are used at Jerusalem by the Israelite in sacrificial feasts. With regard to the same tithes in every third year, see Deut. xiv. 28, 29 ; xxvi. 12, 15 : they are given to the needy and the Levites. No mention is made in Deut. of the tithes of cattle. Comp. on the contrary Num. xviii. 21-32.
¶ Viz. in treating of the more recent sacerdotal laws. ** Deut. x. 8.

but also as members of the supreme court of justice at Jerusalem, whose decisions every Israelite was bound to respect and obey.* It was not part of the Deuteronomist's plan to regulate the duties and occupations of the priests more minutely. He enters upon the holy rites and seasons only so far as is necessary to instruct every Israelite in what he has to do. He especially insists that every one shall offer up his sacrifices in the temple at Jerusalem, and that the sacrificial meals shall be held there.† This applies also to the annual feasts held in honour of Jahveh. He knows of three such: the feast of unleavened bread *(mazzoth)*, that of weeks, and that of tabernacles;‡ he gives his directions for each one in particular.§ The first-mentioned feast begins with the killing and eating of the passover; sheep and oxen, presumably the unpolluted male first-born of these animals, which were put aside for or dedicated to Jahveh,|| were used for this purpose; the meal of the passover, like the eating of unleavened bread for seven consecutive days, served as a memorial of the exodus from Egypt.¶ The feast of weeks, at which, no doubt, the first-fruits of the grain-harvest were given to the priests,** was also kept by free-will offerings, which were used in social repasts in the sanctuary.†† And finally, the feast of tabernacles—no further explanation is given of the meaning of this name—after the conclusion of the vintage, is the great joyous festival at which the people thank Jahveh for the blessing received from him.‡‡ It will be observed that the Deuteronomist enters into some detail only with respect to the feast of unleavened bread; his regulations concerning it may be partly new; he evidently leaves the two other feasts as they were---always with this one exception, that the "appearing before Jahveh's face"§§ is always synonymous in his writings with "the going up unto the place which Jahveh

---

* Deut. xvii. 8-13. † Deut. xii. 26, 27; xiv. 22, seq.; xv. 19, seq.
‡ Deut. xvi. 16, 17. § Deut. xvi. 1-15. || Deut. xv. 19-21.
¶ Deut. xvi. 1-8. ** Deut. xviii. 4; xxvi. 1-11. †† Deut. xvi. 9-12.
‡‡ Deut. xvi. 13-15. §§ Exod. xxiii. 17; xxxiv. 23.

shall choose."* Of the great day of atonement, and of the new moon, and especially that of the seventh month, the Deuteronomist makes no mention at all: the significance of this silence, however, cannot be shown just yet.

Before we review the rest of our author's regulations, let us pause a moment to make a general observation suggested by his laws relating to the public worship of Jahveh. We can compare some of them with the practices of earlier times. An unmistakable difference is then brought to light. But we are still more struck with the close connection between his precepts and those already existing, with the regular development of the older laws or customs in conformity with the principles upon which they were founded. He simply goes a few steps further in the direction which had already been taken before his time. Thus, *e.g.*, in his regulations as to the priests: it may be asserted without exaggeration, that the exclusive competency of the Levites to minister at sacrifices had been in preparation ever since the days of Solomon,† and that the Deuteronomist, in announcing it, followed the logic of facts.‡ The same is true of the limitation of public worship to the temple at Jerusalem, for it had already been attempted by Hezekiah, before the Deuteronomist made it a law. Thus it may be said to be probable that the feast-legislation of Deuteronomy also stands in the same relation to the practices and rules of that day, which we can gather, in some measure, from the Book of the Covenant§ and a few other laws,‖ but yet do not know accurately enough to speak of them with absolute certainty. The *three* high feasts, already prescribed in the Book of the Covenant, had become so thoroughly ratified by custom about 620 B.C., that the Deuteronomist could retain them, and could consider himself absolved from the duty of giving express reasons for their celebration. Hence it follows that Jahveh was regarded at that time as the Lord of nature,

---

* Deut. xvi. 16.   † Vol. I. p. 338, seq.   ‡ Comp. Vol. I. p. 386, seq.
§ Exod. xxiii. 14-17.   ‖ Exod. xiii. (1. 2) 3-10 (11-16); xxxiv. 18-23.

the giver of harvest, and the source of fertility, not only by the prophets—we knew that before—but also by the priests and by the people who visited the temple, or the high places. But our attention is particularly attracted by the deuteronomic law concerning the feast of unleavened bread.* This feast— probably at variance with its original meaning†—had already been connected in earlier times with Israel's exodus from Egypt, in the same month of Abib, in which the feast was celebrated.‡ This explanation is quite in the spirit of Deuteronomy, where an attempt is even made to attach an historical association also to "the feast of weeks," or "of the first-fruits."§ Therefore the author adopts it, and even gives it prominence.‖ But, at the same time, he goes further in the same direction than any of his predecessors. While they had already connected the dedication of the first-born of man and beast to Jahveh—not with Jahveh's being, but—with the death of the first-born of the Egyptians,¶ the Deuteronomist unites the passover with the feast of unleavened bread, *i.e.*, he orders that the male first-born of oxen and sheep shall be slaughtered and eaten at that feast as a thank-offering.** By this combination he promotes, as forcibly as possible, the *historical* interpretation of the two practices, which, indeed, was quite in harmony with the direction in which the idea of Jahveh had long been developing itself: the more spiritually it was conceived, the more natural did it become to connect incidents in the history of Israel with the ceremonies which in reality were connected with Jahveh's attributes as a nature-god. But another remarkable phenomenon presents itself here. While the Deuteronomist, in the first place, makes no mention at all of

---

* Deut. xvi. 1-8.
† Comp. on this point and on the whole of this subject Note III. at the end of this chapter.   ‡ Exod. xiii. 3-10; xxiii. 15; xxxiv. 18.
§ Deut. xvi. 12: "And thou shalt remember that thou wast a bondsman in Egypt, and thou shalt observe and do these statutes."
‖ Deut. xvi. 1, 3, 6. In v. 3, the unleavened bread is called "bread of affliction."
¶ Exod. xiii. 11-16.   ** See above, p. 27, n. ‖ and ¶.

the dedication of the first-born *sons** (and the first-born of *unclean* animals)† to Jahveh, he speaks somewhat ambiguously, in the second place, of the sacrifice of the passover. He cannot conceal the fact that this sacrifice was killed and eaten on the evening of the first day of unleavened bread :‡ this must have long been customary in his day. But, at the same time, he transfers the name of passover to all the sacrifices of oxen and sheep which were offered up during the seven days of the feast.§ It is as if he made a point of rendering the sacrifice of the first day a subordinate part of a larger whole, and thus of diminishing in some measure its significance. May not the one be connected with the other? The Deuteronomist lived at a time when the sacrifice of the first-born to Molech was very common : || does he, perhaps, think it safer for this reason to say nothing about the dedication of the first-born to Jahveh, and to place in the shade this point of resemblance between the service of Molech and the worship of Jahveh? Did he see no opportunity as yet of explaining the sacrifice on the first day of the unleavened bread so as to make it agree entirely with the spiritual interpretation of Jahveh's being, as the author of the law in Exod. xii. did after him? It is not in our power to answer these questions with complete certainty. But it seems to me that the obscurity which remains here, confirms and recommends the hypotheses already advanced as to the original meaning of these practices.¶

We will return to the precepts of the Deuteronomist. Participation in the public worship of Jahveh, according to him, is only one of the characteristics of the servant of Jahveh. As one of Jahveh's people he is called to purity. That which the author prescribes in this respect is evidently borrowed largely from custom. He expresses the principle in these words:

---

* Comp. Exod. xxii. 29 b; xiii. 2, 11-16; xxxiv. 20 b.
† Comp. Exod. xiii. 13; xxxiv. 20 a.   ‡ Exod. xvi. 4, 6, 7.
§ Deut. xvi. 1-3. || Vol. I. pp. 251, 377; Vol. II. p. 3.
¶ See further Note III. at the end of this chapter.

"Ye are the children of Jahveh your God . . . . . ; ye are a people sacred unto Jahveh your God; for Jahveh hath chosen you to be a peculiar people unto himself out of all the nations that are upon the earth."* For these reasons, then, Israel must abstain from " every abomination ;" first of all from eating the flesh of animals which are looked upon as unclean,† or of an animal that has died a natural death.‡ That this prohibition has a religious foundation, is evident from what is added : " thou shalt give the thing that dieth of itself to the stranger that is in thy gates (has settled among you), that he may eat it ; or thou mayest sell it to an alien, for thou art an holy people unto Jahveh thy God."§ Unless I be mistaken, the Deuteronomist gives us a piece of priestly *thorah*|| in this regulation. It has been remarked that his law concerning clean and unclean is incomplete compared with that in the book of Leviticus,¶ and yet agrees with it in language and manner ; it is therefore inferred that he had this law in Leviticus before him, and borrowed from it what seemed to him most important. Another view, however, is more probable. It was not the intention of the Deuteronomist to include the priestly *thorah* in his book ; those who wish to know more of it he refers to the priests themselves.** But with regard to the clean and unclean animals he makes an exception, because his law, intended for the people, would have been too incomplete, had it embraced no rules on this subject, which constantly presented itself in daily life. Now it is most natural that he should give these precepts relating to clean and unclean in the language of the priests, who had established them, and that the younger sacerdotal law should be more copious than his and yet should resemble his in form. This interpretation, at the same time, throws some light upon the peculiar character of these regulations as to cleanness. The reason why men ab-

---

* Deut. xiv. 1, 2; comp. vii. 6.   † Deut. xiv. 3-20.   ‡ Deut. xiv. 21 a.
§ Deut. xiv. 21 b. || Comp. Vol. I. pp. 340, seq.   ¶ Chap. xi.
** Deut. xxiv. 8.

stained from some sorts of food, was originally no other than this, that they excited repugnance or disgust and suggested the idea of uncleanness. The customs born of this naturally became connected with religion, and in such a manner that abstinence from all that was unclean came to be regarded as the characteristic of the people of Jahveh, as a sign of its "holiness" or dedication to Jahveh. But these customs would have lacked all stability and would not have developed into a perfect system, if the people had been left to themselves in this particular. The priests took this matter into their own hands, and charged themselves with its regulation. We can gather from Deut. xiv. 1-21, how far they had completed this their task in the second half of the 7th century B.C.*—There are other precepts also in Deuteronomy which must be regarded from this point of view of "holiness." This is the case with the prohibition to disfigure the face while mourning for the dead ;† the regulation that men may not put on women's clothes, and vice versâ ;‡ the prohibition to unite things of different sorts in clothing or in agriculture.§ The customs condemned here existed among other nations and probably belonged to their religious practices: the people of Jahveh must avoid them and thus distinguish itself from the rest of the nations. The Israelites must also take care of the cleanness of the land: when the land has been defiled by the blood of a man who has been slain, it is to be purified ;‖ the corpse suspended upon a cross is to be taken down and buried before the evening.¶

But the Israelitish lawgiver does not confine himself to subjects of this nature. He also regulates the political, civil and domestic life and the moral life in general. The Israelite knows as little of what we call the separation of church and state as of a separation between religion and daily life. It does not surprise us, therefore, that the Deuteronomist also in-

---

* Comp. also Note IV. at the end of this chapter. † Deut. xiv. 1 b.
‡ Deut. xxii. 5. § Deut. xxii. 9-11. ‖ Deut. xxi. 1-9.
¶ Deut. xxi. 22, 23.

cludes in his writing a number of regulations that have nothing to do with religious duties in their stricter sense. We must pay attention here to these regulations as well. In the meantime we can confine ourselves to the main points more than we could before, even were it for the simple reason that the Deuteronomist is less original in this portion of his work than in the laws concerning religious worship. Some commandments he takes unaltered from former collections of laws, and especially from the Book of the Covenant, and perhaps also from another collection, which he has before him especially in chapters xxi.-xxv.; others he merely enlarges to a certain extent, either working them out in fuller detail or assigning reasons for them;* others again simply confirm existing customs and practices. The following are those which seem to me to be most noteworthy.

In the seventh century B.C. the kingly office had already existed for a long time. The Deuteronomist does not allow himself to be hindered by the plan which he has chosen from stating his ideas on this subject.† The king—he says—must be an Israelite; he is to guard against the trade in horses with Egypt, for fear that too intimate an intercourse with that land may result in Israel's return thither; he is not to take many wives, lest his heart turn away; he is not to multiply his gold and silver too much; he is to cause the priests to give him a copy of "this law" (Hilkiah's book of the law), and is to read in it constantly, in order thus to know and accomplish Jahveh's will. More than one feature in this law is most remarkable. The author shows here, at once, that he either belongs himself to "the priests the sons of Levi," or intends to trust his book of the law to their custody.‡ But no less striking is the author's aversion from Solomon, which is plainly visible here. The warnings against trade with Egypt, polygamy and great riches, are

---

* Comp. *e.g.* Exod. xxi. 2-11 with Deut. xv. 12-18; Exod. xxiii. 6, 8, with Deut. xvi. 18-20. In Deut. xxi.-xxv. the enlarging hand of the Deuteronomist himself is clearly visible, chap. xxi. 21, 22, sq.; xxii. 3; 5 b; 21 b; 22 b; 24 b; xxiii. 4, 5; 17; 21; xxiv. 7; 8, 9; 22; xxv. 12.

† Deut. xvii. 14-20.   ‡ Comp. Deut. xxxi. 9 and 10-13

borrowed from the tradition concerning the wise king, and are directed against the errors into which he fell. The isolation which Israel would have to endure in order to realize the ideal of the Deuteronomist, was indeed diametrically and irreconcilably opposed to the principles of Solomon's government.*

Another power in the Israelitish state was prophecy. The Deuteronomist's observations and directions regarding it are worthy of attention. How highly he estimates the prophets, is plainly evident from the well-known chapter in which he compares them with the soothsayers of the heathen, and shows their superiority.† He insists strongly upon Israel's obligation to listen to the prophets whom Jahveh shall send. Should a prophet dare to utter in Jahveh's name words which the latter has not put in his mouth, or to prophesy in the name of other gods, he forfeits his life. But—the Deuteronomist makes his readers ask—how can we tell that the prophet's words are not inspired by Jahveh? If—runs the answer—they are not confirmed by the result, they are not the words of Jahveh. But it by no means escapes his notice, that this rule cannot be applied conversely. It is on this account that it is said elsewhere,‡ that the prophet or dreamer whose sign comes to pass, must be regarded as a false prophet and put to death, if he attempts to lead his fellow citizens into idolatry. Fidelity to Jahveh and his service is thus the positive characteristic of Jahveh's envoy.

More than one precept refers to the administration of justice. In imitation of earlier lawgivers, the Deuteronomist urges impartiality in judgment.§ He desires that there shall be judges in every city,‖ and proceeds elsewhere from the supposition that the "elders of the city" discharge that office.¶ A high court of justice sits at Jerusalem, composed chiefly of

---

* Comp. above, Vol. I, p. 341, seq. † Deut. xviii. 9-22; comp. Vol. I, p. 211, seq.
‡ Deut. xlii. 2-9. § Deut. xvi. 19, 20 (i. 17 ; x. 17), comp. Exod. xxiii. 6-8.
‖ Deut. xvi. 18.
¶ Deut. xix. 12 ; xxi. 2, 3, 6, 20, 21 ; xxii. 15, 16, 18 ; xxv. 7-9.

priests; it was, as we learn from another source,* instituted by Jehoshaphat; the Deuteronomist earnestly exhorts the people to submit to the decisions of this court.† We need not consider here his special precepts with respect to the punishment of this or that crime. But our attention is strongly attracted by the general rule which he lays down: "the fathers shall not be put to death with the children, nor the children with the fathers: every man shall be put to death for his own sins."‡ It is historically certain that originally other principles were in force in Israel. We read more than once of a punishment executed upon the children for the evil committed by their father.§ Compared with this earlier practice, the precept of the Deuteronomist is a sign of great progress. Does it originate from him? Was he the first who endeavoured to bring the administration of justice into harmony with the more humane principles which had gradually penetrated into the life of the nation? We think this probable, when we observe that his conception of Jahveh's punitive justice also differs from that of his predecessors. It is true that he lets stand in "the ten words" the threat: "Jahveh thy God is a jealous god, visiting the iniquity of the fathers upon the children and upon the third and fourth generation of them that hate him."‖ But when he gives his own ideas on this subject, he says: "Jahveh repayeth them that hate him to their face, destroying them: he giveth him that hateth him no respite; he repayeth him to his face"¶ —without mentioning any judgment against the children. There is an indubitable connection between this modified interpretation of Jahveh's justice and the prohibition to punish the innocent with the guilty. We are the more ready to ascribe them both to the Deuteronomist, or, at all events, to the time in which he lived,** since it also appears from other

---

* 2 Chr. xix. 8-11. † Deut. xvii. 8-13. ‡ Deut. xxiv. 16.
§ Num. xvi. 25, seq.; Josh. vii. 24, 25; 2 Sam. xxi. 1-14. ‖ Deut. v. 9.
¶ Deut. vii. 10.
** Amaziah confined himself to punishing his father's murderers and spared

sources,* that then and shortly afterwards many began to oppose the common conception of Jahveh's justice. It is evident that men first of all mitigated the human administration of justice and then pictured to themselves Jahveh in their own likeness.†

The spirit of equity and clemency which marks the precept of the Deuteronomist of which we have just treated, is also visible in some of his other regulations. Observe, *e.g.*, how he modifies and extends‡ the older law concerning the release of the Hebrew male and female slaves after six years of service.§ Read also his commandments and exhortations in reference to "the year of release."‖ It was decreed in the Book of the Covenant, that the land should not be cultivated in the seventh year, and that all that grew in that year, as well as the fruit of the vine and olive-tree, should be left for the poor.¶ The Pentateuch itself testifies that this precept was not observed before the exile.** The Deuteronomist, too, does not repeat it, probably because he despairs of its performance. But he prescribes that in the seventh year debts shall not be demanded, and at the same time exhorts the people, in spite of this, to lend the needy all that he requires, even upon the approach of "the year of release." His legislation bears witness, in general, to concern for the lot of the poor, the fatherless and the widow, whom he recommends as urgently as possible to the charity of those of larger means.†† The way in which he excites the Israelites to humanity towards their male and female

---

their children (2 Kings xiv. 5, 6), but that he acted thus upon the strength of the law, is an opinion which is only guaranteed by the historian who utters it.

* Jer. xxxi. 29, 30 ; Ezek. xviii. 1, seq.; comp. below in reference to the book of Job. † Comp. Deut. x. 17, with xvi. 19, 20 ; i. 17. ‡ Deut. xv. 12-18.

§ Exod. xxi. 2-6. ‖ Deut. xv. 1-6, 7-11. comp. xxxi. 10-12.

¶ Exod. xxiii. 10, 11. ** Lev. xxvi. 34, 35, 43, comp. 2 Chr. xxxvi. 21.

†† Deut. xiv. 29 ; xvi. 11, 14. Comp. also Deut. xxiii. 15, 16 (the runaway slave not to be given up) ; 19, 20 (comp. Exod. xxii. 25 ; usury forbidden); xxiv. 6, 10-13 (comp. Exod. xxii. 26, 27 ; concerning taking in pledge) ; 14, 15 (care for the day-labourer); 17, 18 (justice to the lowly) ; 19-22 (liberality towards them).

slaves, by reminding them of the bondage in Egypt,* is truly touching. His solicitude extends even to dumb animals.†

It will be observed that in these precepts the Deuteronomist gradually passes from the domain of legislation to that of ethics. He gives some further commandments which are really exhortations, and the breaking of which certainly was not punished. Some of his regulations seem to be even impracticable,‡ so that one involuntarily asks, whether they are not merely intended either to deter the reader from this or that sin, or to present an idea in a conspicuous form. We have already remarked that the proscription of the Canaanites§ must be considered from this point of view, so that it cannot surprise us, if we meet with other precepts of the same nature. The origin, too, of the Deuteronomic legislation readily explains this somewhat double character. As we pointed out before,‖ it was compiled with a view to its practical adoption. But yet it was not the work of a practical statesman, who in drawing up his laws always makes the question of their practicability the main point. Their author was a prophet or a priest, perhaps both. His first aim was to express his notions of Jahveh and the Jahveh-worship in such a way that they would meet with acceptance. Therefore we should form a wrong idea of his writing, if we went on enumerating his particular ordinances, and thus received the impression that these were his principal object. No, the very arrangement of his book reminds us that by so doing we should mistake his intention. As he begins with earnest and pressing exhortations,¶ so he ends with promises and threats. Even the formularies that he recommends**—for it is nothing more than a recommendation, and not really a commandment—for the use of the Israelites who have dedicated their first-fruits and

---

* Deut. v. 14 (comp. Exod. xxiii. 12); also v. 15; xv. 15; xvi. 12; xxiv. 18, 22. † Deut. xxii. 6, 7; xxv. 4.
‡ See the law of war, Deut. xx.; also the precepts Deut. xxi. 18-21; xxii. 13-21; xxiii. 10-15; xxiv. 5.   § p. 24.   ‖ p. 19, seq.
¶ Deut. v.-xi.   ** Deut. xxvi. 1-11, 12-15.

tithes to Jahveh, have no other tendency than to cultivate in them sentiments becoming the pious servant of Jahveh, the true Israelite. The exhaustive discourse which closed the book in its original form,* is purely parenetic. The author himself announces that his aim is not so much to retain or alter this or that custom, as to win over his contemporaries to his interpretation of Jahveh's relation to Israel, and of the duties which result from it. It is true, when they have been moved by his exhortations and warnings to adopt that interpretation, he requires and expects them to maintain it, if need be with rigour and by force, and not to allow apostasy to escape unpunished. This results, naturally, from the identification of state and church which we have already observed in him,† or in other words from the theocratic character of his convictions. But as Josiah begins his violent revolution by making the people accept "the covenant" between Jahveh and Israel, so the command that the Israelite shall "love Jahveh his god with all his heart, with all his soul, and with all his might,"‡ lies at the basis of the deuteronomic legislation, and therefore the stimulation of that love is the beginning and the end of the book in which this legislation is contained.

Were history to teach us that with Josiah's reformation began the period of subjection to the written law—the legal period—we could not be surprised. The reformation started from the book of the law found by Hilkiah, and that book of the law itself laid claim to unqualified authority and to Israel's unconditional submission to its precepts. "What thing soever I command you, observe to do it: thou shalt not add thereto, nor diminish from it," are the words which the Deuteronomist puts into Moses' mouth.§ If this command had been carried out, men would have confined themselves thenceforward to the study and the explication of the law, and would have considered

---

* Deut. xxviii.   † pp. 32, seq.   ‡ Deut. vi. 5.
§ Deut. xii. 32, comp. iv. 2.

its further development superfluous, or even illegal. But this was not the case. Nearly two centuries were yet to pass, before the legal period in the history of Israel's religion could commence. Quite other matters than the calm exposition and application of the book of the law found by Hilkiah were to occupy men's minds. The sequel of this history will show us what they were.

First, however, we will once more glance at the book of the law and its author. It has not been preserved to us in its original form, as we have already remarked,* but has been included in the Pentateuch. A not unimportant part of that Pentateuch is of much later date than the Deuteronomic law, and cannot have been united with it into one whole until after the Babylonish exile. But the prophetic narratives concerning the first men and their descendants and the patriarchal and Mosaic times were in existence, and probably, as we have seen, included "the ten words" and the Book of the Covenant. The same prophetic narrators had also compiled the history of Joshua. The new book of the law had not followed all these accounts blindly, it is true, but yet it had adhered to them so closely, that an attempt could be made to blend it with them. Of course, we could not be sure that this took place shortly after Josiah's reformation, if the chapters that join the real book of the law to the older narratives† did not so greatly resemble that book itself, that we must actually ascribe them to one and the same author.‡ We believe, therefore, that before long the Deuteronomist again took his book in hand, and incorporated it with the prophetic historical narratives of that day. He then wrote the address which we now read in Deut. i. 1—iv. 40, in which the history of the journey in the desert is recapitulated and made the ground of an exhortation to the people. For our purpose, the conclusion of that discourse,

---

* pp. 15, seq.   † Deut. i.-iv. ; xxxi. seq.
‡ Comp. W. H. Kosters, de historie-beschouwing van den Deuteronomist, met de berichten in Genesis-Numeri vergeleken, pp. 16-30

Deut. iv. 1, seq., is of special importance. All stress is there laid upon the superiority of Jahveh's law to the practices of the heathen.* So earnest a warning is given against likenesses of Jahveh,† that we involuntarily ask, whether the circumstances of the time did not give rise to the renewed inculcation of the law that forbade them. The final chapters of Deuteronomy were written upon the same occasion, almost in their present form. Some things occur in it that belong to the older prophetic narrative;‡ the two poems also, "the song" and "the blessing of Moses,"§ were already in existence. But the Deuteronomist included all this and added to it much from his own hand. Thus, among other things, the hortatory discourse in Deut. xxix. xxx. was written then, a counterpart to Deut. xxviii., but—perhaps, under the influence of the disasters that befell Israel after the year 620 B.C.—of more sombre colouring. Most probably the Deuteronomist went still further and compiled the history of Joshua. The narratives relating to the conquest‖ and the final address of the aged leader¶ are indeed founded on older documents, but here and there show very plainly the hand of the Deuteronomist. Thus, among other things, the account of Joshua "utterly destroying" the Canaanites,** according to Jahveh's command to Moses, comes from him. The repeated assurance that the Israelites, like their leader, faithfully kept Jahveh's commandments and were consequently blessed by him in all that they undertook,†† is also undoubtedly from his pen. Thus he kept steadily in view the great end for which he had laboured, and made the history of the previous centuries, as described by his predecessors, also serviceable for the preaching of the great truth that Israel's prosperity entirely depended upon its fidelity to Jahveh.

But however important it may be to trace out the way in

---

* Deut. iv. 6, seq. † Deut. iv. 15, seq. ‡ Especially in Deut. xxxi. 14, seq.
§ Deut. xxxii. 1-43; xxxiii. Comp. Vol. I. p. 378, seq. ‖ Josh. i.-xii.
¶ Josh. xxiii. xxiv. ** Josh. x. 28, seq.; xi. 12, seq.
†† Josh. i. 3, seq.. 6, seq., 17, 18; iii. 7, 10; iv. 14; v. 2, seq.; ix. 11 b; xi. 15-20, &c.

which the Mosaic party endeavoured to make use of literature to promote the realization of their plans, we must now fix our attention upon the wider and turbulent scene of political events. For 13 years more Josiah occupied the throne of David (621-608 B.C.). Scarcely a single fact has been handed down to us from these years. But we venture to assert that it was a time of excitement and strained expectation. Josiah had been able to accomplish successfully his great undertaking, the purification of Judah and Jerusalem. The joyous feast of the passover with which it concluded, was followed by other festivals in honour of Jahveh; the temple, which was now served by a much more numerous priesthood than before, was faithfully attended; the altars and shrines of the false gods had been laid waste and remained so. Is it a wonder that the king and those of his opinion felt sure of Jahveh's blessing, nay, looked forward to fresh and unknown signs of his favour? The promises of the book of the law were surely no less positive than its threats? Political circumstances seemed to encourage in every way the expectation that Israel would again become mighty and great. During the reign of Sennacherib, Hezekiah's contemporary, the Assyrian empire had sustained some heavy blows; then the Medes, among others, had revolted, about the year 710 B.C., and the great king at Nineveh had not succeeded in subduing them again. On the contrary, about the middle of the 7th century B.C., the Medes became dangerous to their former masters. Shortly after Josiah had ascended the throne, their king Cyaxares laid siege to Nineveh (634 B.C.). It is true, he was obliged by the invasion of the Scythian hordes to raise this siege,* but it was easy to foresee that he or his successor would renew the attack. However that might be, the Assyrian empire was much weakened and the king could not think of maintaining his power in the more distant provinces, to which the former kingdom of the ten tribes also belonged. It does not surprise us, therefore, to find Josiah

* See above, p. 10, seq.

appearing as a reformer in "the cities of Samaria" as well,* whether it were as early as his 18th year, or—which is quite as probable—subsequently. There was no one to prevent him from acting there as lord and master, and, if he could rely upon the promises of Hilkiah's book of the law, it was Jahveh's intention, now that Israel hearkened to his voice, to bring back the glorious days of David.†

Let it not be imagined that we infer too much from the mere account of Josiah's operations in Ephraim, and ascribe to him designs which perhaps he never entertained. The last act of his reign proves incontestably that we judge him rightly. In the year 610 B.C. Nineveh was again besieged, this time by the Medes and Babylonians in league together. In the same year Psammetichus, king of Egypt, died and was succeeded by his son Necho. If Psammetichus had already tried to enlarge his kingdom at the expense of Assyria, Necho was not the man to miss the golden opportunity that now presented itself: he proposed to seize Syria and Palestine, the Assyrian provinces that bordered on his own kingdom, and thus to obtain his share of the spoil, even if he did not help to bring down the giant. By the second year after his accession to the throne he was on the march to Syria with a large army. Probably it was transported by sea and landed at Acco, on the Mediterranean, whence it was to proceed overland. But in carrying out this plan he encountered an unexpected obstacle: Josiah went to meet him with an army and attempted to prevent his march to Syria.‡

Josiah's motive for opposing Necho is obvious enough. He could not look on with unconcern while the Egyptian king extended his authority over Syria and northern Palestine. He had everything to fear from such a neighbour. It could not be long before he would also attempt to incorporate little

---

* 2 Kings xxiii. 15-20; above p. 13.
† Comp. also my paper: *De dood van Josia*, in *Nieuw en Oud*, New Series, 1866, pp. 257-273.   ‡ 2 Kings xxiii. 29; 2 Chr. xxxv. 20.

Judah into his kingdom. In spite of this, Josiah's war against Necho remains an ill-advised, nay, a senseless undertaking. He was no match for mighty Egypt. Had he but endeavoured to form an alliance with the kings of Syria! But no, without anyone's help he tries to keep back Necho's army. We can only account for this imprudent act by connecting it with the expectations which had been raised by the new book of the law. Josiah must have firmly believed that Jahveh would fight for his people and defeat the Egyptian ruler. From what Jeremiah tells us of the attitude of the prophets in the reigns of Jehoiakim and Zedekiah, we must infer that many of them strengthened the king in his intention not to endure an encroachment such as that of the Pharaoh.* The Chronicler relates that Necho himself endeavoured to dissuade Josiah from the unequal contest.† But it was no good. The decisive battle was fought in the valley of Megiddo: Judah was defeated; Josiah perished.‡

Josiah's death filled his subjects with bitter sorrow, which showed itself in loud lamentations.§ No wonder, indeed; for those who were like-minded with Josiah could bear witness of him: "like unto him was there no king before him, that had turned to Jahveh with all his heart, and with all his soul, and with all his might, according to all the law of Moses; neither after him arose there any like him."|| Nor could his opponents deny him the praise, that, true to his principles, he had acted with vigour, had strengthened the kingdom, and had extended Israel's power as far as in him lay. His death was therefore a great, an irreparable loss. Besides this, the fact could not be concealed, that after the defeat at Megiddo a new Egyptian slavery was imminent. But with many of the Israelites grief at the loss of such a king and at the lot that awaited the

---

* See below on this subject.   † 2 Chr. xxxv. 21.
‡ 2 Kings xxiii. 29, 30; 2 Chr. xxxv. 22-24.
§ 2 Chr. xxxv. 24, 25; Zech. xii. 10, comp. Jer. xxii. 10, 11, 18.
|| 2 Kings xxiii. 25.

fatherland, was mingled with a still more bitter feeling of disappointment. How utterly different had been their ideal of the result of Josiah's undertaking! How suddenly and rudely were they awoke, as from a fair dream! Had Jahveh's arm been shortened, then; or could his promises no longer be relied upon? Thus doubt went hand in hand with sorrow, and Judah's dismay was as deep as it was general.

It was in truth a difficult problem that the pious servant of Jahveh had to solve in those days. His conception of Jahveh's justice — we noticed it above* — required a perfect accord between lot and life: prosperity was connected with the observance of Jahveh's commandments, misfortune with resistance to him; this indissoluble union revealed itself in the fate of the nation as well as in that of the individual Israelite. Whenever that rule was departed from, or, as in this case, altogether subverted, belief in Jahveh's justice was imperilled. But it was much too deeply rooted to yield to one blow. By all sorts of ways men sought to decide the dispute that arose, and so to interpret the undeniable truth, that it should no longer contradict their faith. During the years which elapsed between Josiah's death and the fall of Jerusalem (608 to 586 B.C.), parties, or varieties of one and the same party, actually formed themselves, which differed from each other especially in the interpretation of Jahveh's justice in connection with Israel's fortunes. We shall pay attention to this shortly. But soon after Josiah's death, unless I be mistaken, the same problem was seriously considered in its application to the individual, and handled in the writings of the Israelitish "wise" men. At first their reflections had no influence worth mentioning upon the course of religious development. Yet they are remarkable enough to make us take cognizance of their results. By doing this we shall prepare ourselves for the better comprehension of the battle which was fought in the domain of politics and religion.

* Vol. I, p. 60, seq.

As early as the eighth century B.C. many of the "wise" had joined the prophets, and had brought the lessons derived from experience into harmony with the higher religious truth proclaimed by those intrepid champions of Jahvism.* It cannot surprise us, therefore, that the Chokmah-literature of the seventh century B.C. shows evident traces of this prophetic influence. It will be worth our while, however, to dwell for a few moments upon this phenomenon: the independence evinced by some of the wise acquires greater significance, when we find that the Chokmah usually followed the paths in which prophecy had preceded it. We remarked before, that the Deuteronomist clearly distinguishes himself from his predecessors among the prophets by the tone which he adopts: he is as much in earnest as they, but he is characterized besides by a certain fervour and conscientiousness, that make him press and persist, repeating, if need be, what he has already said once. Now in the seventh century B.C. proverbial poetry also had its Deuteronomist, the author of Proverbs, chap. i. 7—ix. It cannot be said that, compared with the wise who were before him, he brought new truths to light. Jahvism is his basis as it was theirs. "The fear of Jahveh is the beginning of wisdom:"† this is the theme of his exhortations, and he does not disown it for a single moment. His belief in Jahveh's justice, in the reward of those who fear God, and in the punishment of the ungodly, is unwavering, and is expressed as strongly as possible.‡ For provident and selfish reasons, it is true, but yet with emphasis, he exhorts men to honour Jahveh with gifts to the temple and to the priests.§ If in this alone he goes further than his predecessors, he also distinguishes himself from them by his doctrine of wisdom. He represents it as a person and introduces it acting and speaking.‖ In itself this personification is by no means strange. After the wise had delivered their lessons and

* Vol. I, p. 387, seq. † Prov. i. 7 a.
‡ Prov. ii. 21, 22 ; iii. 31-35 ; iv. 18, 19 ; v. 21-23. § Prov. iii. 9, 10.
‖ Prov. i. 20, seq. ; viii., ix.

proverbs in "the gate" for centuries together, men may easily have come to derive their doctrine from one source and to reduce it to one principle. But the form in which this is done deserves all our attention. Wisdom is regarded as an attribute of Jahveh, or rather, in accordance with the personification, as his companion and helper at the very creation of the world.* Hence it is that she reveals herself in all creation and can be perceived by man.† But at the same time it follows from this, that it is "Jahveh who giveth wisdom and that knowledge and understanding come out of his mouth."‡ This divine wisdom can testify of herself:

"Counsel is mine and sound wisdom,
I am understanding; I have strength;
By me kings reign
And princes decree justice;
By me princes rule
And nobles, even all the judges of the earth."§

The idea that true wisdom can only come from Jahveh is so firmly impressed upon the poet, that he considers wisdom of small account, so soon as it is regarded as the work of man. Hence the antithesis:

"Trust in Jahveh with all thine heart
And lean not on thine own understanding.
Know him in all thy ways
And he shall smooth thy paths.
Be not wise in thine own eyes,
Fear Jahveh and depart from evil."‖

But if so, we can understand how it is, that wisdom appears here purely in a prophetic form, and that exhortations and warnings are put into her mouth which have the greatest resemblance to what Jahveh himself utters through the prophets, and especially in Deuteronomy. To seek her and to

---

* Prov. viii. 22, seq. † Prov. iii. 19, 20. ‡ Prov. ii. 6.
§ Prov. viii. 14-16. ‖ Prov. iii. 5-7.

follow her, is, indeed, the same as to become a worshipper of Jahveh; the blessings which she confers upon her friends, the misfortunes which befall those who despise her, are the blessings and misfortunes which elsewhere are connected with fidelity to Jahveh and with apostasy from him.* To all this let there be added the conformity with Deuteronomy in tone and style.† Is it not very evident that the wise man by whom the first part of the book of Proverbs was written, joins hands with the priest-prophet whom we have learnt to know as the author of Deuteronomy, and works in his own sphere so entirely in the spirit of the latter, that the boundary between Chokmah and prophecy is more than once crossed?

Yet the individuality of the Chokmah was not lost. About the year of Josiah's death an unknown author wrote, perhaps in the desert of Judah, near Thekoa, the birthplace of the prophet Amos, that wonderfully beautiful poem, the book of Job. This is not the place to discuss it thoroughly. We can only consider it from the point of view of religious development. There is indeed no lack of guides to a true perception of the drift of the whole and of its details, and to a right estimation of the æsthetic value of the book.‡ Referring the reader to those guides, I confine myself here to that which falls within the limits of our subject.

When we attribute to the poet of the book of Job an individuality distinct from prophecy, it must not be understood that this "wise" man remained true to Solomon's example and, consequently, a stranger to the later and more spiritual development of Jahvism. The contrary is the case. He is a monotheist in the most absolute sense of the word. This appears not only from what he says in direct reference to

---

* Prov. i. 20-33; viii. 32-36; ix. 5, 6, 11. † Comp. my *Hk. O.* iii. 95, 96.

‡ Comp. in addition to my *Hk. O.* iii. 110-172, the article *Job* in the *Bijb. Woordenboek*, ii. 147-160 (by Veth); J. C. Matthes, *het boek Job vertaald en verklaard* (2 vols. Utrecht; 1865); the papers by Hoekstra and H. Oort, in the *Gids*, 1856, i. 585-642; 1867, i. 219-236; and the poetical rendering of the book of Job by ten Kate.

Jahveh, but also from the remarkable fact that he puts these sublime ideas into the mouths of men who are not Israelites, and makes Jahveh reveal himself to them.* Moreover, the persons who are introduced here as speaking, use throughout —one single place excepted—not the name Jahveh, but the older and more general designations, *El, Shaddai, Eloah*. War between Jahveh and the other gods exists no longer for the poet, it lies far behind him. This is so true, that men have been able to point, not without some show of justice, to the calm of his monotheism as a proof that he cannot have been a contemporary of Jeremiah, who all his life long had to contend against the worshippers of false gods; nay, we should admit this argument, had we to regard the poet as a representative of the sentiments of his day, in which case we should have to place him after the exile. His monotheism of course involves a very pure conception of Jahveh's being and the perfect recognition of his majesty and virtues. He is preeminently the pure one:

> "Shall mortal man be more just than God,
> A man more pure than his Maker?
> Even in his servants he putteth no trust,
> And he findeth folly in his angels!"†

the all-seeing and all-knowing one:

> "The kingdom of the dead is naked before God,
> And the gulf is without veil."‡

and the all-mighty one:

> "Who doeth great things, wholly unsearchable,
> Wonders without number;
> Who poureth out rain upon the earth
> And sendeth out waters upon the fields;

---

* Job xxxviii. seq.
† Job iv. 17, 18. Here and in the following quotations the author generally followed the translation of Dr. Matthes. ‡ Job xxvi. 6.

> Who will set up on high those that be low,
> And make happy those that mourn;
> Who disappointeth the devices of the crafty,
> So that their hands perform nothing real;
> Who taketh the wise in their own craftiness,
> And causeth the counsel of the cunning to fail."*

But it is unnecessary to go on in this strain. Let us simply remark, in addition, that the morality advanced by the poet is proportionate to the sublimity of his notion of God. As one proof out of many, I will name the beautiful chapter in which Job protests his innocence and enumerates various sins from which he is conscious that he is free :† even desire he would have imputed to himself as a sin ;‡ and, no less, want of pity towards the poor, the fatherless and the widow,§ and the unjust treatment of his male or female slaves, for have not both he and they one Creator and Maker ?|| All the rest agrees with these few instances.

No, the difference between the poet of Job and the prophets lies elsewhere, in the attitude of each with regard to the doctrine of recompense. How the prophets interpreted this doctrine, need not be repeated here; besides, we shall soon witness the conflict that they waged over it, although they agreed on the main point. The author of the Jobeid denies that God's retributive justice clearly manifests itself in the unequal fortunes of mankind, and above all that we are at liberty to decide upon a man's religious and moral character from his lot, whether it be prosperity or adversity. This is done by the three friends of the unhappy Job, who appear in the poem as the representatives of the popular belief. Their endless arguments amount to this, that the justice of God's dispositions cannot be doubted, that a man's life and his lot in life *must* correspond. If this connection be not at once appa-

---

* Job v. 9-13, comp. xii. 7, seq., &c. † Job xxxi.
‡ Ver. 1.   § Vers. 16, seq. || Vers. 13-15.

rent, it is because the sin of which the calamity is the punishment has remained unnoticed by or hidden from others. Or else the punishment has been deferred for a time, and will be accomplished afterwards upon the sinner himself or upon his children. Against these dogmas, which sometimes are also recommended by their similarity to the tradition of centuries, Job, in the depth of his abasement and misery, advances this one argument alone : the testimony of his conscience, which does not reproach him for any sin of which his great sufferings could be the penalty. Appealing repeatedly to this internal judge and to God, of whose cruelty he bitterly complains, Job repulses his friends' attacks, and at last silences them. They retire; he remains master of the field, and, no longer disturbed by their contradictions, can now reflect aloud, as it were, first upon the relative truth of their assertions and upon the inscrutableness of God's wisdom,* and then upon his fair past, his present adversity, and the testimony of his conscience.† But although he somewhat limits in the course of these reflections one or two things that he has said before, he does not arrive at a solution of the problem, nor at an insight into the wherefore of God's enigmatical dispensations. On the contrary, at the very end of that soliloquy he assumes a tone of deep grievance against God :

"O that one heard me!
Lo! here is my signature:
Let the Almighty give me an answer to it!
And the accusation-roll which my enemies wrote,
Verily, I will carry it upon my shoulder,
And bind it on me as a crown!
The number of my steps I will declare unto him,
Bold as a prince, I will approach him."‡

But now—for Elihu's arguments§ do not belong to the original book—Jahveh himself appears upon the scene to answer

* Job xxvii, xxviii. † Job xxix.-xxxi.
‡ Job xxxi. 35-37. § Job xxxii.-xxxvii.

Job. Will he dispel the obscurity and vindicate his government of the world? By no means. Both his addresses* are intended to show that Jahveh's might and wisdom manifest themselves in nature, and vain man is incapable of comprehending what God does, much less of altering it or improving upon it. Proof upon proof is furnished of God's supremacy. The first address, which concludes with the question:—

"Shall the fault-finder contend with the Almighty?
Let him that accuseth God give answer to this!"†

is enough to humble Job, who says:—

"Behold, I am too vile: what shall I answer thee?
I will lay mine hand upon my mouth.
Once have I spoken—but never again,
And twice—I will do so no more!"‡

Once again Jahveh speaks, now more particularly to make him observe God's might, and his own nothingness, in the wonderful structure of the hippopotamus and the crocodile. Deeply ashamed, Job asks forgiveness for his presumption:—

"I know that thou canst do everything,
And that for thee no plan is infeasible. . . . .
I have spoken without searching,
Things too wonderful for me, which I knew not. . . .
I had heard speak of thee,
But now mine eye hath seen thee:
Therefore I retract and I repent
In dust and ashes."§

The designs of the Almighty and All-wise are inscrutable to vile mortals: this is the result of the Jobeid. There is nothing left but faith, or, rather, blind submission to God's dispensation.

What a remarkable confession! By the mouth of this pious man, Israelitish Jahvism declares itself powerless to account

---

* Job xxxviii.-xl. 2 and xl. 6—xli. † Job xl. 2. ‡ Job xl. 4, 5.
§ Job xlii. 2-6.

for the truth which it cannot deny. On the one hand, its doctrine of recompense is gainsaid by experience time after time. Yet, on the other hand, it cannot be abandoned, for this, to the Israelite, would have been equal to denying God's justice, *i.e.* God's very existence. Nothing remains, therefore, but to hold fast to both hypotheses, in spite of their mutual antagonism. This dilemma is far from satisfactory. But there is no way of getting out of it. The epilogue of the poem* is a striking emblem of the difficulty in which the poet, and with him many a pious man of thought, was placed. He would have hurt the feelings of his readers, if he had allowed Job to die in his misery. He has no choice, therefore, but to describe his restoration to his former prosperity. That is to say: he must apply to the life of his hero that very doctrine of recompense which he does not entirely reject in his poem, it is true, but the universal applicability of which he has denied, nay, attacked as vigorously as possible. And let us not forget that it is by no means any flaw in his argument that reduces him to this necessity. On the contrary, it is just because he has grasped and rendered the facts as experience presented them to him, that he is forced to end with this concession. Therefore we repeat the observation with which we began : it was a difficult problem that the pious servant of Jahveh had to solve in those days. We ought to bear this in mind in the sequel of our investigations, which now return to political events and their influence upon religious development.

After the victory in the valley of Megiddo and the death of Josiah, Necho was master of the kingdom of Judah. Before he arrived there, " the people of the land" made Jehoahaz, a younger son of Josiah, king, presumably because he was more attached than his elder brother to his father's policy. At all events, Necho hastened to depose him and send him to Egypt: He was superseded by Eliakim, henceforward called Jehoiakim.†

* Job xlii. 7-17.   † 2 Kings xxiii. 31-35 ; 2 Chr. xxxvi. 1-4.

At first Jehoiakim was a vassal of Egypt, and it does not appear that he made any attempt to escape from this servitude. But it was not long before events occurred elsewhere in Asia that entirely changed his position. Nineveh had fallen; the Medes and the Chaldeans or Babylonians now ruled over the former territory of the Assyrians; Syria and Palestine fell to the share of the Babylonians. Of course, the Egyptians were not inclined to let them have undisputed possession. A battle was fought at Carchemish (Circesium), on the Euphrates, between the armies of Necho and Nebuchadnezzar, who then commanded in the name of his father, Nabopolassar, but very shortly afterwards succeeded him. The Egyptians sustained a crushing defeat (604 B.C.).* This decided the fate of Western Asia, including Judæa. A year or two after the victory at Carchemish, Jehoiakim had to submit to the Chaldeans (602 B.C.).† From that period all thoughts in Judæa were centred upon the possibility of deliverance. It does not appear that Jehoiakim himself and his successors took the initiative in the repeated attempts to shake off the yoke of the foreigner. The impression we receive is rather that they were pushed forward by the national desire for independence which showed itself strongly among the chief men and the courtiers, as well as among the populace of Jerusalem, led by the priests and by the much greater portion of the prophets. Three years after his submission, Jehoiakim declared his independence (599 or 598 B.C.).‡ Probably Nebuchadnezzar had his hands too full at this moment to march against him at once. He confined himself to ordering ravaging incursions into Judah's territory.§ Before he could proceed to more decisive measures, Jehoiakim had died and had been succeeded by his son Jehoiachin (Jechonia, 597 B.C.). Upon the latter descended the punishment for his father's revolt. After a reign of three months, he had to surrender with his capital to Nebuchadnezzar. The

---

* Jer. xlvi. 2. † 2 Kings xxiv. 1. ‡ 2 Kings xxiv. 1.
§ 2 Kings xxiv. 2.

latter deemed a severe chastisement necessary to keep the turbulent people under restraint : Jehoiachin himself and a number of the chief citizens of Jerusalem, the kernel of the nation, were carried prisoners to Babylon; the temple was plundered of part of its treasures; Mattaniah, a son of Josiah, ascended the throne as Zedekiah.* But even these violent measures turned out to be inadequate for the object in view. The great majority of the people and its leaders could not accommodate themselves to the subjection to the Babylonish conqueror. As early as the fourth year of Zedekiah's reign, an alliance with the neighbouring peoples (Edomites, Moabites, Ammonites, Phœnicians), the first step toward a rebellion against the Chaldeans, was prepared (594 B.C.).† For reasons unknown to us, this plan was not then carried out, but the feeling remained the same. The friends of liberty naturally turned their eyes to Egypt: without help from that quarter they could not possibly succeed. It may be that Necho was disinclined to involve himself in another war with the Chaldeans. At all events, it is worthy of notice that Zedekiah's revolt coincides with the accession of Necho's successor, Hophra (589 B.C.).‡ Nebuchadnezzar was not the man to be deterred by the prospect of a rupture with Egypt from punishing the rebels. On the 10th day of the 10th month of Zedekiah's ninth year his army appeared before Jerusalem (588 B.C.).§ Hophra, true to his promise, made an attempt to relieve the city, and compelled Nebuchadnezzar to raise the siege for a time. But his army must have been beaten. At all events, Jerusalem was soon surrounded again. At length, a year and a half after the first appearance of the Chaldeans under the walls—on the 9th day of the 4th month of Zedekiah's eleventh year (586 B.C.)—the city was captured. Severe judgment was dealt to the king,

---

* 2 Kings xxiv. 8-17; 2 Chr. xxxvi. 9, 10.   † Jer. xxvii., comp. li. 59-64.
‡ Comp. my *Hk. O.* ii. 168, n. 10.
§ See ibid. p. 200, sq., where the passages of which use is made in the sequel of this sketch, are quoted. Compare generally 2 Kings xxv. 1-21; Jer lii. 1-30.

who had tried in vain to save himself by flight. When the
city and the temple had been plundered, they were given up to
the flames. Again a number of the inhabitants of Jerusalem
and of the rural districts were carried away into exile. Gedaliah the son of Ahikam was appointed governor over those that
remained, and established himself at Mizpah. At first he
seemed to meet with some success in his attempts to reunite
the scattered Judæans. But the jealousy of the Ammonitish
king, Baalis, worked the destruction of even this small remnant
of the kingdom of Judah. Ishmael the son of Nethaniah, in-
stigated by Baalis, killed Gedaliah, and although the interven-
tion of other captains prevented him from making the Judæans
migrate to Ammon, in accordance with his plan, yet, after this
atrocity, further residence in Judæa was not to be thought of.
Such, at least, was the opinion of most men. They were afraid
of being charged with and punished for the murder of Gedaliah, and resolved to migrate to Egypt.* The aged prophet
Jeremiah was obliged to accompany them against his will, and
died there. A comparatively few scattered inhabitants in the
rural districts were all that were now left in Judæa. The
Israelitish nation had ceased to exist in its native land.†

These were momentous times in the history of the kingdom
of Judah. The spectacle they present to us is interesting in
itself. A small nation, warmly attached to its independence,
struggling to preserve it, and to win it back when lost, but
succumbing in that struggle: who could witness this scene
with indifference ? But this period becomes doubly interesting
to us, when we notice the commotions and mutual strife of the
religious parties. Our information in this regard is tolerably
complete. The historians can tell us nothing more of the last
four kings of Judah than the monotonous: " he did that which
was evil in the sight of Jahveh, according to all that his fathers

---

* In 581 B.C. ? Comp. II. Oort, *Jeremia in de lijst van zijn tijd*, pp. 160, sq.

† The events subsequent to the fall of Jerusalem we know from Jer xl. 1.—xliii·
7; comp. 2 Kings xxv. 22-26.

had done."* All that we can infer from this is, that there was a material difference between them and Josiah their predecessor; wherein that difference lay, this adverse verdict does not inform us. But we are able to consult other sources. The prophet Habakkuk and the unknown writer whose oracular utterances are contained in chaps. xii.-xiv. of the book of Zechariah, belong to this period. Jeremiah, who made his first appearance in the thirteenth year of Josiah (626 B.C.), lived to see the fall of Jerusalem and the events that succeeded it. In the fourth and fifth years of Jehoiakim's reign (604 and 603 B.C.) he began to write down his addresses.† From that time, with Baruch's assistance, he continued to commit to writing his own prophecies and the narrative of his adventures, which also throw light upon the political and religious condition of the people. Shortly after the destruction of Jerusalem, the prophecy of Obadiah was brought to its present form. The Lamentations too, the last alone excepted, were composed then. Among the exiles who had lived on the banks of the Chebar since 597 B.C., Ezekiel appears as a prophet as early as the year 592 B.C.; before he was carried off he served as a priest in the temple at Jerusalem, and afterwards he was well informed of what went on in his native land; we have him to thank for more than one important piece of information. And finally, it is as good as certain that some of the penitential psalms belong to this period. Of no other period of Israel's history do we possess such abundant and trustworthy evidence.

The first significant fact that we learn from these eyewitnesses, is the revival of idolatry. Habakkuk mentions it but once—we shall see why presently—if, at least, we may assume that this sin also is included in the "iniquity" and the "grievance" of which he complains.‡ The author of Zech. xii.-xiv. is more lucid. He looks forward longingly to the time when "Jahveh of hosts shall cut off the names of the idols out

---

* 2 Kings xxiii. 32, 37; xxiv. 9, 19; 2 Chr. xxxvi. 5, 9, 12.
† Jer. xxxvi. ‡ Hab. i. 3, 4.

of the land, so that they shall no more be remembered."*
When he states further, that many prophets are actuated by
the "unclean spirit," one is led to conjecture that they encouraged the service of the strange gods, or even prophesied in
their name.† It is Jeremiah especially, however, who enters
into details upon this subject. It is not always possible to
determine when he is speaking of the past, and when of his
own contemporaries. But this in itself is full of significance,
for it proves that no real difference existed between the state
of affairs before the eighteenth year of Josiah's reign, and that
of which the prophet was a witness under Jehoiakim and his
successors. He does not hesitate, either, to say to his hearers:
"Your fathers have forsaken Jahveh and followed after other
gods . . . . *but ye have done worse than your fathers.*"‡
Sometimes he confines himself to the complaint that his contemporaries serve "other gods," "the Baalim," or "Baal"—
equal in his mouth to "the false gods"—and burn incense to
them.§ At other times he mentions particularly the worship
of the false gods on hills and under green trees.|| He would
not have proved so indignant at the Molech-worship,¶ which
was practised largely on the topheth in the neighbourhood of
Jerusalem, if all traces of it had been wiped out. It would
seem that the temple at Jerusalem was again polluted with
idols,** and that the burning of incense to "the host of heaven"
was resumed.†† And "the queen of heaven" especially, *i.e.*
the moon-goddess, Astarte, is zealously worshipped by men
and women, with all the ceremonies pertaining to her service.‡‡
Jeremiah had still to combat this form of idolatry in Egypt.
The inhabitants of the kingdom of Judah had served this goddess "in the cities of Judah and in the streets of Jerusalem."

---

* Zech. xiii. 2. † Zech. xiii. 2-6. ‡ Jer. xvi. 11, 12.
§ Jer. ix. 12, seq.; xiii. 10; xviii. 15; xxii. 9.
|| Jer. xiii. 27; xvii. 2, seq., comp. ii. 20; iii. 6, 13.
¶ Jer. vii. 31; xix. 4, 5, 11-13; xxxii. 35, comp. 30.
** Jer. vii. 30; xxxii. 34. †† Jer. xix. 13. ‡‡ Jer. vii. 16-19.

Nay, they themselves declared that from the moment that they ceased to honour her (openly and officially), *i.e.* from the eighteenth year of Josiah's reign, all sorts of misfortunes had befallen them.* If Jeremiah, in an oracle uttered before Josiah's reformation, but not written down till after it, could speak in this way :—

"As a thief is made ashamed when he is found,
So stands the house of Israel ashamed,
They, their kings, princes, priests, and prophets,
Who say to a stock, 'Thou art my father!'
And to a stone, 'Thou hast brought me forth!'
For they have turned their back unto me, and not their face,
But in their trouble they will say, 'Arise and save us!'
But—where are thy gods that thou hast made thee?
Let them arise, that they may save thee in thy trouble!
For as numerous as thy cities have thy gods become, O Judah!"†

he repeats these last words in the reign of Jehoiakim, and adds :—

"According to the number of the streets of Jerusalem have ye set up altars to the 'shameful thing,'
Altars to burn incense unto Baal!"‡

When we open Ezekiel's prophecies, we find Jeremiah's statements confirmed. Our attention is especially attracted by his description of what took place in or around the temple at Jerusalem.§ It has been suspected, not without reason, that he refers to earlier times, and particularly to the reign of Manasseh. But when we reflect how Ezekiel speaks of his contemporaries,‖ it is difficult to believe that an end was put to these practices under Zedekiah. He too makes mention more than once of the Moloch-worship.¶ He expressly adds

---

* Jer. xliv. 7-9, 17, seq.
† Jer. ii. 26-28 ; comp. iii. 6, seq. ; iv. 1 ; v. 7, 19.   ‡ Jer. xi. 13.
§ Ezek. viii., comp. Note I. at the end of this chapter.   ‖ Ezek. xx. 30, seq.
¶ Ezek. xvi. 20, 21 ; xx. 30, 31 ; xxiii. 37-39.

that those who dedicated their sons and daughters to the false gods by fire, afterwards appeared in Jahveh's sanctuary, and so defiled it.* Jeremiah also knows frequenters of the temple who at the same time burn incense in honour of Baal†—with him, as has been said, a general name for the false gods. Therefore both bear witness—and we should assume it even without their assurance—that the worshippers of the other gods did *not* intend to substitute them for Jahveh, and thus to sever the connection between him and Israel. Like their forefathers, they only repudiated the *exclusive* Jahveh-worship, of which the prophets, whose evidence we have collected, were the vigorous defenders. Their Jahvism, however, partly in consequence of increased intercourse with other countries, was even more mixed than that of the common multitude in the 8th century B.C. And, moreover, this mixed Jahvism, the prophets assure us, was not the religion of the few, but of the majority of the people.

We should mistake at once the nature and the extent of these phenomena, were we to imagine that they can be explained by pointing to the statement of the historian, that Josiah's successors " did that which was evil in the sight of Jahveh." In any case it would devolve upon us to explain the nature of this " evil-doing." But even if we succeeded in so doing, such an appeal to the example and influence of the kings would still be quite unsatisfactory. However great we suppose their power to have been, and however strong the pressure that they brought to bear, they remain insufficient to account for the sudden restoration of the service of the false gods. But besides this, Jehoiakim and Zedekiah—the other two only reigned three months each—were, unless we are altogether deceived, not at all powerful princes, who applied themselves to alter the religious condition of the nation, or would have been capable of effecting a change. Josiah was

---

* Ezek. xxiii. 38, 39. † Jer. vii. 9, 10, comp. 6.

the man of zeal and power who had tried to do so, and had really succeeded. His successors did nothing more than—let things alone. But this, of itself, was enough to revive the old forms which Josiah had opposed. So little had the violent measures of that pious king effected, so deeply rooted in the majority were the craving to serve and the habit of serving other gods besides Jahveh. It is far from improbable that during the sole domination of strict Jahvism in the second half of Josiah's reign, the Mosaic party increased in number. To this extent the reformation gained its end. But in other respects Jeremiah was not wrong, when he asked:—

"Shall the Ethiopian change his skin,
Or the leopard his spots?
Shall ye also do good,
Who have been taught to do evil?"*

Ezekiel even goes so far as to ascribe to his contemporaries the intention to become " as the nations, as the families of the countries, serving wood and stone"—although he assures them at the same time that Jahveh shall compel them " with a mighty hand and a stretched out arm and with fury poured out" to acknowledge him as their god, "until all the house of Israel serve him upon his holy mountain."† Can words declare more plainly, that *as yet* exclusive Jahvism is not the religion suited to the minds and the hearts of the Israelites? that when left to themselves, they walked in the ways of the heathen?

But this "left to themselves" is a supposition opposed to the reality. The Mosaic party—as we have already said—continued stronger than ever, and did not lose sight of its aim. From this time its different varieties claim our attention, for we perceive at the first glance that its unity is broken.

Like Isaiah and Micah, but in a much higher degree, Jeremiah and Ezekiel are opposed to " the prophets." Jeremiah, especially, wages unceasing war against them, and pays back with interest in reproaches and accusations the treatment that he

* Jer. xiii. 23. † Ezek. xx. 32-40.

receives at their hands. From the fact that he does not charge them with idolatry, at all events in his later prophecies, we unhesitatingly conclude that they were not guilty of it. In one passage* he himself compares the prophets of Samaria with those of Jerusalem; of the former he says that "they prophesied in Baal's name and caused Jahveh's people Israel to err," and of the latter, that they "commit adultery, walk in lies, and encourage the evil doers, so that they do not return from their wickedness." In fact, Jeremiah's great complaint against the Jahveh prophets of his time is, that instead of preaching repentance as he does, they set their hearers at ease and predict them a glorious future. "Sword and famine shall not rage in this land," they say.† And again, "Ye shall not see the sword, and famine shall not hurt you, for Jahveh shall give you unbroken peace in this place."‡ To those who despise Jahveh—so he describes their preaching in another passage—they say, "Jahveh hath said, 'Ye shall have peace;'" to every one that walks in the wickedness of his own heart, "No evil shall come upon you."§ Ezekiel also reproaches them that they speak of "peace," where there is no peace.‖—We learn best how to interpret all this from Jeremiah's meeting with Hananiah the Gibeonite. In the fourth year of Zedekiah's reign, while plans of rebellion against Nebuchadnezzar were being laid, Jeremiah appeared in the temple with a yoke, the symbol of slavery, on his neck. He earnestly warned the people against the rash step which it was proposed to take: no blessing would rest upon the enterprise; on the contrary, it could not but result in the destruction of the state.¶ This prophecy of misfortune was answered by Hananiah. He too spoke in the name of Jahveh of hosts, but his prediction was of quite another purport: Jahveh shall break the yoke of the king of Babylon; within two years the holy vessels that Nebuchadnezzar has taken from the temple, shall be brought back,

---

* Jer. xxiii. 13, 14, comp. 27.   † Jer. xiv. 15.   ‡ Jer. xiv. 13.
§ Jer. xxiii. 17.   ‖ Ezek. xiii. 10, 16.   ¶ Jer. xxvii.

and Jehoiachin with the rest of the exiles shall return to his native land.* Jeremiah was ready with his reply: if he (Jeremiah) had spoken of war, and famine and pestilence, his predecessors had also prophesied in the same spirit; Hananiah, who foretold quite another future, could not be recognized as an envoy of Jahveh, until events had confirmed his words.† But Hananiah will not allow himself to be driven from the field: he snatches the yoke from Jeremiah's neck and breaks it to pieces in the presence of all the people in the temple: "So," he says, "shall Jahveh break the yoke of Nebuchadnezzar king of Babylon from the neck of all nations in two years."‡ For the moment Jeremiah was unable to answer him: it was not until afterwards that he repeated his prediction, and then declared also, that Hananiah, as a punishment for his deception, would die that very year. "And Hananiah the prophet died the same year, in the seventh month."§

Before we try to understand the contest of which this incident makes us witnesses, let us see what supporters the two parties had. The great majority sided with Hananiah, nay, more than this, Jeremiah fought almost alone. He pours out bitter complaints at the charges and ill-treatment to which he is exposed.‖ One of his allies, Urijah the son of Shemaiah, who prophesied against the city and the land "according to all the words of Jeremiah," was obliged in Jehoiakim's reign to flee to Egypt, to save his life, but was fetched back and put to death with the sword.¶ At the same time Jeremiah himself, in consequence of the discourse which has been preserved to us in the seventh chapter of his prophecies, was accused of blaspheming Jahveh's sanctuary by talking of its approaching destruction. It was "the priests and the prophets" who brought this charge against him, "the princes of Judah" who investigated it. When Jeremiah repeated his prediction in

---

* Jer. xxviii. 1-4. † Jer. xxviii. 5-9.
‡ Jer. xxviii. 10-11. § Jer. xxviii. 12-17. Comp. my *Hk. O.* ii. 196, n. 5.
‖ Chap. xi. and elsewhere. ¶ Jer. xxvi. 20-24.

their presence and declared that Jahveh had put it into his mouth, the princes refused to pronounce sentence of death upon him, and there stood up men from among "the elders of the land," who, pointing to the example of Micah,* maintained the prophet's right to threaten even the holy city and the temple.† For the moment this feeling prevailed. But the opposite party did not abandon the persecution. While Jehoiakim was still on the throne, it would seem, Jeremiah was arrested upon one occasion by the governor of the temple and was not released till the next day‡—an occurrence that drew bitter complaints from him.§ When, in Zedekiah's reign, he exhorted the exiles who had been carried away with Jehoiachin to submit calmly, the Jerusalem priesthood received letters urging them to do their duty and imprison Jeremiah.‖ At length, during the last siege of Jerusalem, Jeremiah was deprived of his liberty, and did not regain it till after the conquest. The narrative of his sufferings during this period belongs to the story of his life, which cannot be told here.¶ I have given enough of it to show that Jeremiah pulled against the stream, while his opponents were backed by the people and their leaders.

This does not, indeed, surprise us. Hananiah and, in general, the prophets who agreed with him, were merely the representatives of the popular desires and expectations. Full of faith in Jahveh's might, penetrated with the conviction that he stood in the most intimate relation to Israel, gazing on the temple dedicated to him, in which the smoke of sacrifices ascended in his honour,—they were convinced that the humiliation of Jahveh's people could but be transitory. In the series of disasters which commenced with the death of Josiah, they could see nothing but signs of an approaching change. And especially after the removal of Jehoiachin and the partial plundering of the temple, the deliverance and glorification of Israel seemed to them to be

---

* Mic. iii. 12, comp. Vol. I, p. 40.   † Jer. xxxi. 1-19.   ‡ Jer. xx. 1-6.
§ Jer. xx. 7-13, 14-18.   ‖ Jer. xxix. 24-32.
¶ Comp. my *Hk. O.* ii. 200, seq.; Oort, *Jeremia*, pp. 127, seq.

at hand. Would Jahveh suffer his sanctuary to be desecrated by strangers and his people to be oppressed any longer? In their eyes this was an absurdity. His justness would not allow it. The Chaldean would soon receive his due, and Israel would reap the fruits of the zeal with which it had observed the commandments of Jahveh's law since Josiah's reformation.

But—surely they could not talk of having observed the law? Was it not openly broken by very many of them? Our preceding investigations show that we must reply in the affirmative. Some of the divergences, indeed, were so glaring, that every one who belonged to the Mosaic party must have seen them, and consequently have desired that they should be discontinued. But it is easily conceivable, that there were some who thought this of minor importance and considered judgment upon the Chaldeans much more urgent. It seemed to them that it was necessary *before all things* that Jahveh should maintain his honour and avenge the desecration of Zion. This judgment would include at the same time the purification of Israel, so far as was requisite. In fact, we can very well imagine that earnest men held these opinions, and in prophetic ecstasy gave utterance to their ideas of the state of affairs at that time and of the immediate future as Jahveh's word. And what is more, we have documents to prove it. Habakkuk and the author of Zech. xii.-xiv, may not have encouraged the rebellion against Nebuchadnezzar, and may thus have distinguished themselves from Hananiah. But their expectations have a greater resemblance to his than to the sombre views of Jeremiah.

There is a slight difference of opinion as to the year in which Habakkuk's prophecy was written: he must have made his appearance either immediately after the battle of Carchemish (604 B.C.), or a few years later, not long after Jehoiachin's removal (597 B.C.); the latter is the more likely. He is not blind to the sins of his nation. But he has scarcely begun to lament over them,* before he interrupts himself and points to the much greater abominations of which the Chaldeans have been guilty, and which they still commit.† Will Jahveh let these iniquities go unpunished, he, "who is purer of eyes than to behold evil?"‡ It is impossible! And before long he learns from Jahveh that the judgment is approaching: "it will surely come and not tarry."§ He seems already to hear the nations that were conquered by the Chaldean crying, Woe! unto him, and rejoicing in his fall.‖ It is true that his heart trembles at the thought of the terrible things that are at hand, and of which Judah will receive its share, but he does not doubt the final issue for a moment:

> "Thou (Jahveh) wentest forth for the salvation of thy people,
> For the salvation of thine anointed.¶
> *   *   *   *   *
> I will leap for joy in Jahveh,
> I will rejoice in the God of my salvation.
> Jahveh the Lord is my strength;
> He maketh my feet like hind's feet,
> And maketh me to walk upon mine high places." **

So the oppressor is punished and Jahveh's people escape the danger which threatens them.††—This is what Habakkuk writes. If a man such as he adopted this tone, is it to be wondered at, that the people and their leaders added the deed to the word, and, as often as an opportunity presented itself, instead of "waiting quietly for the day of trouble,"‡‡ rushed to arms to hasten the hour of their deliverance?

The writer of Zech. xii.-xiv., who perhaps appeared a few years later, held opinions akin to those of Habakkuk. Was he, like Micah, a countryman? We should infer this from the idea which he forms of the future. In his eyes, Jerusalem had been

---

* Hab. i. 2-4. † Hab. i. 5-17. ‡ Hab. i. 13.
§ Hab. ii. 3. ‖ Hab. ii. 6-20. ¶ Hab. iii. 13 a.
** Hab. iii. 18, 19 a. †† Hab. iii. ‡‡ Hab. iii. 16.

guilty of a great sin, on account of which her citizens, headed by the house of David, would humble themselves deeply with loud lamentations.* Perhaps it is for that reason that Jahveh "shall save the tents of Judah first, that the glory of the house of David and of the inhabitants of Jerusalem do not magnify itself against Judah."† A great catastrophe is at hand. The nations gather themselves together against Jerusalem and make war upon her. At first they seem to succeed in their object; the city is taken and plundering begins. But at this moment Jahveh appears, to fight the nations. In the midst of terrible natural phenomena he executes judgment upon them. Jerusalem and the temple are spared, and remain the centre of the worship of Jahveh.‡ The prophet does not deny—the very description of the city's distress proves it—that the people of Jahveh, and especially the population of Jerusalem, are sinful and unclean. Yet he does not despair of the accomplishment of the great events which he announces. He looks forward to the time when idolatry and the prophetic order, of which he evidently has a very low opinion, shall be rooted out,§ and a stream of living water shall purge David's house and Jerusalem's inhabitants,|| and spread fruitfulness also over the whole land.¶ Thus it is a new, a regenerate Jerusalem that will remain after the judgment.** From that time forward the nations of the earth shall go up thither every year to keep the feast of tabernacles in Jahveh's honour: those who stay away shall be severely punished; the whole city shall be sacred to Jahveh, and become, as it were, his temple.†† There is much that is fantastic in this description; much too that remains an enigma to us, because we only half know the circumstances of the time. But we certainly are not mistaken in our estimation of the author's standpoint, when we place him half way between Habakkuk and Jeremiah. He is more distressed than the

---

* Zech. xii. 10-14.   † Zech. xii. 7. comp. 5.   ‡ Zech. xii. xiv.
§ Zech. xiii. 2-6. || Zech. xiii. 1.   ¶ Zech. xiv. 8.
** Zech. xiv. 9-11.   †† Zech. xiv. 16-21.

former by the wickedness that he sees in his contemporaries; therefore his idea of the future, or rather of the events which will introduce it, is less brilliant. But he too—and therefore we called his opinions akin to those of Habakkuk—expects that before long Israel will be exalted. He too considers her safety guaranteed by Jahveh's justice, and by the relation in which he stands to her.

Now in what does the difference between these men and Jeremiah consist? It cannot be said that they hold another creed. How can that be possible? Habakkuk and the unknown author of Zech. xii.-xiv. uttered the very same conviction that had been declared about a hundred years before by Isaiah.* Jeremiah will also agree with him. No, the difference between Jeremiah and his contemporaries arises from his views and estimation of the religious-moral condition of the people. As we have already pointed out,† his opinion of this condition is most unfavourable. He is not misled by appearances. He does not allow the fact that the multitude regularly frequent the temple to persuade him that they are true to Jahveh. His eyes are fully open to the manifold sins of the people, the extortions of the great, the theft, murder, adultery and false swearing which he sees around him.‡ Let it not be imagined that, inspired with a sort of misanthropy, he takes a delight in seeing and exposing all this wickedness. On the contrary, it is a source of deep sorrow to him, for he loves his nation with all his heart, and would gladly give his life to rescue her from the error of her ways. "Oh," he cries, "Oh, that my head were waters and mine eyes a fountain of tears, that I could weep day and night for the slain of my people."§ Jeremiah's feelings were extremely sensitive, and, had it been possible, he would have avoided the spectacle of Israel's sins and meditation upon their deplorable consequences. It speaks well for him, therefore, that in spite of this and the opposition

* See Vol. I., p. 40. † Comp. pp. 57, sq.
‡ Jer. vii. 5, 6, 9, and elsewhere. § Jer. viii. 23.

which he had to expect, he accepted his vocation and came forward as a prophet. This sensitiveness naturally made the internal struggle more severe. If at first he flattered himself with the hope that his preaching would work a change for the better, he must gradually have given up that hope. The sad events that followed Josiah's death must have robbed him of all that was then left of these cheerful anticipations. At all events, when, four years afterwards, he caused his prophecies, which already extended over a period of twenty-three years, to be written down, he evidently took it for granted that he should not succeed.* But could he, then, simply acquiesce in all this? Could he accept the subjection of his people, first by the Egyptians and then by the Chaldeans, as he would any other dispensation of Jahveh? On the contrary, it was just this that cost him the most bitter agony. One of two things must happen. Either Jahveh must mitigate in some measure the rigour of his demands, and be content with a half-dedication of Israel to his service, or Israel's chastisement, the foretaste of which was already being felt, would be accomplished in full and her independent existence would cease. According to Jeremiah it is the latter alone that can happen.

It was not without a cruel struggle that he brought himself to this. Nay, even after this conviction had been forced upon him, he fought against the duty of asserting it publicly. Read his bitter complaint:

"Thou hast deceived me, Jahveh, and I allowed myself to be deceived;
Thou hast overcome me and hast prevailed;
So am I become a derision the whole day long, they all mock me!
For whenever I speak, I must shout, and cry 'violence' and 'spoil';
For the word of Jahveh is a reproach unto me, and a derision the whole day long.

* Jer. xxxvi. comp. xxv. 1, seq.

And if I say, 'I will not make mention of him nor speak
any more in his name'—

Then it becomes in my heart as a burning fire shut up in
my bones,

And I weary myself to keep it within me, but I cannot
do it."*

In truth, we are not surprised to hear him complain in this way. He drew down derision and persecution upon his head; but, besides this, he had the appearance of being a traitor to his country. When, under Jehoiakim and especially Zedekiah, the fire of rebellion was smouldering and occasionally burst into flame, he did not cease to exhort the people to submission and humiliation, or to shake the courage of the rebels by his prophecies of misfortune. We do not for a moment suspect the purity of his intentions. But it is a fact, that during the siege of Jerusalem (588-586 B.C.), he did all that lay in his power to make the defence fail, and that his preaching was practised by those who—deserted to the enemy.† It was a sad, I had almost said, a humiliating part that Jeremiah found himself called upon to play. Is it to be wondered at, that in a moment of despair he cursed the day of his birth?‡

But while we admit this candidly, and judge Jeremiah's opponents leniently on this account, we wish at the same time to give him the praise which is his just due. From the point of view of Jahvism he was the great man. He had comprehended Jahveh's being and the rigour of his moral requirements, and they had made so deep and indelible an impression upon him, that he could deny them no longer. Therefore, however painful it may have been to him, he held fast to what, in our estimation, forms the real significance and the lasting value of the Jahvistic idea. The Jahvism of the rest was, in truth, subordinate to their patriotism; Jeremiah's stood above it; when the difficult task of choosing between the two was

---

* Jer. xx. 7-9.   † Comp. Jer. xxi. 9; xxxviii. 2, 17, 23.
‡ Jer. xx. 14-18.

imposed upon him, he preferred to be a bad citizen to his country rather than an unfaithful servant to Jahveh. We have drawn attention more than once to the intimate connection between Israel's religion and her nationality. In ordinary times these two could live together in peace. But there was always the possibility of a conflict between them, and, under certain circumstances, it was unavoidable. We easily perceive now, that the destiny of Israel's religion to become the property of mankind could not be accomplished unless the ties between this religion and the people among which it was born and grew up, were loosened. This gives a special interest to the repeated struggles between Jahvism and Jewish nationality, for they belong to the history of the world. We do not say that Jeremiah wished to sever that bond: we are about to perceive that the contrary is true. But he prepared this separation, as far as he was able and circumstances permitted. If his contemporaries, who encouraged the national cravings, gained the applause of the many, he had to bear their reproach, but then he lived and laboured for the future and for mankind.

But we must hasten to quit the domain of general considerations and return to facts. In attempting to show what Jeremiah at last achieved, by virtue of his conception of Jahveh's being, we run the risk of giving an incorrect idea of what he himself desired and taught. We repeat: Jeremiah did not sever the bond between Jahveh and Israel; it never even entered his thoughts to do so; it could not enter his thoughts. When necessity demanded it, he did not consider his belief in Israel's existence as a nation and in the inviolability of the temple too precious to sacrifice to the pure conception of Jahveh's being. That is all. Others had already preceded him on that road,* but he had the courage and the self-denial

---

* Mic. iii. 12; iv. 10. Comp. also Am. v. 27; Hos. ix. 3, &c. It must not be forgotten, however, that these threats date from an earlier period, long before Josiah's reformation.

to go on in their footsteps, when the loss of the goodwill of the people, nay, even of the better disposed, was connected with it, when his life was endangered by it. For the rest, he was not able, even less able than his predecessors, to imagine Jahveh without Israel and Israel without Jahveh. As yet there was but one people that knew and served "the living god;"* its destruction would at the same time have been that of Jahvism. This, therefore, was not to be thought of. Jeremiah too believed — nay, was forced to believe — in a future for his people, in the restoration, therefore, of its independent existence as a nation. It certainly will not be superfluous to consider somewhat more minutely the form which these expectations assumed in his mind.

In the collection of prophecies which Jeremiah dictated to his servant Baruch in the 4th and 5th years of Jehoiakim's reign, he also set forth his ideas as to the future of the heathen.† Let us begin by making ourselves acquainted with them. These utterances against the heathen are generally marked by a certain uniformity and by their close resemblance to the earlier prophets, whose predictions are sometimes borrowed word for word. The fate that Jeremiah announces to those nations—Egyptians, Philistines, Moabites, &c.—is sad: Nebuchadnezzar will invade and subjugate them, and some he will even utterly destroy. But with respect to Egypt, Moab, Ammon and Elam, a hope is expressed at the end, although only in a single word, that "Jahveh will turn their captivity"— give them back their former prosperity.‡ The prophet repeated this prediction some time afterwards§ in reference to Judah's neighbours—partly, therefore, to the same nations—but he made it depend upon a condition, to which we shall revert immediately.‖ First we must examine Jeremiah's ideas as to the future of his own nation.

Whatever he may have thought before of the judgment that

---

* Jer. xxiii. 36, comp. x. 10. † Jer. xlvi.-xlix.
‡ Jer. xlvi. 26; xlviii. 47; xlix. 6, 39. § Jer. xii. 15. ‖ Jer. xii. 16, 17.

was awaiting Judah, when he summed up his labours of 23 years in the 4th year of Jehoiakim's reign, as we have already mentioned, he felt certain that his nation would be carried away into exile.* But while he expressed this conviction, he added immediately afterwards, that its existence as a nation would only cease temporarily. Judah shall serve Nebuchadnezzar *seventy years*—was then his prediction.† Subsequently, in a letter to the exiles, this was repeated,‡ while about the same time it was asserted that Judah and her neighbours would serve *Nebuchadnezzar, his son and his grandson*, until Babylon's time should also have come.§ We gather from these passages, that Jeremiah pictured to himself a long exile for Judah. Seventy is a round number, and the prophet himself did not intend it to be taken literally.|| When that time has elapsed, judgment will be executed upon Babylon: it is true that Jeremiah calls Nebuchadnezzar "Jahveh's servant,"¶ but only in so far as he carries out the divine sentence; he and his people remain responsible for their actions and shall not escape their well-deserved punishment. The fall of Babylon and the restoration of Israel will be simultaneous. From all quarters of the world, wherever they have been carried, the children of Israel will return to their native land,** Ephraimites as well as the tribe of Judah, in fact the former will return first. This agrees with the comparatively favourable verdict which the prophet pronounces upon the exiles from the kingdom of the ten tribes.†† In one of his oldest prophecies‡‡ he places them much above the men of his own tribe. This preference is certainly not based upon a minute comparison of the religious-moral condition of the two kingdoms. It arises rather from the very dismal impression that "treacherous Judah"—as he calls her in contradistinction from "backsliding Israel"—has made upon

---

* Jer. xxv. 9, seq.   † Jer. xxv. 12.   ‡ Jer. xxix. 10.   § Jer. xxvii. 7.
|| Comp. my *Hk. O.* II. 217, sq. and *Nieuw en Oud*, New Series, II. 269, seq.
¶ Jer. xxv. 9; xxvii. 6; xliii. 10.   ** Jer. xxiii. 7, 8, and elsewhere.
†† Jer. iii. 11, seq.; xxxi. 4-6.   ‡‡ Jer. iii. 6—iv. 2

the prophet, an impression so sad that he cannot imagine Ephraim's depravity to be still greater. But it is also connected with the fact that at that time the Ephraimites had already been in exile for more than a century. This excites Jeremiah's pity, and he readily believes in their inclination to repent. For the same reasons, in the beginning of Zedekiah's reign, he places Jehoiachin and his fellow exiles very far above their brethren in Judah, upon whom the judgment had not yet been accomplished.* We are not surprised, therefore, that the Ephraimites take precedence in Israel's restoration to national existence, and that Judah returns after them and joins them. They have all repented together of their former errors, which are now no longer remembered, for "Jahveh shall cleanse them from all their iniquity which they have committed against him, and pardon all the sins which they have sinned against him."† Jahveh and his people start afresh, as it were. "The days come, saith Jahveh, that I will make a new covenant with the house of Israel and with the house of Judah; not according to the covenant that I made with their fathers in the day when I took them by the hand to bring them out of Egypt, for my covenant they brake, although I was their master, saith Jahveh. But this is the covenant that I will make with the house of Israel after those days, saith Jahveh: I will put my law in their inward parts and will write it in their hearts, and will be their god and they shall be my people. And they shall teach no more every man his neighbour and every man his brother, saying, 'know Jahveh!' —for they shall all know me, saith Jahveh, from the least unto the greatest; for I shall forgive their iniquity and remember their unrighteousness no more."‡ The people thus restored and regenerate will be again ruled by David's descendants. It is said generally that "their (Israel's) head shall be of themselves and their governor shall proceed from the midst of them; I, Jahveh, will cause him to draw near, and he shall approach me; for who is he that hath engaged his heart to approach unto

---

* Jer. xxiv. † Jer. xxxiii. 8. ‡ Jer. xxxi. 31-34.

me? saith Jahveh."* Here, therefore, the prophet excludes all foreign dominion, and states at the same time that the king of Israel, dedicated to Jahveh, shall have free access to him. Elsewhere he unequivocally expresses his anticipation that this king will be a descendant of David: "I will set up shepherds over them which shall feed them, and they shall know fear and dismay no more, neither shall they be lost, saith Jahveh. Behold, the days come, saith Jahveh, that I will raise unto David a righteous branch,† and he shall reign as king and prosper, and shall execute judgment and justice in the land. In his days Judah shall be saved and Israel dwell safely, and this is the name whereby men shall call him [all Israel], 'Jahveh is our righteousness.'"‡ And in another passage, "they shall serve Jahveh their god, and David their king, whom I will raise up unto them."§ It is only apparently that mention is made here of a single Davidic king. The prophet expects that the princes of this race—the shepherds whom he named in the first instance‖—will succeed each other without interruption and will all, without distinction, answer to the description which he gives, for in each of them David their forefather will live again. Under their rule Israel will enjoy uninterrupted prosperity. Her enemies shall be rendered harmless and shall set foot in the land no more.¶ Jerusalem shall be rebuilt** and greatly enlarged,†† even as her population shall be much more numerous than before.‡‡ The cities of Judah and the streets of Jerusalem shall again echo, as in former times, with "the voice of joy and the voice of gladness, the voice of the bridegroom and the voice of the bride, the voice of them that say, 'praise Jahveh of hosts, for he is good, for his mercy endureth for ever.'"§§ There shall be an abundance of corn and wine and oil and sheep and oxen; the

---

* Jer. xxx. 21.
† Perhaps more correctly, "righteous sprout" (zémach), i.e. offspring.
‡ Jer. xxiii. 4-6.   § Jer. xxx. 9.   ‖ Jer. xxiii. 4.
¶ Jer. xxxiii. 9, and elsewhere.   ** Jer. xxx. 18.   †† Jer. xxxi. 38-40.
‡‡ Jer. xxxi. 27, 28.   §§ Jer. xxxiii. 10, 11.

virgin shall rejoice in the dance, both young men and old together; for Jahveh will turn their mourning into joy and make them rejoice according to their sorrow.* The temple—we scarcely need say—will again be the centre of the worship of Jahveh. The priests will be satiated by Jahveh.† Watchmen upon mount Ephraim will cry, "Come, let us go up to Zion, to Jahveh our god!"‡ In harmony, however, with the new state of things which will commence after the restoration, not only the temple, but the whole of Jerusalem will then be dedicated to Jahveh.§ "When ye"— the prophet had already said in Josiah's reign||—"be multiplied and fruitful in the land, in those days, saith Jahveh, they shall say no more, 'The ark of the covenant of Jahveh;' neither shall it come to mind, neither shall they remember it nor miss it, and it shall not be made again. At that time they shall call *Jerusalem* the throne of Jahveh."

When we hear Jeremiah utter such anticipations as these, we call to mind how his contemporary the author of Zech. xii-xiv,¶ and even Isaiah and Micah,** had announced the participation of the heathen in this glorious Jahveh-worship. This idea also is not wanting in Jeremiah. Having called Jerusalem "the throne of Jahveh," he immediately adds, "all nations shall be gathered unto it on account of the name of Jahveh."†† "To thee"—he says elsewhere‡‡—"to Jahveh shall the nations come from the ends of the earth and shall say, 'our fathers have only inherited lies, vanity, and among them (among these good for nothing gods) there is none that helpeth.'" The restoration of the tribes carried away by Nebuchadnezzar—as we have already said§§—depends upon their willingness to "learn the ways of Israel and to swear by the name of Jahveh, as they formerly taught Israel to swear by Baal;" if

---

* Jer. xxxi. 12, 13.   † Jer. xxxi. 14.   ‡ Jer. xxxi. 6.
§ Jer. xxxi. 40. || Jer. iii. 16, 17a ; comp. Vol. I., p. 233, n.†
¶ See above p. 66.   ** See Vol. I., p. 66, seq.   †† Jer. iii. 17 b.
‡‡ Jer. xvi. 19.   §§ Above p. 71.

they fulfil this condition, " they shall be built in the midst of Jahveh's people."* It cannot be said, however, that Jeremiah attaches much value to this prospect. He considers the conversion of the heathen by no means certain,† and in his exhaustive description of Israel's future‡ he confines himself to the prediction, that " they shall fear and tremble at all the good and all the prosperity that Jahveh will give unto his own."§ He is evidently so full of what his own people has to expect in the immediate future and thereafter, at its restoration, that he does not trouble himself with the future of the heathen.

I have purposely given Jeremiah's anticipations somewhat fully. He is in all respects worthy of an important place in the history of the Israelitish religion. Our tolerably extensive knowledge of his fortunes and of the time in which he laboured, causes him, more than any other prophet, to stand before us in person, with his peculiar, strongly marked characteristics. Jeremiah, so to speak, is a living figure. The same is true, therefore, of his ideas and views of the future: however strange and mixed they may seem to us, they present themselves at once as the natural expression of the real living man, and as the fruit of his belief and experience. Thus we have him to thank, that the Israelitish religion, at the important crisis in its history which we have just approached, lies before us as a reality. But there is another reason for which it was necessary to pay more attention to Jeremiah. He exercised a most important influence, not during his lifetime, but after his death, not upon his contemporaries, but upon those who came after him. We have explained his views without involving ourselves in the question, whether events proved him to be in the right and his enemies in the wrong. In our estimation, the purity of his principles, and not the precision of his political insight, decides his merit. But with the men of his time, of course, it was

---

* Jer. xii. 16. † Jer. xii. 17. ‡ Jer. xxx.–xxxiii. § Jer. xxxiii. 9.

very different. If he, the prophet of misfortune, had been contradicted by events; if Nebuchadnezzar had not laid waste Jerusalem and the temple—we should probably never have possessed his prophecies. But as it is, he became a great man, and preeminently the prophet, in the eyes of his contemporaries, and still more so in the eyes of their children. The hope of restoration pronounced by him soon passes into the consciousness of the people, and, partly at all events, on this very account, is realized. The men in whose midst he worked in his last days, flee to Egypt and disappear there without leaving any traces. But his prophecies are brought to Babylon and here do not fail to take effect. The exiles on the Chaboras and elsewhere accept his legacy. *After seventy years* they return to their native land. Upon them devolved the beautiful but difficult task of realizing the rest of the prophet's expectations as well. The future of Israel and of Israel's religion is in their hands.

We now turn, therefore, to Babylonia and the exiles who there await the time of their deliverance.

NOTES.

See pp. 4 n 3, and 58 n §.

Chapters viii. to xi. of Ezekiel's prophecies belong together and describe to us, according to chap. viii. 1, what Ezekiel saw and heard in an ecstasy into which he fell on the 5th day of the 6th month of the 6th year of his captivity, while "the elders of Judah" sat before him in his house. Now it has already been shown in *Hk. O.* ii. 295, seq. (comp. p. 270 n 9), that the dates, &c., in the titles of Ezekiel's prophecies are of no historical value: they are in great part fictitious and are employed as a literary form. Therefore we must consider that the prophet draws us here a picture of the idolatry in Judah, in the form of an ecstatic vision, which is represented as having occurred to him, apparently to announce, but in reality to vindicate, the judgment that had already descended upon Jerusalem and the temple. It will now be perceived how difficult it is to decide whether and to what extent Ezekiel is faithful to historical truth in this description. With respect to various, not unimportant, particulars, there consequently remains some uncertainty, which I do not consider myself able to clear away entirely, but yet wish to explain somewhat more fully.

(1.) Haevernick's opinion (*Comm. über den Proph. Ezech.* p. 97-104), that only one form of idolatry, and this a feast to Adonis, is described in chap. viii. 5-16, has been rejected with perfect justice by the rest of the exegesists, and among them by Keil. The prophet does not intimate by a single word that the ceremonies which he sketches are subdivisions of one *cultus*. The climax in chap. viii. 6, 13, 15, also pleads against this view. There are therefore four forms of idolatry that occur here: (1) The worship of "the image of jealousy, that provoketh [Jahveh] to jealousy," (chap. viii. 5-6, comp. 3), *i.e.* of an image of a false god, perhaps a symbol of Ashera (comp. 2 Kings xxi. 7; xxiii. 6); (2) The worship of animals, with figures of which the walls of a secret chamber were ornamented (chap. viii. 7-12); it is suspected, on the strength of the accounts of the Ancients, that Egyptian idolatry is meant here; the figures represent "all the filth-gods of the house of Israel" (chap. viii. 10); perhaps, therefore, although we may think of Egypt, we must not do so of her exclusively; (3) The mourning over Tammuz, *i.e.* Adonis, performed by women (chap. viii. 13-15); comp. Keil, *der Prophet Ezechiel*, p. 75, sq. (4) Prayer to the sun at sunrise (chap. viii. 16).

(2.) Does Ezekiel believe that all these idolatrous customs— whether it were in the reign of Zedekiah, or earlier—took place *in and around the temple at Jerusalem?* This is denied by Keil (*l.c.* p. 72). According to him, the locality belongs to the literary form: to render it quite plain how very much Israel was sinning by her idolatry, Ezekiel makes the latter take place in the very centre of the Jahveh-worship, where he makes (chap. viii. 11) seventy elders, the representatives of the whole people, and (chap. viii. 16) twenty-five men, the representatives of the priesthood, appear and commit their abominations. That at all events some of these ceremonies were practised in the houses of the Judæans, is evident from chap. viii. 12, where we read, " Seest thou what the ancients of the house of Israel do in the dark, *every man in his chambers adorned with figures?*" This unequivocally teaches us that the worship of animals took place in the houses of the great, and therefore not in the temple. Such is Keil's opinion. The liberty which he makes Ezekiel take, does not seem to me to be too great: I think it quite conceivable that, contrary to reality but in harmony with the idea he wished to represent, he made the sanctuary at Jerusalem the scene of all the abominations. But would he, in that case, have indicated the different sides and courts of the temple so minutely as he now does in chap. viii. 3, seq.? Is it not evident from the distinctions which he makes, that he has the real temple in view, and thus also the rites which actually occurred there? As regards chap. viii. 12, it would follow from this passage, that the Judæan of high rank had *more than one* chamber adorned with figures in his house: can this have been Ezekiel's meaning? must we not allow to Hitzig that the text is corrupted? His emendation (*Der Proph. Ezech.* p. 61), partly according to LXX., consists in striking out the words which produce difficulty; it seems very hazardous. But even if it cannot be decided for certain what the prophet wrote, in no case can chap. viii. 12 be employed to reject the conclusion to which all the rest of the description leads.

(3.) Does Ezekiel describe the idolatry which was practised in the temple in his time, whether it were in the 6th year of his captivity, or while he still lived at Jerusalem, but in either case after Josiah's 18th year? Or does he refer to earlier times, and particularly to the reign of Manasseh? To arrive at certainty in this respect, let us first study chap. viii. 11; xi. 1, 13. Among the seventy elders who take part in the second form of idolatry, we find Jaazaniah ben Shaphan; to the twenty-five men who stop at the east gate of the temple, belong Jaazaniah ben Azur and Pelatiah ben Benaiah; when Ezekiel—in the vision—prophesies against these twenty-five men, the last-mentioned is struck dead by divine judgment. What are we to think of these names? Do they indicate contemporaries of Ezekiel, who distinguished themselves by their zeal among the upholders of idolatry? Is *e.g.* Shaphan the father of Jaazaniah (chap. viii. 11) the same as Shaphan the Scribe, whom we know from the narrative of Josiah's reformation (2 Kings xxii. 3, seq.)? These questions are usually answered in the affirmative. If the accuracy of that answer could be proved, the case would be at once made out: Ezekiel would then treat of facts and persons of his own days. But this proof has not been, and cannot be, furnished. It may be assumed equally well, that the three names belong to the literary form, and are only intended to render the picture more striking—in the same way that the sudden death of Pelatiah is, doubtless, related for no other purpose (comp. chap. xi. 13 *b*). Thus it appears to me that the proper names do not decide the point in question *for us*—however much light they may have thrown upon Ezekiel's meaning *for his contemporaries.*—Chap. viii. 17 seems to me less ambiguous. After the prophet had seen all the abominations, Jahveh asks him, "Hast thou seen it, O son of man? Was it not enough for the house of Judah to commit the abominations which they have committed here, that they [now, in addition] have filled the land with wrong, and have again provoked me — — — ?" The words "which they have committed here," and especially the antithesis between "to commit the abominations," and "to fill the land with wrong," are in favour of the hypothesis that the idolatry belongs to the past, or at all events was practised in the past in the forms in which it was described here. In that case Ezekiel would here make up the account of his nation, as he does in chap. xx.-xxiii. (comp. *Hk. O.* ii. 274-6), and delineate in particular the worship of strange gods in all its compass and diversity.

The reader will now understand why, when use was made above of Ezek. viii., the applicability of that chapter to Manasseh's time was represented, not as quite certain, it is true, but yet as extremely probable.

II.—*See p. 9, n.* ‡.

The provisions of the Book of the Covenant concerning the Jahveh-worship are in every sense worthy of further explanation.

A prominent position must be given to the fact, that the author of that book sets his face against the service of other gods, and stirs up and exhorts the Israelites to worship Jahveh alone. See Exod. xx. 23; xxii. 20; xxiii. 13; 24-33. According to the Authorized Version, chap. xxii. 28 runs, "Thou shalt not revile the gods, nor curse the ruler of thy people." This has been interpreted as if it were forbidden here to treat the gods of other nations insultingly. This is incorrect: such a prohibition is opposed to the notions of the ancient Israelites. Nor can "the gods" (Hebr. *Elohîm*) be interpreted in the sense of "judges." Translate, "Thou shalt not curse God, nor revile the ruler of thy people." We find the same combination of God and ruler (or king) in 1 Kings xxi. 10, 13.

The Book of the Covenant permits sacrifice to Jahveh in more than one place. Read Exod. xx. 24: "Make me an altar of earth, and sacrifice thereon thy burnt-offerings and thy thank-offerings, thy sheep and thy oxen; *in all places where I shall establish the remembrance of my name* (or, where I shall make my name remembered), *I will come unto thee and bless thee.*" This evidently speaks of more than one place where the

Israelite praises Jahveh—and this, as the context shows, by means of sacrifices—and Jahveh accepts that praise and answers it with his blessing. In accordance with this, mention is made in verse 24a of an altar of earth, and in verse 25 of an altar of stone, and directions are given there as to the manner in which each sort of altar must be made. The sense of verse 24b becomes much plainer, however, if we slightly improve the text, according to the Syriac translation and the thargûm of Jerusalem, and read, " in all places *where thou shalt praise my name*, &c." This emendation is strongly recommended by the idiom (comp. for hizkîr, among others, Exod. xxiii. 13), and no less by comparison with the other old translations, from which it is clearly evident that the text has been altered in various ways, to make it agree with the younger laws, which only recognize one altar, at Jerusalem. (Comp. Geiger in *Zeits. der D. M. G.* xix. 603, sqq.)

In the meantime it is thought that this interpretation of Exod. xx. 24, is contradicted by other passages of the Book of the Covenant. Men point to chap. xxi. 14, where mention is made of " mine altar," in the singular. But comp. Exod. xx. 26, in connection with verses 24, 25, which passage proves that chap. xxi. 14 must be understood as referring to one of the altars of Jahveh. Appeal is also made to chap. xxiii. 19a, " the first of the first-fruits of thy land thou shalt bring into the house of Jahveh thy god." But exactly the same thing applies to this passage: the lawgiver could express himself thus, although several temples to Jahveh existed at the time. If, as is probable, he was acquainted with the temple at Jerusalem, and had this especially in view, he still does not absolutely exclude sacrifice in other places. And further, when chap. xxiii. 14 speaks of three feasts in honour of Jahveh, and verse 17 of appearing before (or seeing) Jahveh's face three times, this can be just as well understood to mean a visit to the smaller sanctuaries, the " high places," as a festival in the temple at Jerusalem.

Rather do passages occur in the Book of the Covenant which remain inexplicable, unless we suppose them to refer to a larger number of Jahveh-sanctuaries and to the priests who served there. See chaps. xxi. 6, xxii. 8, 9. According to the States-translators, these passages speak of "the gods." Of course they did not mean false gods, but *judges*, who, they believed, are called "gods" (*Elohim*) because judgment is considered to proceed from God and to be delivered in his name. This interpretation has been upheld quite recently by Knobel and Keil. But Graf is perfectly right in rejecting it (*Z. d. D. M. G.* xviii. 309-14). In the three passages cited above he translates *Elohim* by *God*, and shows that they refer to an act done or a decision taken at the holy place, before Jahveh's face and with the co-operation of the Jahveh-priest. The Hebrew slave who voluntarily entered into servitude for life, had to make his declaration to that effect in the sanctuary, in order to add to the solemnity of his act (chap. xxi. 6). The questions mentioned in chap. xxii. 8, 9, cannot be decided by the ordinary judge, by the "elders of the city," (see above p. 34); therefore they are settled by the priest, at the sanctuary—presumably with the urîm and thummîm, *i. e.* by sacred lot (Vol. I. p. 97, seq.). Chap. xxii. 11, also, indicates "the oath of (or by) Jahveh" as a means of settling a dispute. The reason why *God* (*Elohim*, with the article) is employed in the passages referred to, and not Jahveh, is no other than this, that in proceedings of this nature the name of the god is not concerned: the decision proceeds from *the deity*, quite in a general sense, and thus from Jahveh, not in his capacity as Israel's god, but as god, and nothing more. Now it is obvious—and this is why we have referred in this note to these texts—that Exod. xxi. 6, xxii. 8, 9, could not possibly be put in practice, if the Israelite had to go for that purpose to the one sanctuary, whether it was at Shiloh or at Jerusalem. Precepts such as these suppose that every one had a sanctuary of Jahveh in his immediate neighbourhood, or at all events had not to travel very far to reach such a sanctuary.

In other words, the centralization of worship, either in the one tabernacle, or in the temple at Jerusalem, is unknown to the author of the Book of the Covenant.

Graf's explanation is objected to by Dr. J. Werner (*Z. d. D. M. G.* xix. 306), and this on the strength of 1 Sam. ii. 25. He translates, "if one man sin against another, *the judge* (Hebr. *elohim*) decides, but if a man sin against Jahveh, who shall set himself up as judge for him (Jahveh)?" No evidence can be brought against the accuracy of this interpretation, which diverges from the ordinary one in the last words. But how can it serve as a proof that *elohim* is here = *the judge?* Why could not we translate *god*, and think of the *oracles* in the Jahveh-sanctuaries? The meaning then becomes: transgressions against men, however serious they may be, are judged by the Jahveh-priest and repaired by paying the penalty imposed by him, but a sin against Jahveh cannot be repaired by any means whatever; it must be expiated, and that by the severe punishment which Jahveh himself will execute upon the offender.

III.—*See pp.* 13, *n.* ††; 29, *n.* †; 30, *n.* ¶.

The ideas put forward in these passages as to the feast of unleavened bread and the passover, require some further explanation. A thoroughly complete treatment of this extremely involved problem must not be expected here; the main points alone can receive attention.

I. The passover-feast of Josiah (2 Kings xxiii. 21-23) is regarded above (p. 13) as historical, at variance with the opinion held by Redslob (*Die bibl. Angaben über die Paschafeier*, p. 33) and Dozy (*De Israëlieten te Mekka*, pp. 139, 140). They hold 2 Kings xxiii. 21-23, to be a subsequent interpolation, tending to represent the more recent, in fact post-exile, passover as having been already known and solemnly kept in Josiah's days, and thus to facilitate its introduction. In support of this opinion they point to verse 21, where Josiah says, "Keep the passover unto Jahveh your god, as it is written in *this book of the covenant*"—although the book of the covenant has not been mentioned since verse 3 and verses 4-20 treat exclusively of the rooting out of idolatry. They also refer to verse 24, where, conversely, the said book is indicated with great diffuseness by the formula, "the words of the law which were written in the book that Hilkiah the priest had found in the house of Jahveh"—as if that book had not been spoken of immediately before. Both these difficulties disappear if we regard verses 21-23 as an interpolation.—I have already intimated above (Vol. I. p. 95) that this argument does not seem to me to be convincing. After having stated in 2 Kings xxiii. 1-3, that on the basis of Hilkiah's book a covenant was made between Jahveh and the people, the author goes on to relate how the stipulations of this covenant were put into execution. In verses 4-23 he describes how public worship was instituted according to the words of Hilkiah's book of the law, and this (1) (verses 4-20) by the complete abolition of idolatry and illegal Jahveh-worship, which are described here *uno tenore;* (2) by the solemn celebration of the feast of the passover, which the book of the law prescribed (verses 21-23). In verse 24 he passes to another subject, viz. the abolition of the idolatrous practices, images, &c., which belonged to household worship (comp. Thenius, *die Bücher der Könige*, p. 434, sq.) It cannot be said, therefore, that verses 21-23 break the sense or are misplaced. Now as for the expression in verse 21, it proves that I was right just now in regarding verses 4-20 and verses 21-23 as subdivisions of one whole: verse 21 refers straight back to verse 3, and shows that the author, after having sketched the negative side of the introduction of the Law, now goes on to the positive introduction of its principal commandments; for this reason " *this book* of the covenant" is mentioned again in verse 21. And as for verse 24, the expression is certainly unnecessarily long, but not more so than in verse 3 compared with verse 2; and moreover the author of Kings generally writes very diffusely, and, as we have observed above, he enters in verse 24 upon another subdivision of his subject, so that it is not without reason that he employs the full formula to indicate the book of the law.

If, therefore, the proofs of the subsequent interpolation of 2 Kings xxiii. 21-23 are inadequate, it is certain, on the other hand, that a passover was already held in honour of Jahveh before the captivity, nay before Josiah's time, even if it was not kept at Jerusalem, as first prescribed in Deut. xvi. 1-8, and thus in Hilkiah's book. Ezekiel mentions the passover (chap. xlv. 21-24), and he does it as if he considered it already known to his readers. In Deut. xvi., too, it is not only commanded, but also represented as a thing generally known. Nay, even in Exod. xxxiv. 25, the words of the Book of the Covenant (Exod. xxiii. 18 b), "the fat of my feast-offering shall not remain until the morning," are reproduced with this alteration, "the sacrifice *of the feast of the passover* shall not remain until the morning." Therefore, unless it be thought that these texts may also be regarded as later interpolations, there is not the least ground to deny 2 Kings xxiii. 21-23 to the author of the portions of the chapter that precede and follow it. Thus it will surprise no one that, instead of looking upon Deut. xvi. 1-8 as a proof of the later origin of the Deuteronomic law, I have, on the contrary, advanced that pericope, in its connection with 2 Kings xxiii. 21-23, as evidence for the identity of Deuteronomy with Hilkiah's book of the law.

II. In what chronological order do the laws relating to the feast of unleavened bread—henceforward called mazzôth for shortness' sake—and to the sacrifice of the passover follow each other? After considering carefully what has been put forward on this subject by, among others, Hupfeld *(de vera et primit. fest. apud Hebr. ratione)*, Riehm *(die Gesetzgebung Mozes' im Lande*

Moab), and lately by Graf *(Die gesch. Bücher des A. T.* pp. 32-37), I am of opinion that they must be arranged in this way:—

1. Exod. xxiii. 15 (mazzôth; no mention of the sacrifice of the passover);
2. Exod. xiii. 3-10 (ditto; but in verses 2 and 11-16, the dedication of the first-born);
3. Exod. xxxiv. 18 (ditto; but mention is again made in verses 19, 20, of the dedication of the first-born; while verse 25 speaks of "the sacrifice of the feast of the passover");
4. Deut. xvi. 1-8 (mazzôth and sacrifice of the passover; immediately preceded in chapter xv. 19-23 by commandments relating to the first-born of sheep and oxen);
5. Exod. xii. 1-28, 43-50; Lev. xxiii. 5-8 [also 10-14]; Num. xxviii. 16-25; ix. 1-14 (all of which laws belong together and connect mazzôth with the sacrifice of the passover).

The most debatable point in this arrangement is the placing of 4 before 5—with respect to which I refer my readers to Graf. Riehm alleges (*Stud. u. Krit.* 1868, p. 362, sq.) against him, that the celebration of the passover in the houses of the Israelites, according to 5, is obviously older than that at the sanctuary, according to 4. It must indeed be admitted that the Deuteronomist introduces something new, when he removes the sacrifice of the passover to Jerusalem. But it does not follow from this that the laws named under 5 are older and were known to him. Let it be taken into consideration, that especially the first and second of these laws, Exod. xii. 1-28, and 43-50, exhibit a double character; they are promulgated at the exodus from Egypt, and therefore serve partly to ordain the first paschal sacrifice and partly to regulate the yearly passover. Of course, at the first paschal sacrifice a sanctuary, &c. was out of the question. But as far as the annual passover is concerned, the lawgiver, unless I be mistaken, really takes the celebration in

the city of the temple for granted (comp. Exod. xii. 16; also
Lev. xxiii. 7, 8, 10-14; Num. ix. 6, seq., throughout which the
celebration at the sanctuary seems to be assumed). The celebration prescribed in Exod. xii. is more ancient than that of
Deut. xvi. in one respect alone: in the commandment that the
lamb of the passover must be eaten in the evening by the
members of one family indoors. Should I succeed in showing,
however, that the Deuteronomist was acquainted with this custom, but, for reasons sufficient for himself, does not expressly
mention it, then this objection to the higher antiquity of Deut.
xvi. 1-8 will have been cleared away; for then an old custom
will have been elevated into a law in Exod. xii., although by a
younger lawgiver. Thus the very weighty arguments advanced
by Graf and others (see also Geiger, *Jüdische Zeitschrift*, iii.
178, sqq.) in favour of the later origin of the laws named under
5, will retain their full force.

III. From the list of the laws relating to mazzôth and passover
given above, it is most clearly evident, *a.* that mazzôth originally stood alone; *b.* that this feast, at a comparatively early
date, and at all events in the eighth century B.C., was interpreted
as a memorial of the deliverance out of the land of bondage.
It is not probable in itself, that this fact will have been
celebrated by such a feast. But besides this, it is obvious
that the lawgivers are puzzled, when they have to explain the
connection between the eating of unleavened bread and the
exodus. The oldest laws abstain from any attempt to do this
(1, 2, 3). The Deuteronomist gives two explanations: *a.* he
calls the mazzôth "bread of affliction" (chap. xvi. 3 a); *b.* he
writes, "for thou camest forth out of the land of Egypt in
haste" (chap. xvi. 3 b)—presumably an allusion to Exod. xii.
34, 39 ("the people took their dough before it was leavened;
their kneading-troughs being bound up in their clothes
upon their shoulders;" of this same dough they afterwards
baked unleavened cakes, "for they were thrust out of Egypt
and could not tarry.)" The youngest lawgiver, it would seem,

is acquainted with both these explanations; see Exod. xii. 8 (the bitter herbs with the mazzôth reminds us of "the bread of affliction"); 11 (the preparation for the journey described here reminds us of Deut. xvi. 3 b; nor is the expression "in haste" wanting). It will surely be admitted that the old-testament conception of mazzôth, both in itself and on account of the difference in the way in which it is worked out, is not at all probable and can hardly be original. But then whence comes the custom of eating mazzôth for seven consecutive days in the spring? We do not know for certain. Let any one who desires to become acquainted with the contradictory answers to this question consult Knobel, *Exod. u. Levit.* p. 103, sq. and the authors named there; also M. Duncker, *Gesch. des Alterthums I.* 311, 765 sq. (3e Ausg.). Without making any definite choice from among the various explanations, I would draw attention to the precept in Lev. ii. 11, that meat-offerings for Jahveh must always be unleavened. Unleavened bread therefore was looked upon as pure, and its use was eminently fitted to symbolize the dedication of the people to Jahveh. This agrees with the fact that mazzôth is a spring-feast and is kept at the beginning of a new year. But I repeat, this explanation, in my opinion, is far from certain. This alone is certain, that, whatever may have been the original meaning of mazzôth, attempts were made at a very early date to connect that feast with the remembrance of the exodus, and thus to turn it into a Jahveh-feast in a still narrower sense, into a theocratic feast.

IV. To comprehend the meaning of the passover-sacrifice, we must keep in view the decrees of the various lawgivers in reference to the dedication of the first-born to Jahveh. Arranged chronologically they are as follows: Exod. xxii. 29b, 30; xiii. 2, 11-16; xxxiv. 19, 20; Deut. xv. 19-23; Lev. xxvii. 26, 27; Num. xviii. 15-18; iii. 11-13; 40-51; viii. 5-22 —with this proviso, that the precepts in Leviticus and Numbers are almost, if not quite, contemporaneous. These laws by no means agree with each other: comp. *Hk. O.* i. 34, 35. Setting aside what does not directly concern our present subject, I will devote my attention to the following points.

(1.) According to the Book of the Covenant, there is no manner of connection between the dedication of the first-born and any one of the three yearly feasts. It is expressly said (Exod. xxii. 30) of the first-born of oxen and sheep, that they must be given to Jahveh eight days after their birth, *i.e.*, therefore, at all seasons of the year. When the first-born sons were "given to Jahveh" and in what that "giving" consisted, the lawgiver does not say (v. 29). We may suspect that they too had to be eight days old. It is also natural to connect this with the circumcision on the eighth day (Gen. xvii. 12; Lev. xii. 3). See further under VI.

(2.) On the other hand, we see very plainly in Exod. xiii. xxxiv.; Deut. xv., the endeavour to connect the dedication of the first-born with mazzôth. Comp. above under II. In Exod. xiii. a law relating to mazzôth (verses 3-10) stands between a short precept and a longer law relating to the dedication of the first-born (verses 2, 11-16). In Exod. xxxiv. the commandment to keep mazzôth (verse 18) is separated by the precepts about the first-born (verses 19, 20) from the commandments relating to two other high feasts (verse 22). Deut. xvi. 1-8 is immediately preceded by the law concerning the first-born of oxen and sheep (Deut. xv. 19-23). For the moment I will pass over what follows from this. At any rate the phenomenon is remarkable.

(3.) Whereas all the rest of the laws assign the first-born of man as well as of beasts to Jahveh, the Deuteronomist speaks exclusively of the first-born of oxen and sheep (chap. xv. 19-23). The fact cannot be denied, but — is it of any significance? or must we attribute it to accident? It seems to me that the Deuteronomist is purposely silent with respect to the dedication of the first-born sons. He had more than one opportunity of speaking of it, not only in chap. xv., but also in chap. xviii. 4—that is to say, if the custom of redeeming the first-born by paying a sum of money to the priest already existed in his time (comp. Num. xviii. 15-18). Ezekiel too mentions the dedication of the first-born sons but once, in chap. xx. 25, 26, where he speaks of " the statutes of Jahveh, that were not good, and the judgments whereby they could not live;" in regulating the incomes of the priests, chap. xliv. 29, 30, he only assigns to them the first-fruits of the field. I admit, however, that this reasoning is not conclusive. But if it can be shown what the Deuteronomist's motive was for keeping silence as to the dedication of the first-born sons, then it will become highly probable, if not certain, that there has been no accident in this case. Therefore see below under VI.

V. In explaining the paschal sacrifice, we have to notice both the manner in which it was offered and the meaning of the name which it bears. But for particular reasons the practices decreed in Exod. xii. 1-28 afford us but little light. This law, namely, tends definitely to connect the paschal sacrifice with the events which occurred at the exodus, and therefore cannot be followed, unless we could either regard this interpretation of the passover as the original one, or could be sure that the lawgiver did not allow himself to diverge in the least from existing customs. Neither one nor the other is the case. Therefore we turn to the name *phésach* (of which the New Testament *pascha* is the Aramaic form). Dozy (l. c., p. 139) has inferred from the proper name Thapsacus (from the verb *phĕsach*, Hebr. *phasach*) that the primitive meaning of phésach is no other than a *going over*, a *passage*, in accordance with which he assumes that the paschal sacrifice was intended to keep alive the remembrance of the passage of the Jordan. But when we consult the Old Testament, it becomes evident that the meaning of the *Hebrew* verb, however closely it may be allied to the sense expressed by the Aramaic verb, as appears from the name Thapsacus, does not coincide with it entirely. In the law relating to the paschal sacrifice the Hebrew verb clearly means to *spring* or *pass over*, and therefore to *spare*.

See Exod. xii. 13, 23, 27. However much liberty the author of that law may have allowed himself, he must have employed the verb *phasach* in the same sense as that in which the Israelites used it, at least if he wished to be understood by them. In fact, *phásach* does occur at least once again in the Old Testament —1 Kings xviii. 21 is surely of a different nature—in the same sense, in Isaiah, chap. xxxi. 5. We read there, "as birds fluttering [over their young], so will Jahveh of hosts defend Jerusalem, defending and saving, *sparing* and delivering." And besides this, the Hebrew words which are derived from *phasach* (and especially *phisséach*, cripple) do not contradict the supposed original meaning of this verb. Thus we have to consider that *phésach* is equal to a *passing over*, an *exemption*. This is the opinion of the great majority of exegetes.

VI. It may be assumed to be probable that the interpretation of the paschal feast which is advanced in Exod. xii. is not very far from the original meaning of that sacrifice: to gain acceptance for his explanation, the lawgiver was obliged to adhere as much as possible to existing ideas and customs. From this point of view, the hypothesis that the paschal sacrifice is a substitutional sacrifice, *that the animal sacrificed takes the place of the first-born son, to whom Jahveh is considered to have a right and to lay claim*, deserves special recommendation. We are not surprised that this supposition has met with defenders before now, and has lately been maintained by M. Duncker, in the work referred to, p. 310, sq., 765, sq. Independently of these examples, it has forced itself upon me also, in studying the whole of this subject anew. Let the following serve to elucidate and recommend this view.

Originally, the father of every family, on the eighth day after the birth of his first-born son, offered up to Jahveh a redemption-offering, which was called *phésach* for the reasons just indicated: viz., it induced Jahveh to *pass over* or *spare* the child, to which he had a claim, and which therefore ought really to have been offered up to him [Exod. xxii. 29, and above, IV. (1.)]. From its very nature, this offering was of a private character; it was not and could not be congregational. Now it must gradually have become the custom, *a.* to offer such an exemption-sacrifice *annually*, and *b.*, in connection with this, to combine it with one of the feasts that recurred annually, with mazzôth. We find evident traces of this combination in Exod. xiii. xxxiv. (above, IV. 2). Probably the paschal offering consisted of a lamb or a he-goat. Was it originally offered to Jahveh as a burnt-offering? This is not unlikely, but it must gradually have become customary, that the members of one family should eat the paschal lamb together, and that then the first-born of oxen and sheep that the past year had produced should be eaten at sacrificial meals on the following days of mazzôth. This is what the Deuteronomist found in existence. He made this alteration in it, that he removed mazzôth, and therefore also the sacrificial meals just mentioned, to Jerusalem. But at the same time he places those meals in the foreground—as was pointed out on p. 30—and the eating of the paschal lamb in the background; why he did so is there shown. The priestly lawgiver, Exod. xii. 1, seq., is the first who can entirely restore the paschal sacrifice to its right position, while and because he interprets and represents it in a purely historical sense, and thus alters considerably its original meaning. The same lawgiver makes another alteration besides this. He decrees, namely, that every first-born son, as belonging to Jahveh, must be redeemed from the priest (Num. xviii. 16), and, moreover, that the priest is entitled to the first-born of oxen and sheep, after deducting what goes to the altar (verses 17, 18). Both these innovations are introduced in the interest of the priesthood and find in this their explanation. The first, if our interpretation of the paschal sacrifice be correct, was a sin against the rule, *ne bis in idem*. But there is nothing strange in this, after all the modifications that the original dedication of the first-born to Jahveh had undergone in the course of centuries.

Our hypothesis is recommended by the fact that it accounts

for the diversity of the laws, and for the peculiar phenomena which present themselves in the deuteronomic precepts about mazzôth and phésach (chap. xvi. 1-8), and for the Deuteronomist's silence with regard to the dedication of the firstborn sons. So long as this dedication had not yet been explained historically, it constituted a real difficulty for a man such as the Deuteronomist. Therefore he says nothing about it, and when he mentions the paschal sacrifice, which was so intimately connected with that dedication, he abstains from all further explanation of its meaning.

Let the reader himself judge, whether other attempts to solve this intricate historical problem answer reasonable expectations better than this one.

IV.—*See p. 32, n. **

In reference to "clean and unclean," a paper by Veth in *de Evangelie-Spiegel*, 1862, pp. 257, seq., 353, seq., is worthy of perusal. His idea of the reasons why some animals were looked upon as unclean, is the same as that advanced above, (p. 32); comp. also Knobel, *Exod. u. Levit.*, p. 431, sqq.

My remarks upon Deut. xiv. and Levit. xi. must be illustrated here somewhat more fully.

The capability of distinguishing between clean and unclean belonged in Israel to the *priests*; it was especially their task to give *instruction* (thorah) in this matter to all who desired it. This is evident, not only from the laws relating to cleanness and purification in Levit. xii.-xiv., where the assistance of the priest is always called in, but also from passages such as Ezek. xliv. 23; Hagg. ii. 11, seq. And other passages as well, which simply mention the thorah of the priest, we have no hesitation in taking to refer to his directions upon the same subject, *e.g.* Mal. ii. 6, 7; Deut. xxxiii. 10, &c. (comp. Vol. I. p. 340, seq.).

The conjecture that Deut. xiv. 1-21 is a piece of priestly thorah, thus brings its own recommendation with it. It is confirmed by the agreement in style between this pericope and the elohistic (priestly) portions of the Pentateuch. Mark the formula "after his kind" (Deut. xiv. 13-15, 18), and the expression "creeping things" (verse 19), and not only these, but also the whole character and the style of the deuteronomic law relating to food. It is not without reason that Riehm writes (*Stud. u. Krit.* 1868 p. 359): "In 3 Mos. 11 ist das Gesetz Bestandtheil einer Gesetzsammlung, deren charakteristisches Gepräge auch ihm eigen ist; im Deuteronomium steht es dagegen in einer Gesetzsammlung, deren charakteristisches Gepräge ihm so fremd ist, das die Annahme der Entlehnung aus einer älteren Urkunde [comp. Graf, *die gesch. Bücher des A. T.* S. 22, 67] nicht abzuweisen ist. Dazu komt dasz mehrere der für die Formulirung des Gesetzes charakteristischen Ausdrücke (die im Deuteronomium eben nur in ihm vorkommen) der aus der Genesis wohlbekannten Schreibweise des Verfassers der Grundschrift angehören."

Yet I cannot agree with Riehm's opinion that Lev. xi. is older than Deut. xiv. Deut. xiv. 21, compared with the rest of the ordinances relating to the same subject, pleads against it—besides the general arguments for the more recent origin of the priestly legislation. The precept in Deut. is almost the same as that of the Book of the Covenant, Exod. xxii. 31. But it differs from Lev. xvii. 15, 16 (where the prohibition extends also to "the stranger"), and from the same passage and Lev. xi. 40, where the eating of carrion is so far allowed, that a not very severe penalty is provided, submission to which was all that was required, if, for any reason, *e.g.* from poverty, a man did not wish to leave the carrion uneaten. According to the priestly legislation, the priest alone has to abstain from eating carrion (Lev. xxii. 8). Who does not perceive that here the deuteronomic law is older and more original than Leviticus? The author of the enactments in

Lev. xvii. 15, 16; xi. 40, finds himself forced by custom to make concessions; of a religious precept he makes, so to speak, a police-regulation; in doing this, he makes it apply also to the stranger, who is exempted in Deut., because the religious grounds did not exist in his case.—If this view of Deut. xiv. 21, be admissible, we apply it without hesitation to the preceding verses as well: verses 3-20 are no more younger than Lev. xi. 1, seq. than verse 21 is younger than Lev. xi. 40.

The twofold result thus far obtained (1. Deut. xiv. 3-20, displays the characteristics of the priestly legislation; 2. this pericope is older than Lev. xi.) serves to confirm an hypothesis which I put forward in 1861 in my *Hk. O.* i. 84, seq. The Elohistic laws in Exodus, Leviticus and Numbers embrace " the tradition which had been preserved and committed to writing by the priests and Levites concerning the lawgiving of Moses, in so far as the latter regulated religious service and all that was connected with it;" thus they did not originate at one period, but successively, and were repeatedly worked up and re-edited, according to the wants that arose. In agreement with this hypothesis, I already at that time took some of the priestly laws to be younger than the parallel decrees in Deuteronomy (*l.c.* pp. 146-8, 152-5). Since then, by further study and by the excellent work of K. H. Graf, *Die gesch. Bücher des A. Testaments,* I have been led to the conviction, that the priestly legislation in Exod.—Numbers was not brought to its present form until after the exile, and therefore in its entirety is younger than Deuteronomy. But this opinion, which will be justified more fully in the sequel of this History, is not opposed to my earlier hypothesis as to the successive origination of that legislation, and must be combined with it. The decrees of the priestly law were not *made* and *invented* during or after the exile, but *drawn up.* Prior to the exile, the priests had already delivered verbally what—with the modifications that had become necessary in the mean time—they afterwards committed to writing. A set terminology, a definite mode of expression, gradually formed itself for these "instructions" (comp. Graf, *l.c.* p. 93). The committal to writing of the priestly thorah, also, will not have been deferred until the period of the second temple or even till the days of Ezra. It is true, there did not exist before that time any complete system of priestly lawgiving, but detached priestly laws, priestly advice upon this or that subdivision of the questions that belonged to the domain of the staff of the temple, cannot have been wanting. Now such a priestly "Gutachten" as this is adopted by the Deuteronomist in chap. xiv, and especially in verses 3-20 of that chapter. Thus both the priestly (Elohistic) character of that document and the want of completeness which it shows in comparison with Lev. xi. are most natural: when the priests wrote down their thorah about clean and unclean animals nearly two centuries after Josiah's reformation, their system was more finished and developed, and thus they were obliged to treat the same subject at greater length.

CHAPTER VII.

THE ISRAELITISH EXILES IN BABYLONIA.

ABOUT the year 580 B.C. Judæa presented a sad spectacle. Jerusalem and Solomon's temple lay in ruins. Nebuchadnezzar had thrice caused a number of the chief inhabitants of the land to be carried away.* The remainder, although still many in number, formed but a pitiful remnant of the former kingdom of Judah. Part of them had grown wild and led the lives of freebooters.† Others busied themselves with agriculture,‡ but they had much to suffer from the bands of Chaldean soldiers that roved about the land, and from the neighbouring tribes, who took advantage of Israel's abasement to extend their territories.§ After the murder of Gedaliah, who at first stood at their head as the governor appointed by the Babylonish king,‖ they appear to have had no regular government. They were also deprived of almost all spiritual guidance. It is true, a few prophets still raised their voices among them after the fall of Jerusalem,¶ but these men do not appear to have made much impression: if we remember how the grey-haired Jeremiah was treated by his countrymen, first in Judæa and afterwards in Egypt, we could scarcely expect it. The priests of Jahveh had almost all been carried away, and, after the destruction of the temple, would have had much less influence than before. In a word, the hope that those who were left in Judæa would work the regeneration of Israel** was of short duration; even in those who cherished it at first, subsequent events gradually weakened and at last stifled it altogether.

---

* 2 Kings xxiv. 14-16; xxv. 11; Jer. lii. 28-30.   † Jer. xl. 7, seq.
‡ 2 Kings xxv. 12; Jer. lii. 16.   § Lam. v. 1, seq.   ‖ Above, p. 55, seq.
¶ Obadiah (comp. *Ilk. O.* ii. 339, seq.) and, probably some years after him, the author of Isa. xxiv.-xxvii. (comp. *l.c.* ii. 145, seq.).   ** Ezek. xxxiii. 23-29.

This time also the light was to arise in the East. We do not know with certainty the number of the exiles carried off by Nebuchadnezzar: the returns given in the Old Testament are evidently incomplete.* But that their number was very considerable, can be gathered from the number of those who afterwards went back. For their intrinsic worth, even more than for their numerical strength, these exiles had a right to be regarded as the real representatives of the kingdom of Judah and thus of all Israel. The repeated rebellions against the Chaldeans were kindled by the Judæans of the highest rank. Upon them in the first place, therefore, the conqueror's revenge necessarily fell. A few men of high position were even punished with death,† but by far the most of them were condemned to banishment. To the first body of exiles there belonged, as will shortly appear more fully, prophets, opponents of Jeremiah, and priests. After the fall of Jerusalem it was again the most enlightened who were sent into exile. It was therefore *the kernel of the nation* that was brought to Babylonia.

Our information as to the social condition of the exiles is very defective. Even to the question, where they had to settle, we can only return an imperfect answer. We meet with a colony of exiles, companions of Jeconiah, at Tel-abîb, in the neighbourhood of the river Chebar, usually supposed to be the Chaboras, which runs into the Euphrates not far from Circesium, but considered by others to be a smaller river, nearer to Babylon.‡ It lay in the nature of the case, that the second and third company of captives received another destination. Even had it been possible, prudence would have opposed their settling in the immediate vicinity of their predecessors. We are not surprised therefore that Ezekiel, who lived at Tel-abîb, does not mention their arrival there. Where they did go we

---

* 2 Kings xxiv. 14-16; xxv. 11 (Jer. lii. 15); Jer. lii. 28-30. Comp. Note I. at the end of this chapter.   † 2 Kings xxv. 18-21 (Jer. lii. 10 b, 24-27).

‡ Ezek. iii. 15; i. 3, &c. Comp. *Hk. O.* ii. 258, n. 2, and Schenkel's *Bibel-lexikon*, i. 508, sq.; ii. 558, also 247.

are not told. The historian says "to Babylon,"* to which place, according to him, the first exiles (597 B.C.) were also brought;† probably he does not, in either passage, mean only the capital of the Chaldean kingdom, but rather the province of that name, to which the city of course belonged. But wherever they may have settled, the exiles had to live. How did they support themselves? Some undoubtedly tilled the land or pursued their former handicrafts.‡ But all would not be in a position to do this. These were naturally led to take part in the trade that was carried on, upon a large scale, in their new dwelling place. At first they could have occupied only subordinate parts in it. But we may assume it to be probable, that they speedily showed their natural aptitude for commerce, and that many of them soon managed to acquire some wealth.

It follows from this that they enjoyed a certain amount of liberty in the land of their exile. Such was indeed the fact. Probably they were not all upon an equally favourable footing in this respect. The instigators of the rebellion would for some time be subjected to a strict surveillance, and perhaps even had to work as slaves. But there was no occasion to treat the whole of the exiles in this way. Nebuchadnezzar's purpose, the prevention of fresh disturbances, having been attained by their removal from Judæa, he could now leave them to develop their resources. It was even for the interest of the districts in which they settled, that their development should not be obstructed. Many unnecessary and troublesome conflicts were avoided and the best provision was made for the maintenance of order, by leaving them free, within certain limits, to regulate their own affairs. So the elders of the families and tribes remained in possession of the authority which they had formerly exercised.§ Nay, it would not surprise us, if the foundations were already laid of the organization which we

---

* 2 Kings xxv. 7, (Jer. lii. 11) of Zedekiah ; Jer. xxxix. 9 ; xl. 1, 4, of the rest of the exiles. † 2 Kings xxiv. 15, 16.

‡ Comp. 2 Kings xxiv. 14, 16 ; also Jer. xxix. 5. § Ezek. viii. 1; xiv. 1; xx. 1.

meet with centuries afterwards in Babylonia. Then the Jews who were established there formed an independent community, governed by a chief of their own, the *Resh Galutha* ("head of the exiles"), just as at Alexandria an officer chosen from among them, the Alabarch, represented them before the magistrates of the land, and was, as it were, responsible for them. If this organization was at least prepared as early as the first years of the captivity, then we can easily comprehend how it is that, at the return under Cyrus, Zerubbabel, a descendant of David, and Joshua, a priest, place themselves at the head of the exiles and exercise their authority without meeting with contradiction. We may then see in this a proof that the families of distinction, the princes and the chief of the priests were acknowledged by the Chaldeans as the natural leaders of their fellow countrymen and were not obstructed in the exercise of their power.

But we will abstain from farther conjectures on this subject. However full of interest it may be, a deeper study of it is not absolutely necessary for the right comprehension of the religious condition of the exiles, with which we now have to do.

As was to be expected, we find among the captives the same diversity of convictions that existed in the kingdom of Judah after Josiah's death.* It is sometimes imagined that the calamities which befell the nation under Jehoiakim and his successors, brought about an immediate change in its relation to Jahvism. These misfortunes, and especially the final catastrophe, were foretold by the prophets and thus confirmed the prophets' unfavourable opinion of the religious and moral condition of the kingdom: must not their effect have therefore been that many men repented and entered upon the path into which Jeremiah, for example, desired to lead them? But this expectation, however natural it may be to all appearance, is not confirmed by the evidence of history, and, in fact, has no adequate foundation. To be able to regard the fall of Jerusalem

---

* Above, p. 55, seq.

as a judgment of Jahveh upon his faithless people, as Jeremiah did, it was necessary that the Judæans should start from the same promises as the prophet. But, as we perceived before, this was not the case. Their stand-point was a different one, and consequently their view of the events also differed from his. We can prove this from the documents themselves.

It is evident, in the first place, that the worship of the strange gods remained in existence.* Jeremiah had to continue the struggle against idolatry in Egypt. The Judæans who had emigrated thither still kept up the worship of " the queen of heaven," and were not at all ashamed of it. When the prophet pointed to the disasters which had afflicted their native land on the very account of their infidelity to Jahveh, they were not at a loss for an answer. "All that hath gone forth out of our mouth"—they said†—"all our vows we will certainly perform, burning incense unto the queen of heaven and pouring out drink-offerings unto her, as we have done, we, and our fathers, our kings and our princes, in the cities of Judah and the streets of Jerusalem: then (when we did this) we had plenty of bread, and it was well with us, and we saw no evil. But from the time that we left off to burn incense and pour out drink-offerings unto the queen of heaven, we have wanted all things, and have perished by the sword and by the famine." It will be observed that these men, as well as Jeremiah, regarded and explained the events from their own religious point of view. Things were no better among the exiles in Babylonia. One of their number, the prophet Ezekiel, reproaches them repeatedly with their idolatry, and especially adverts, with deep abhorrence, to the sacrifice of children to Molech.‡ Nay, he even puts these words into their mouths: "we shall be as the nations, as the families of the countries, serving wood and stone."§ There are reasons for taking this description to be somewhat exaggerated, but it could not have been given at all,

---

* Comp. above, p. 57, seq., where the testimony of both Jeremiah and Ezekiel is given. † Jer. xliv. 17, 18.

‡ Above, p. 58, seq. § Chap. xx. 32.

if the exiles, without any exception worth mentioning, had been addicted to exclusive Jahvism.

We also meet again among the exiles with the party of the political Jahvists—as we can fitly call Jeremiah's antagonists.* It had started the resistance to Nebuchadnezzar; upon it therefore, in the first place, fell the punishment, the captivity. At first it was not disheartened by it. While Zedekiah reigned at Jerusalem, prophets appeared among those who had been carried away with Jeconiah : Ahab, Zedekiah ben Maaseiah, and Shemaiah, who consoled their fellow-captives with the prospect of a speedy deliverance. Their words met with such ready acceptance that Jeremiah thought it necessary to write to the exiles and exhort them to have patience.† I pass over the question, whether he is right in accusing, in this letter, the first two of these prophets of immorality.‡ Their colleague, Shemaiah, did not hesitate to come forward for the cause which he upheld. In a letter which he sent to Zephaniah and other priests at Jerusalem, he imputed it to Jeremiah as a crime that the latter had said to the exiles, "It will last still a long time! Build houses and dwell in them; plant gardens and eat the fruit of them." In his opinion, the priests of Jerusalem ought to have interfered and imprisoned the prophet.§ With such great confidence did this party come forward in Babylonia.

Some of Jeremiah's friends also had undoubtedly already gone thither into exile with Jeconiah. We gather this from the favourable verdict that the prophet passed upon the first exiles,‖ and from his letter itself, which surely would not have been sent, unless the prophet had reckoned upon a friendly reception for it, at all events from some. The course of events necessarily strengthened these adherents of Jeremiah. So long as Jerusalem yet stood, it was in a certain sense easy to believe in the inviolability of Jahveh's seat. After the fall of city and temple, before a single presage of their approaching restora-

---

* Above, p. 60, seq. † Jer. xxix. 1-23. ‡ Verses 21-23.
§ Verses 24-32. ‖ Chap. xxiv.

tion had yet shown itself, it was but natural that only a few could be induced to expect that restoration shortly. At that time, therefore, the explanation which Jeremiah gave of these sad events must have recommended itself to many who hitherto had not sided one way or other in the fierce struggle between him and his opponents. And this the more, because he too announced the regeneration of Israel, even though it were after a long lapse of time and as the fruit of the people's conversion to Jahveh.*

It is not improbable that an attempt was made as early as the first years of the captivity to give visible shape to that conception of Israel's history, of which Jeremiah had been the interpreter, and at the same time to disseminate it among the people. The opinion has been advanced recently from more than one quarter, that the Deuteronomist not only worked up his own laws into one whole with the older historical narratives relating to the patriarchs, Moses and Joshua,† but also treated in his own spirit the later history of Israel, during the period of the Judges and under the Kings.‡ The books of Judges, Samuel and Kings, with the exception of a few additions of still later date,§ would then be the work of the Deuteronomist, and would thus also, it speaks for itself, have been written shortly after the fall of Jerusalem. We need not involve ourselves here in an examination of this opinion. Thus much is certain, that in the books just mentioned, the spirit, at all events, if not the hand, of the Deuteronomist appears plainly here and there—and especially in the judgments passed upon the actors and in the views respecting the direction of Israel's fortunes by Jahveh.|| Whether it be assumed that this conception was

---

* Above, p. 72, seq. † Above, p. 39.

‡ Comp. K. H. Graf. *die gesch. Bücher des A. T.* p. 97, sqq., where, however, the Deuteronomic redaction of Judges and Samuel is overlooked; E. Schrader in de Wette's *Einleitung*, 8e. Ausg. § 218-223, and the writers quoted there.

§ Schrader (p. 353) names as such, 2 Kings xxv. 22-30; 1 Kings iv. 24, 25; (hebr. v. 4, 5).

|| Comp. my *Hk. O.* i. 201, 215, (upon Judges); 239, seq. (upon Samuel); 274 seq. (upon Kings).

really put into writing under the fresh impression of the fall of the kingdom, or its written redaction be placed somewhat later, in either case we may consider that, from the very first, there was no lack among the exiles of men who followed in the footsteps of the Deuteronomist and his fellow-thinker Jeremiah, and appealed to *history* in proof of their mission from Jahveh. They could not have employed a more powerful means than this of recommending their views and causing them gradually to pass into the consciousness of the people.

Our sketch of the religious condition of the exiles during the first period of their abode in a strange land would end here, were it not that, even before the taking of Jerusalem by Nebuchadnezzar, a man had risen among them, who merits all our attention. We have already mentioned more than once the name of the prophet Ezekiel. It is true that less even than almost all the other prophets can he be regarded as the representative of his age. It is true, he stands fighting at his post alone—in such a way that we see his spirit revive, not in his immediate successors, but in a younger generation. But in spite of this—or is it on this very account?—he attracts our notice in a high degree, and deserves to be sketched as accurately as possible, both in his relation to his contemporaries and to posterity.

Ezekiel the son of Buzi was a priest in the temple at Jerusalem, when, in the year 597 B.C., Jeconiah was punished by Nebuchadnezzar for the revolt of Jehoiakim, his father and predecessor, and was carried off to Babylonia with the chief inhabitants of Jerusalem. Why this lot also befell Ezekiel, we do not know: he could scarcely have taken an active part in Jehoiakim's rebellion; but other priests besides him were sent into exile;* and it may have been purely by accident that he was among their number. Unless we be mistaken, this captivity was a terrible blow to Ezekiel. He was one of

* Jer. xxix. 1.

those priests who were wholly engrossed in the duties of their office, and attached great weight to every portion of them. To him the temple was, in the full sense of the word, the dwelling of Jahveh; the priest's calling seemed to him to be a very high one, his responsibility very great. Is it a wonder that he resigned himself to sombre meditations in the comparative solitude and inaction to which he found himself condemned on the banks of the Chebar? It was impossible for him to agree with those of his companions in misfortune, who, believing the words of their prophets, anticipated a speedy return and the approaching restoration of Israel's independence. His nature had no propensity for such optimism; he was rather accustomed to look at the dark side of things. But besides this, for him at least Jeremiah's words had not echoed in vain. With that preacher of repentance, whom he may have heard more than once in the court of the temple, he saw in the sins of the people the cause of the disasters that had befallen them, and from earnest repentance alone did he expect the dawn of better times. He was firmly convinced therefore, that the cup of misery was not yet full, and that—he and his fellow exiles would not return to Jerusalem, but—the men of Jerusalem would come to them. Perhaps I should express myself too strongly, were I to say that Israel's apostasy *embittered* him. But true it is, that his sentiments at that time were quite different from those of Jeremiah, for instance, in whom sadness was the prevailing tone. Was it because he, Ezekiel, was himself the victim of his people's error and found himself deprived by it of the office which he loved and valued as the highest privilege? Enough that he judged his contemporaries severely and did not show the least inclination to excuse their conduct out of pity for their lot.

When we open Ezekiel's prophecies and note the exactness of the dates with which they are provided, we imagine at first that we are in a position to follow him in his career step by step. According to these headings,* he made his appearance as a prophet in the 5th year after his banishment, and at that time, and in the 6th, 7th and 8th years, spoke out more or less at length upon the fate that was hanging over king Zedekiah and the population of Jerusalem and Judæa. He then, according to a second series of headings,† just before the fall of Jerusalem and immediately after that event, committed to writing his expectations with regard to the future of Ammon, Moab, Edom, Philistia, Tyre, Zidon, and Egypt, and added to these one more prophecy, in the 27th year of his captivity. (570 B.C.)‡ And finally, the predictions concerning Israel's restoration (chap. xxxiii.—xlviii.), according to the dates of the first and last,§ were written down between the year of the taking of Jerusalem, the 11th of his exile (586 B.C.), and the 25th year after his banishment (572 B.C.). In the meantime, phenomena occur in the prophecies themselves, that forbid us to accept this chronology as literally correct. I need only give here the results of the researches which have been made elsewhere‖ into this subject. We possess, then, in the book of Ezekiel, a review, written by the prophet himself with great freedom and no less skill, both of his public preaching and of the outcome of his meditations upon Israel's lot and future. It may be historical, that in the 5th year after his banishment (592 B.C.) he felt himself seized by the hand of Jahveh, and then for the first time addressed his fellow-captives as an envoy of the god of Israel.¶ Also, he may have written down a few prophecies, especially those against some heathen nations,** in the years to which they are referred, just as we now possess them. But when, at least 25 years after the beginning of his exile,†† he sat down to give, for the benefit of his contemporaries and posterity, an account of his labours and to lay bare

---

* Chap. i. 2 ; viii. 1 ; xx. 1 ; xxiv. 1.
† Chap. xxvi. 1 ; xxix. 1 ; xxx. 20 ; xxxi. 1 ; xxxii. 1, 17.
‡ Chap. xxix. 17—xxx. 19, (according to others, chap. xxix. 17-21).
§ Chap. xxxiii. 21 ; xl. 1.   ‖ *Hk. O.* ii. 295-306.   ¶ Ezek. i. 2.
** Chap. xxvi. seq., xxix. seq.   †† Chap. xl. 1 ; xxix. 17.

the ideas which he had formed of the future, he did not then consider himself bound—even supposing that he was in a position to do so—to report literally what he had said on various occasions. It was enough for him to reproduce his chief thoughts correctly. Let us then try, in our turn, to form an idea of what went on in his mind.

We are surely not mistaken in believing that Ezekiel often meditated deeply upon the sins of his people. At all events, the description of them occupies a considerable portion of his oracles. For our present purpose, his conception of Israel's conduct in general is at least as important as the accusations which he brings against his contemporaries in particular. More than once he lays open, as it were, the register of Israel's sins—nowhere so expressly, however, as in the 20th chapter of his prophecies. "Wilt thou judge them, son of man, wilt thou judge them? Cause them to know the abominations of their fathers!"—so runs the beginning of this castigation. In Egypt— the prophet goes on to say—Jahveh had declared himself ready to deliver Israel and to bind Israel to himself. But the condition which he imposed, the forsaking of the idols, had not been complied with. Yet, to save his name from disgrace, he had fulfilled his promise once given and had led Israel out into the wilderness.* There Jahveh had revealed himself to his people, had made known to them his ordinances and had introduced the Sabbath as a token of the covenant made with him. Again the Israelites had been refractory and had proved themselves worthy of destruction. But once more their god had forgiven them, and had promised fertile Canaan to the next generation.† But even this new generation had not submitted to Jahveh's laws. Hence it was that the future dispersion of Israel among the heathen was already announced in the desert; hence it was too that Jahveh had "given to the Israelites statutes that were not good, and judgments whereby they could not live,"

---

* Chap. xx. 5-9. † Verses 10-17.

and had especially prescribed the dedication of the first-born, which in after times was to be made use of to justify the sacrifice of children.* Yet out of mercy, on this occasion also, the actual sentence of destruction was not executed.† So now Canaan was given to the Israelites for an inheritance. But here also they went on sinning, for they allowed themselves to be seduced by the Canaanites into taking part in their idolatry on the "high places"—the name of which (*bamah*) Ezekiel derives from the curiosity with which the first Israelitish inhabitants of the land had observed and enquired into the practices of the natives.‡ The prophet now turns to his contemporaries, to upbraid them that they had followed in the footsteps of their forefathers, nay, had made a formal resolution to forsake Jahveh and to become as the heathen. Terrible punishments will come upon them, and with this result, that at last it will be possible to assemble in the holy land a people that has dedicated itself entirely and with its whole heart to Jahveh and serves him alone.§—In this light does the history of his nation present itself to Ezekiel, as a series of errors, one worse than another, and collectively the incontrovertible proof of Israel's ingratitude and obstinacy. Elsewhere he employs other figures to express the same conception—such as, in chapter xvi. an allegory worked out in detail||—but in his verdict he remains throughout consistent with himself.

If we are to form a true notion of the impression which such a sinful existence as that of Israel made upon Ezekiel's mind, we must bring the sketch which he drew of it into connection with his conception of Jahveh's justice. It is scarcely necessary to say, that it agrees in general with that of his predecessors among the prophets: divergence from it would have been equal to a renunciation of Jahvism. Yet his ideas have

---

* Comp. *Theol. Tijdschrift*, i. 69, seq.   † Verse 18-26.   ‡ Verses 27-29.
§ Verses 30-40. || Comp. also chap. xxiii. where Samaria and Jerusalem are indicated by the symbolical names of *Oholah* ("her tent"); and *Oholibah* (" my tent is in her").

a peculiar tint, the reflection of his personality. The same formality and severity that characterize himself, he also attributes to Jahveh. The prophet is convinced that fidelity to Jahveh and apostasy from him are followed at once by Jahveh's blessings and punishments. The piety of the righteous man always results in good to him, but to him alone, and so long as he perseveres in it, but not a moment longer. In the same way, the godless man, and he alone, is punished for his sins, but his repentance too is immediately followed by reward. Ezekiel devotes a long discourse to the development of these ideas.* At the outset he mentions the proverb which we also know from Jeremiah: "the fathers have eaten sour grapes, and the children's teeth are set on edge"†—but only to combat it with all the earnestness that is in him. This earnestness is also shown by the application of these ideas to his own person and office. He is deeply penetrated with the responsibility which rests upon him. From the moment that he entered upon his office, he feels that he is required to render account of the conduct of those in whose midst he lives. He who slights his warnings has only himself to blame, if just punishment overtakes him. But should any one be lost without having been warned, his blood will be demanded from the unfaithful watchman to whose care he had been consigned.‡ We may not indeed withhold our respect from a man who spoke and thought thus; still a figure such as his is not attractive. He involuntarily reminds us of Calvin. He also has this in common with the reformer of Geneva, that he does not recoil from a single consequence that results from his fundamental principle. That the reality seems to ridicule his conception of Jahveh's government of the world; that it would appear from experience that the consequences both of good and evil—according to his conception, rewards and punishments—are by

---

* Chap. xviii. comp. xiv. 12-23; xxxiii. 10-20.
† Chap. xviii. 2, comp. Jer. xxi. 29.
‡ Chap. iii. 16-21; xiv. 9-11; xxxiii. 1-9.

no means confined to the individual and the term of his life during which he goes on in the same path—all this does not hinder him from holding fast and working out in detail his notion, the only one which he can form, of Jahveh's justice. We repeat: a character such as this may claim our respect, but its onesidedness and its want of depth do not escape our notice.

Besides, this idea of Jahveh's justice is not an independent phenomenon, it is in harmony with the whole of the prophet's idea of God. Even though he be not without faith in Jahveh's mercy and love, still it is much less apparent than his reverence for the highly exalted God and his fear of his majesty. It is as if Ezekiel could not for a single moment forget the infinite distance that separates him from Jahveh. He is constantly addressed by Jahveh as "son of man,"* a designation which does not exclude the intimate relation between the prophet and his sender, it is true, but still places it quite in the shade. More than once he tells us that "the hand of Jahveh came upon him,"† as if, whenever a revelation was made to him, he felt himself seized by an irresistible power. In connection with this, it deserves our notice, that he—for the first time among the prophets—makes the angels act as emissaries to the prophet from Jahveh, and as interpreters of the visions in which the latter reveals himself to him.‡ And the elaborate description of Jahveh's appearance—to Ezekiel himself and at the entry into the new temple§—is also intended to convey a deep impression of Jahveh's unapproachable glory. All this is closely connected. The idea of Jahveh's being becomes purer and more elevated, but at the same time Jahveh draws back, as it were, and a gulf opens between him and mankind. Here, in the prophecies of Ezekiel, we discover the first evident traces of this modification of the notion of God.

* Chap. ii. 1, 3, 6, 8, &c., altogether about ninety times.
† Chap. i. 3; iii. 22; xxxvii. 1; xl. 1.   ‡ Chap. viii. seq.; xl. seq.
§ Chap. i.; x.; xliii. 1, seq.

As we proceed, we shall learn to comprehend it better, and to estimate more truly its great significance.

We return to Ezekiel's conception of Jahveh's justice. The prophet looks upon Israel and the heathen-world from the same point of view. A portion of his book is devoted to a description of the lot that awaits the latter. It is especially—as we were reminded above—the nations and cities with which Israel had been in contact, whose future he sketches. He dwells longest on Tyre and Egypt.* Here also we are struck by his astonishing exactness. The lamentation over Tyre† embraces a complete enumeration of the tribes who traded with the great capital, and of the articles with which they provided her and those which they received from her in exchange. To archæology it is invaluable. But is it not very characteristic, that all these particulars are given us in a prophecy which has no other aim than to announce the utter ruin of Tyre? To explain this diffuseness, however, we must take another thing into consideration, besides Ezekiel's exactness: he evidently lingers with satisfaction over the deep humiliation, or rather the destruction, which he predicts for the proud queen of the seas. Just as the other nations who share her fate, the inhabitants of Tyre had also wronged Israel and had shown in no equivocal manner their joy at the fall of Jerusalem.‡ This the prophet cannot forgive them. He is fully convinced that the God of Israel will punish them for it. For, in spite of his extremely unfavourable verdict upon his own nation, he does not waver for a moment in his belief that Israel is Jahveh's chosen people. Nay, it is precisely because he believes this so firmly, that he is so severe in his demands upon Israel. It is no wonder, therefore, that he does not doubt the punishment of the peoples who have sinned against Jahveh's people, and gladly gives the rein to his imagination in describing their misfortune.

He is no less sure with regard to Israel's future. The last

---

* Chap. xxvi -xxviii. and chap. xxix., xxxii. † Chap. xxvii.
‡ Chap. xxvi; 2 comp. xxv.; 1 seq., 8 seq., 12 seq., 15 seq.

part of his book* is devoted to its description. We already
know that he looks forward to the return of the Israelites to
their native land. We meet again in his prophecies with the
ideas uttered by his predecessors on this subject. Thus, he
believes in the reunion of Judah and Ephraim,† in the restoration of the Davidic monarchy,‡ in the moral regeneration of
Israel.§ But here also peculiar traits are not wanting. Thus,
that regeneration is represented figuratively as the return of
life into dead men's dry bones.|| Thus also—and this diver-
gence from the older prophets does not affect the form merely
—chap. xxxviii. and xxxix. announce a final and decisive
attack of heathendom upon Israel restored. Gog, from the
land of Magog, the leader of a number of nations, viz. Rôsch,
Meshech, Tubal and others, marches upon Canaan to exermi-
nate the inhabitants and enrich himself with their possessions.
But before he passes the borders of the holy land, he is over-
taken by Jahveh's judgment and destroyed with all his followers.
Israel reaps immense spoils, and appears, under Jahveh's protection, to be invulnerable. Ezekiel himself gives us a hint as
to the origin of this conception, when he makes Jahveh speak
to Gog thus: "Thou art he of whom I have spoken in old time
by my servants the prophets of Israel, which prophesied in those
days that I would bring thee against him (against Israel)."¶
To begin with, the reference to the earlier prophets, of which
Ezekiel here gives the first example, is remarkable. But it is
evident at the same time that the prophet, while he acknowledges that those predecessors have been sent by Jahveh,
reserves to himself the right of interpreting their utterances
very freely: we search in vain in the prophecies of earlier date
for the announcement of the attack by Gog upon Israel mentioned here. Moreover, we find in this appeal to Jahveh's

* Chap. xxxiii.-xlviii.   † Chap. xxxvii. 15-18.
‡ In the same passage and chap. xxxiv.; xvii. 22-24.
§ Chap. xxxvi. 16-38; xxxvii. 1-14, &c.
|| Chap. xxxvii. 1-14; comp. *Hk. O.* ii. 289, 290.
¶ Chap. xxxviii. 17; comp. xxxix. 8.

former envoys the proof that the whole picture is the product, not of prophetic enthusiasm, but of calm deliberation and thought. Its form also surely bears witness to this: no trace of elevation of mind, but great copiousness and precision of detail. If Ezekiel's prophecies in general be works of art, this is true in a special degree of this prediction.

If Ezekiel strikes out his own path in these two chapters, he does so much more still in chap. xl.—xlviii, where he sets forth his ideas upon the new order of things which will come into being after Israel's return to her native land. We search the Old Testament in vain for a parallel to this picture. One might call it a complete plan for the organization of the new Israel. Ezekiel first gives a minute description of the temple;* this is followed by his precepts concerning religious worship and the staff of the temple, and concerning the Prince, his rights and obligations;† and finally he regulates the division of the land among the twelve tribes, the residences of the priests and Levites and the arrangement of the temple-city.‡

From more than one point of view this last portion of Ezekiel's book is the most important of all. In the first place, it confirms in the most striking manner our conception of the origin of the laws attributed to Moses. The Jewish tradition tells us that in the first century of the Christian era the canonical authority of Ezekiel's prophecies was still disputed.§

---

* Chap. xl. 5—xliii. 27. Mention is made here in turn of the outer courts and its buildings; the inner court and its chambers; the temple as a whole; the holy cells and the size of the sanctuary. According to chap. xliii. 1-12, Jahveh's glory takes possession of the temple. After this again (verses 13-27) there follows the description of the altar for burnt-offerings.

† Chap. xliv. 1—xlvi. 24. These regulate the duties of the sons of Zadok and of the rest of the Levites; the incomes of the temple and the Prince; the sacrifices, at festivals as well as in general; the Prince's gifts and the preparation of the sacrificial meals.

‡ Chap. xlvii. xlviii. We find here first the description of the spring that rises in the temple and flows through part of the land; then a statement of the boundaries of the land and directions as to its division among the tribes, the priests and the Levites, and finally a decree relating to the gates of Jerusalem.

§ Comp. *Theol. Tijdschrift*, iii. 163.

This does not surprise us. Rather do we wonder that for so long afterwards the conflict between his book and the current opinion as to the age of the Pentateuch remained unnoticed or was thought capable of explanation. For that conflict is indeed most obvious. Let us suppose for a moment that Ezekiel was in possession of the entire Pentateuch. Even then, with a view to Israel's return to the holy land, he might have framed a number of precepts and rules. There was nothing to hinder him, *e. g.*, from decreeing how the temple should be built and arranged: the Solomonic house of Jahveh lay in ruins and would have to be replaced by a new building. Nor would the precepts concerning the division of the land among the twelve tribes and concerning the share of the Prince, the priests and the rest of the temple-servants, have been unnatural or superfluous in that case. But Ezekiel goes further in his regulations. He gives instructions as to the consecration of the altar of burnt-offerings,* the qualifications required for admittance into the priesthood,† the dress and the cleanness of the priests,‡ the festivals and the sacrifices which belonged to them.§ What? we ask upon reading these decrees, was all this necessary? Why does not Ezekiel content himself with a simple reference to the Mosaic laws? For in the present Pentateuch all these subjects are, in fact, regulated, and this generally more fully and minutely than in the writings of the prophet of the exile. No one gives us a satisfactory answer to this question. So we must therefore infer from Ezekiel's regulations that he was not acquainted with the whole of the Mosaic law: Deuteronomy and the still older Book of the Covenant‖ are pre-supposed by him throughout, but nothing beyond these collections.

The accuracy of this conclusion, however, is still open to doubt. In the abstract, the possibility must be granted, that Ezekiel thought this and that decree of the Mosaic laws less adapted to the new state of things which he was describing,

---

* Chap. xliii. 18-27. † Chap. xliv. 10-16, comp. xl. 46; xliii. 19; xlviii. 11.
‡ Chap. xliv. 17-31. § Chap. xlv. 18-25. ‖ Above, p. 8.

and therefore tried to replace them with others. But when we lay his precepts side by side with those of the Pentateuch, it is evident again and again that this is not the relation between them. Ezekiel's regulations have the appearance rather of an older draft, an as yet incomplete and less elaborated sketch, of what has become law in the Pentateuch. We know from Deuteronomy, that at the time of Josiah's reformation all the Levites, without exception, were considered qualified to serve as priests of Jahveh.* Ezekiel is the first to desire other rules *for the future:* after the return of Israel to her native land, "the sons of Zadok" shall be the only lawful priests; they have rendered themselves worthy of this honour by their fidelity to Jahveh; their brethren, the rest of the Levites, have strayed away from Jahveh with Israel, nay, have set the example to Israel in practising idolatry; for this sin they are punished with degradation; in future they shall be employed in and about the sanctuary in subordinate positions.† The younger laws of the Pentateuch go much further: according to the account which they give us, the difference between priests and Levites is founded upon their descent; the former are "sons of Aaron," and as such are exclusively qualified for the priestly office.‡ Had Ezekiel known of these regulations, he would have withheld his historical explanation of the difference in rank between "the sons of Zadok" and the Levites. How could he have thought of putting forward as something new and alleging express reasons for what, according to the laws of the Pentateuch, had existed from the very beginning, and, so long as the election of Aaron and his race by Jahveh retained its force, would have to continue unaltered?

We might go on in this way: every fresh comparison would render it still clearer that Ezekiel's regulations are to the younger, priestly ordinances of the Pentateuch as a preliminary

---

* Above, p. 26. † See the passages indicated on p. 115, n. †.

‡ Exod. xxviii. xxix; Lev. xxi. xxii.; Num. iii. iv.; xviii. 1, seq., and a number of other passages which will be cited in this and the next chapter.

draft is to a definite law. But it seems preferable to reserve this comparison, in so far as it belongs to our subject, until later, when we shall be called upon to handle expressly the priestly documents of the Thorah. The manner in which Ezekiel wished to see the public service conducted is, to a certain degree, a matter of indifference to us. His anticipations and plans do not become of real interest to us, until it appears that they have been realized or even exceeded by the reality. In this latter case they show us the road by which the ultimate purpose, which we learn from the Pentateuch, has been attained. Who would not hail with thankfulness every ray of light which falls upon the highly important, but, unfortunately, in great part hidden efforts of the Jahveh-priests?

There is still another point of view from which Ezekiel's description of the re-born Israel deserves our whole attention. It surprises us at first to meet with such a picture in a book written out of Palestine and at a time when no temple, nay, even no Israelitish state, existed. Nothing can be more natural than that the exiles should have pondered deeply upon the things which were to come. But how can it have occurred to one of them to outstrip time, as it were, and to regulate the service of a temple which was yet to be built? Upon more mature consideration, however, this surprise disappears. The very firmness of Ezekiel's belief in Israel's restoration accounts in some measure for the fulness and minuteness of his draft: he lives and moves in the future, as though it were already present. But besides this, it is easy to explain psychologically, how it was that his mind busied itself in preference with the Jahveh-worship in the temple. He had carried the remembrance of it with him into exile. His estimation of that worship, far from suffering from its temporary suspension, necessarily gained by it: the sacrifices and feasts, with their ceremonial, were fairer in the imagination than in the—often not very elevating and sometimes even degrading—reality. Hence it is that we find in Ezekiel—and why not also in others, who were placed

in the same circumstances as he?—great predilection for the
ceremonies and customs of the Jahveh-worship, which displayed
itself, very naturally, in the collecting and writing down of the
priestly traditions relating to them, and led of itself, as it were,
to the projection of fixed laws.

But even though such considerations as these dispel the
surprise which Ezekiel's undertaking at first occasioned, that
undertaking nevertheless remains most remarkable and worthy
of reflection. We Dutchmen are involuntarily reminded of the
great man, who, while Napoleon's yoke pressed upon our land
with the weight of lead, employed himself in his quiet study in
drafting a " Constitution for the Kingdom of the Netherlands."
To him it was given to witness the realization of his desires
and to powerfully co-operate therein himself. This privilege
was not reserved for Ezekiel. He quitted the scene before
the new day began to glimmer upon the horizon. Yet he did
not think and labour in vain. His words did not make much
impression upon his contemporaries: they appear to have
ridiculed the sombre preacher, his similes and metaphors, his
apparently harebrained visions.* And even the next generation, which lived to see the deliverance, shows but feeble
traces of his influence. But his prophecies were preserved,
and, even if they did not meet with their fulfilment, at all
events exercised great influence upon the regeneration of
Israel about a hundred years after his death.

Let us not anticipate, however. As yet the priestly tendency, which Ezekiel represents, is not the main stream of
Israel's religious history. The exile at Tel-abîb stands aside,
as it were. Jeremiah, to whom he also was much indebted,
was to revive among his nation before Ezekiel's spirit gained
the upper hand. The men who uttered their inspired language
towards the end of the captivity, walked in Jeremiah's footsteps. In order to understand that language, we will first take
a glance at the course of political events.

* Chap. xxxiii. 30-33; comp. *Hk. O.* ii. 259, n. 7.

After a reign of more than 40 years, which upon the whole was very prosperous, Nebuchadnezzar died in the year 561 B.C. Under Evil-Merodach, his son and successor, better times seemed to be dawning for the Israelitish exiles. Jehoiachin, who hitherto had been a prisoner, was treated with favour at the beginning of the new reign, and even admitted to the court.* Perhaps the Israelitish captives expected an improvement in their own condition also from this change of fortune for their former king. In that case, however, their hope was not realized: everything remained as before. But soon phenomena presented themselves, which were to give another direction to their hopes. The usual malady of Eastern monarchies began to declare itself in the Chaldean kingdom in a very alarming manner. After a rule of two years Evil-Merodach was killed and succeeded by his brother-in-law Neriglissar (559 B.C.). The latter reigned four years. After a reign of nine months his son Laborosoarchod fell a victim to a conspiracy, in consequence of which Nabonedus or Nabunita, descended from another family than that of Nebuchadnezzar, now became king (555 B.C.). He does not seem to have been wanting in energy and talent. But he struggled against his fate in vain. The man had already arisen who was to hurl him from his throne. In the year 558 B.C. the Persians, led by Cyrus, the son of Cambyses, had won their independence from the Medes. Before long they subjected their former masters to their authority, so that Cyrus stood at the head of the united Persians and Medes, and soon threatened all Asia. Next to the tribes which had belonged to the Medean monarchy, Croesus king of Lydia was vanquished by him. It was now Nabunita's turn. Cyrus crossed the Tigris and defeated him severely. Nabunita had to save himself by flight, was unable to reach his capital again, and threw himself into Borsippa. The reduction of Babylon, however, where Nabunita's son, Belsharezer or Belshazzar, now commanded, remained for Cyrus a very difficult,

---

* 2 Kings xxv. 27-30 ; Jer. lii. 31-34.

nay, an almost hopeless undertaking. He succeeded in it by a fortunate stratagem: the waters of the Euphrates, which ran through the city, were diverted, so that the Persians were able to enter by the nearly dry bed of the river and to attack the inhabitants unawares. The mighty Babylonish monarchy became a province of the great kingdom of Persia (538 B.C.).

Nothing can be more natural, than that these events should have attracted the attention of the Babylonish exiles in a high degree. Especially those among them who were most attached to Jahveh and his worship must have watched them with the greatest interest. To these men their exile in a foreign land, their removal from Zion, Jahveh's abode, was a great calamity: they were much less able than their fellow tribesmen to adapt themselves to their new surroundings. But beside this, the remembrance of Jahveh's promises, of which Jeremiah especially had been the interpreter, remained alive among them. If the expectations that had been built upon these promises had gradually been lulled to sleep by the long duration of the exile, but little was needed to rewaken them. And very soon after his rise it was evident that Cyrus' plans were wide in their conception and masterly in their execution.

We are not astonished, therefore, that after the year 558 B.C. the exiles began to bestir themselves. How glad we should be to be accurately informed of what took place amongst them. But this wish is idle: historical accounts are altogether wanting. Yet we can form a tolerably complete and accurate idea of what went on in their minds. Unless the Israelites had grown altogether unlike their forefathers, the fermentation among them must have shown itself outwardly in prophetic ecstasy. And this is what indeed happened.

The book named after Isaiah includes, besides the oracles which are really derived from that prophet, Hezekiah's contemporary, a number of other prophecies, which, as appears from their form and contents, date from later times, in fact from our period. Part of them have been inserted between the genuine productions of Isaiah,* but by far the majority are at the end of the collection.† From the fact that they are preceded by four historical chapters,‡ it has been rightly inferred that they were added to the book of Isaiah when the latter, in the intention of the original compiler, was already finished: if he had also attributed chap. xl.-lxvi. to Isaiah, he would have made the historical explanation of part of the labours of the prophet, which is now given in chap. xxxvi.-xxxix, follow chap. lxvi. At any rate it is certain that the author of these last twenty-seven chapters never thought of passing for Isaiah. Not so certain are the answers to the questions: Are these chapters from one hand? Were they written before the fall of Babylon, or—all or part of them—after it? Which is the land of their birth, Babylonia or Palestine? The investigation of these points is yet far from completed. Still I do not hesitate to accept it as proved, that at all events some portions§ were written down in the land of the exile, whether it were in the vicinity of the Chebar, or in the immediate neighbourhood of Babylon, and this before the fall of the Chaldean monarchy. It is especially of these portions that we may confidently make use for our present purpose. Nor do we hesitate to borrow from Isa. xiii. 1—xiv. 23, xxi. 1-10, xxxiv, xxxv, the information which we seek. Besides the light which they themselves afford, these prophecies are of service to us through their affinity with Jeremiah, chap. l., li.: they teach us, namely, that the lengthy oracle against Babylon contained there did not originate from Jeremiah, but was written in his name towards the end of the exile. Very naturally—but in violation of literary good faith—the seer who had announced the return of the exiles in the distant future, is now made to predict their deliverance as immediately at hand.‖

If the chief inducement to all these prophets to come for-

---

* Chap. xiii. 1—xiv. 23 ; xxi. 1-10 ; xxiv.—xxvii. ; xxxiv., xxxv.
† Chap. xl.-lxvi ‡ Chap. xxxvi.—xxxix. § viz. Chap. xl.-xlviii. or xlix.
‖ Comp. also *Hk. O.* ii. 98-144, 151-157, 226-240.

ward, or—for some of them seem to have worked rather as writers than as speakers—to write all these prophecies, lay in the revolt and the first victories of Cyrus, we are not surprised that the approaching fall of the Babylonish kingdom, and, in consequence, the liberation of the Israelites from their captivity, formed the real purport of the predictions. The anticipations cherished and uttered concerning these events, which were the main thing for the contemporary, have lost much of their weight for us and therefore need not be set forth here at length. In describing the fall of Babylon and the journey of the liberated exiles to their native land, the prophets could allow their imaginations full play. But whatever shape their representation of the deliverance assumed, to which moreover the result did not at all respond, the ideas upon which it was based remained the same. The Chaldeans sinned against Jahveh, when they laid waste Jerusalem and the temple and carried away Israel into exile; this insult Jahveh could leave unpunished for a time, it is true, but not for long; he is the just one; moreover he is faithful to the covenant made with Israel: these are thoughts to which these seers give utterance again and again. It is easy to imagine the picture of the future which unrolled itself to their minds on the strength of these convictions. One describes to us the deep humiliation of Babylon's king and the reception given him in the lower world, the *Sheol*, when the spirits awake out of their slumber and cry to him, "How art thou fallen from heaven, O morning-star, son of the dawn! how art thou cast down to the earth, which didst smite the nations!"* Another revels in the description of Babylon's destruction and of the glorious return of the Israelites:

"The ransomed of Jahveh shall return
And come to Zion with rejoicing,
And everlasting gladness is upon their heads:
Joy and rejoicing shall be their portion,
But sorrow and sighs shall flee away."†

* Isa. xiv. 4, seq., 12. † Isa. xxxiv. sq.; xxxv. 10.

A third is never tired of telling of the striving of the nations against the proud city.* Another again makes us witnesses of the abasement of her gods† and of the confusion of her astrologers.‡

In these expectations the prophets who raised their voices towards the end of the exile agree together and do not essentially differ from their predecessors. But we should be mistaken, did we imagine that they confined themselves to repeating, in a modified form, what had already been said before. In our opinion, there is no real or internal connection between the great conquests of Cyrus and the fortunes of the Israelitish exiles in the kingdom of Babylon: the latter, we believe, when they obtained permission to return to their native land, reaped the fruits of events with which at first they had nothing to do. But this was not the standpoint of the pious Israelites in those days. They were thoroughly convinced that it was *for their sakes* that Cyrus appeared and that his enterprises were crowned with such great success. If we place ourselves upon this standpoint, it at once becomes clear to us how the conception of Jahveh's being necessarily became modified and enlarged under the influence of the events of those days. It is true, even before the Babylonish exile the prophets had regarded events of such preponderating significance as, *e. g.*, the victories of the Assyrians and the struggle between the Chaldeans and the Egyptians, as dispensations of Jahveh, and had connected them most intimately with Jahveh's plans respecting his people. But now they became convinced that the condition of the whole of Asia was governed by Jahveh, and was changed in accordance with their wants and wishes. The violent revolution of which they had been interested spectators, was the fulfilment of the promises which he had caused Jeremiah and other prophets to announce. Nothing could be more natural than that they should now form a much grander idea than before of Jahveh's might and fore-knowledge.

* Jer. l. li.   † Isa. xlvi. 1-2.   ‡ Isa. xlvii. 9, 12-15.

It is especially the author of Isa. xl. seq., whom we can call for the sake of distinction the second or Babylonish Isaiah, who reflects in his oracles the influence thus exercised by these great events. Hear how he challenges the servants of the false gods to try their strength with Jahveh:

"Produce your cause, saith Jahveh;
Bring forth your strong proofs, saith the king of Jacob.
Let them bring them forth and declare to us
The things which shall happen.
Declare to us what the former predictions were,
That we may mark them and consider their end;
Or let us hear what is to come.
Declare the things that shall come hereafter,
That we may know that ye are gods;
Do some good or evil,
That we may be amazed and behold it together.
Behold, ye are of nothing and your work is of nothing:
An abomination is he that chooseth you.
 I raised him* up out of the north, and he came,
Out of the east him who calleth upon my name,
That he should trample upon governors as upon mire,
As the potter who kneadeth the clay.
Who hath declared from the beginning, that we may know it,
And beforetime, that we may say, he is right.
There is none that declared it, none that proclaimed it,
None that understood your words.
As the first (I say) to Zion, 'Behold, there they are!'
And I give to Jerusalem one that bringeth good tidings."†

No less strongly does he express himself elsewhere, in a discourse which seems to be addressed to the Israelites who are inclined to idolatry:

"Remember this and show yourselves men,

---

* *i.e.* Cyrus. † Isa. xli. 21-27.

Take it to heart, O ye unfaithful.
Remember the former things from of old,
That I am a Strong One,* and none else,
A Fearful One,† and none is like me,
Who declare the end from the beginning,
And from old what has not yet happened,
Who say, 'My counsel shall stand
And all my pleasure I shall perform;'
Who call from the East an eagle,
From a far country the man of my counsel:
I have spoken it and I will also bring it to pass,
I have planned it and I will also fulfil it."‡

The comparison between Jahveh and the gods of the heathen which we find instituted in these and similar passages, occurs again constantly in the second Isaiah, and always leads to the same result, the utter nullity of the idol. The way in which he identifies the false god with the image of the false god is characteristic. The prophet describes with biting sarcasm the making of such an idol and the folly of those who expect light and help from it.§ Others had already attacked the worshippers of false gods in this way before his time, but no one does it so expressly and fully as he. Here also the influence of contemporary events is unmistakable. On the one hand, the warning against the worship of those images is absolutely necessary in Babylonia, "the land of idols."‖ And, on the other hand, the humiliation of the false gods is the reverse side of the exaltation of Jahveh. In none of the earlier prophets, therefore, do we find so much stress laid upon *Jahveh's oneness* as in the second Isaiah. Its recognition, as we have seen,¶ is not wanting in his predecessors. But they are not in the habit of enlarging upon

---

* Hebr. *El*. Comp. Vol. I., p. 41.   † Hebr. *Elohîm*. Comp. Vol. I., p. 41.
‡ Isa. xlvi. 8-11. See farther also chap. xli. 1-7 ; xlii. 9 ; xliii. 8-13 ; xlv. 19-21 ; xlviii.
§ Isa. xl. 19, 20 ; xli. 6, 7 ; xliv. 9-19 ; xlvi. 6, 7.
‖ Jer. l. 38.   ¶ Vol. I., p. 50, seq.; above, p. 22.

it. In fact, it is enough for them to know that none of the other gods can be compared to Israel's god. Jahveh's envoy to the exiles goes much further in utterances such as these:

"Ye are my witnesses, saith Jahveh,
And my servant whom I have chosen,
That ye may observe it and believe me,
And understand that *I* am he:
Before me there was no god formed,
And there shall be none after me.
I, even I am Jahveh,
And beside me there is none that saveth.
I have declared, and saved, and made known,
While there was no strange (god) among you:
Ye are my witnesses and I am god.
Yea, from of old I am he,
And there is none that teareth out of my hand:
I accomplish it, and who shall hinder it?"*

"Thus saith Jahveh, Israel's king and redeemer, Jahveh of hosts:
I am the first and I am the last,
And beside me there is no god."†

"Thus saith Jahveh, thy redeemer,
And thy creator from thy mother's womb:
I, Jahveh, do all things,
I alone stretch out the heavens
And establish the earth by my might;
(I am he) that frustrateth the tokens of the liars,
And putteth the diviners to shame,
That turneth back wise men,
And turneth their knowledge into foolishness."‡

This strict monotheism necessarily influenced the whole of

---

* Isa. xliii. 10-13. † Isa. xliv. 6.
‡ Isa. xliv. 24, 25. See further chap. xlv. 5, 6, 14, 18, 22; xlvi. 9, &c.

the prophet's religious views. Jahveh is enthroned in awful majesty, above the earth and its inhabitants: what are the latter compared with him?

"All flesh is as grass
And all its goodliness as the flower of the field:
The grass withereth, the flower fadeth,
When Jahveh's breath hath blown upon it;
Surely the people is grass!
The grass withereth, the flower fadeth,
But the word of our god standeth for ever."*

Contrasts such as these also occur elsewhere in this prophet.† There were some among his contemporaries who threw doubt upon the care of so highly exalted a God for the affairs of men, or for Israel in particular. The second Isaiah does not think of doing so. On the contrary, he firmly believes in Jahveh's all-embracing activity. In the same discourse in which he points so emphatically to the infinite distance between mankind and Jahveh, we find this touchingly beautiful encouragement:

"Why sayest thou, O Jacob,
And speakest thou, O Israel,
'My way is hid from Jahveh,
And my right passeth by my god?'
Knowest thou not, or hast thou not heard,
That Jahveh is an everlasting god,
The creator of the ends of the earth,
Who fainteth not, neither is weary,
Whose understanding is unsearchable?
He giveth power to the faint,
And to the weak he sendeth great strength.
Youths become faint and weary,
And young men surely stumble,
But they that wait for Jahveh shall renew their strength

---

* Isa. xl. 6-8.   † Isa. xl. 15, 17, 22, 23, &c.

And spread out their wings as eagles :
They shall run and not become weary,
They shall walk and faint not."*

It will be observed, that as yet the recognition of Jahveh's majesty does not in the least detract from the belief in his gracious nearness to man : "The high and lofty one that sitteth in eternity and whose name is holy" also dwells "in the contrite and humble of spirit, to revive the spirit of the humble and the heart of the contrite."† But the prophet does feel the necessity of making it plain to himself and others, how this absolutely solo Jahveh could place himself in an altogether peculiar relation towards a single people. In proportion as Jahveh became more highly exalted in the estimation of his servants, the choosing of Israel by Jahveh appeared the more singular : was it not at variance with what, precisely as that Only One, he owed to all ? At all events it was very natural that an attempt should also be made to justify logically the universal belief of the Israelites in that choice. The Babylonish Isaiah employed his energy upon this, and arrived at results which more than merit our closer study.

Nothing is further from the mind of our great unknown writer than the idea that from the very beginning Israel has been entitled by her virtues to the distinction which has fallen to her share, or has since proved herself worthy of its continuance by her fidelity to Jahveh. He rather deplores throughout the sins of his nation, and more than once he makes it humbly confess its guilt :

"Who hath given Jacob for a spoil
And Israel to the robbers ?
Hath not Jahveh, against whom we have sinned,
In whose ways we would not walk,
To whose *thorah* we did not hearken ?"‡

---

* Isa. xl. 27-31; comp. also chap. xlix. 14-16.
† Isa. lvii. 15.   ‡ Isa. xlii. 24.

"Transgressor from thy mother's womb is thy name"—he says in another passage.* The confession which the people make is touching:

"Behold, thou (Jahveh) art become wroth, and we have sinned,
Thine anger is everlasting, and we have transgressed.†
We are all as one unclean,
And our virtues as a soiled garment;
So we all faded as a leaf,
And our sins tore us away like the wind;
No one called upon thy name
And stirred himself up to take hold of thee,
For thou hast hid thy face from us
And lettest us perish because of our transgressions."‡

But it is unnecessary to write out any more passages to prove this.§ It is, perhaps, superfluous to add that the deliverance from the exile may also by no means be regarded as a reward for Israel's fidelity. For:

"Not upon me hast thou called, O Jacob!
Nor given thyself trouble for my sake, O Israel!
Thou hast not brought me thy burnt offerings of sheep,
Nor honoured me with thy sacrifices;
I have not caused thee to serve with a meat offering,
Nor wearied thee with incense.
Thou hast bought me no sweet cane with money,
Nor filled me with the fat of thy sacrifices:
But thou hast vexed me with thy sins,
And wearied me with thy transgressions."‖

If the cause of the intimate relation in which Jahveh stands to this one people, and which, as appears from the approaching

---

* Isa. xlviii. 8. † According to an altered reading of the text.
‡ Isa. lxiv. 5b-7.
§ Among others, Isa. xl. 2; xliv. 22; xlvii. 6; xlviii. 4, 18; l. 1; li. 13; liii. 5, 6, 8, 12; lviii. 1, seq.; lix. 2, seq.; 10, seq.; lxiii. 10, 15, seq.
‖ Isa. xliii 22-24, comp. lxv. 1-7.

miraculous deliverance, he will not break off in the future, do not lie in Israel, then it must lie in Jahveh himself. And so in fact it does : to the words just quoted the prophet immediately adds :

> "I, even I am he that blotteth out thy transgressions for mine own sake,
> And remembereth thy sins no more."*

He reverts to this idea again and again.† Now it is Jahveh's *faithfulness* to his promises,‡ then again his *love*, by which the prophet considers the continuance of the relation between Jahveh and his people to be assured. Every one will remember those beautiful words :—

> "Zion said, 'Jahveh hath forsaken me
> And the Lord hath forgotten me.'
> Doth a woman forget her sucking child,
> Having no compassion on the child of her womb?
> Though she should forget,
> Yet will I not forget thee."§

The problem has now been clearly put, it is true, but it is yet far from solved : how is so intimate a connection between the sole God and a single nation—a nation laden with guilt— to be justified? Of course, I by no means assert that the Babylonish Isaiah gives a complete and satisfactory answer to this question, nor even that he puts it exactly in this form. Yet we find in him two ideas which are not only connected with this problem, but also occurred to the prophet, or at any rate were further developed, in consequence of it. I refer to what he says of *the servant of Jahveh* and *his calling as regards the heathen-world*.

To the question, who is "the servant of Jahveh"?—the prophet himself seems to give an unequivocal answer, when he

---

* Isa. xliii. 25.   † Comp. Isa. xlviii. 9-11, and elsewhere.
‡ Isa. liv. 10, and elsewhere.   § Isa. xlix. 14, 15, comp. xliii. 3, 4.

explains that expression by adding to it "Jacob" or "Israel." As, *e. g.*, in the words:

"And thou, Israel, *my servant*,
Jacob, whom I have chosen,
Seed of Abraham, my friend."*

"And now hear, O Jacob, *my servant*,
And Israel, whom I have chosen.
Thus saith Jahveh, that made thee and formed thee,
That helpeth thee from thy mother's womb:
Fear not, *my servant* Jacob,
And Jeshurun,† whom I have chosen."‡

Or where the servant is introduced speaking:

"Jahveh said unto me, 'thou art *my servant*,
Israel, in whom I will glorify myself.'"§

But it is already evident from these passages, and still more so from others which will be quoted immediately, that Isaiah is not thinking of the actual Israel, but of Israel proper, *i. e.* of the kernel of the nation, that really possesses the attributes which ought to characterize the whole. Thus he makes a distinction between Israel in a broad and in a narrow sense. To the latter belong those who are not only descended from Jacob, but also possess the virtues which beseem the chosen people of Jahveh. It lies in the nature of such a form of speech, that it exhibits a certain looseness, and here and there leaves the prophet's meaning somewhat doubtful: in reality also the lines of demarcation between the spiritual Israel and the Israel of the flesh could not be sharply defined. Read, *e. g.*, the beautiful description which is put into the mouth of the servant of Jahveh:

---

* Isa. xli. 8.   † Comp. Vol. I. 379, n. ‡.
‡ Isa. xliv. 1, 2. See further chap. xlii. 19-21, (comp. 22-24); xliv. 21; xlv. 4; xlviii. 20.   § Isa. xlix. 3.

"Hearken, O inhabitants of the coast, unto me,
 And listen, ye peoples from afar.
 Jahveh hath called me from my mother's womb,
 Even before I was born, he made mention of my name.
 And he made my mouth like a sharp sword,
 In the shadow of his hand he hid me;
 He made me a sharp arrow,
 And put me away in his quiver.
 Then said he unto me, 'Thou art my servant,
 Israel, in whom I will glorify myself.'
 And I said, 'I have laboured in vain,
 Without fruit and for nought have I spent my strength:
 Yet—my right is with Jahveh,
 And my reward with my god.'
   But now saith Jahveh,
 Who formed me from my mother's womb to be his servant,
 That he should bring back to himself Jacob,
 And gather to himself Israel,
 While I am honoured in Jahveh's eyes,
 And my god is my strength;
 Thus he said, 'It is too little, that thou shouldst be my
        servant,
 To raise up the tribes of Jacob,
 And bring back the liberated of Israel:
 Therefore have I appointed thee for a light to the nations,
 That my salvation may reach to the end of the earth.
   Thus saith Jahveh the redeemer and holy one of Israel,
 To him whose life is despised, whom the nation abhorreth,
        who serveth the rulers,
 (To him) shall kings look up; (before him) they shall
        stand up,
 The princes, and unto him they shall show honour—
 For the sake of Jahveh, who is faithful,
 Of the Holy One of Israel, who hath chosen thee."*

* Isa. xlix. 1-7: comp. also chap. xlii. 1-7.

It is true, one thing and another occurs here upon which the requisite light will not be thrown till afterwards. But it is undeniable, that the author contrasts a portion, and that the better portion, of the nation with the rest. If we now recall to mind, that at all times some prophets belonged to that kernel of Israel, we are not surprised that here and there "the servant of Jahveh" is pictured or made to speak in such a way, that evidently in the first place Jahveh's envoys are referred to. Thus, *e.g.*, where it is said of Jahveh :

"He confirmeth the word *of his servant*
And performeth the counsel of his messengers,
When he saith to Jerusalem, 'be restored!'
And to the cities of Judah : 'be rebuilt !
And their ruins will I raise up again' "—*

and where the second Isaiah—or one of his younger contemporaries?—sketches himself, as one of Jahveh's interpreters, in particular :

"The Lord Jahveh gave me a tongue of the learned,
That I might refresh the weary with words ;
Morning by morning he wakeneth mine ear,
That I may hear as they that are instructed.
The Lord Jahveh opened mine ear, and I resisted not,
And I turned not away backward.
I gave my back to them that smote,
And my beard to them that plucked out the hair ;
I hid not my face from shame and spitting.
The Lord Jahveh shall help me :
Therefore shall I not be confounded ;
Therefore I make my face as flint,†
And I know that I shall not be put to shame.
He is near that justifieth me :
Will anyone contend with me ? let us then stand up together.

---

* Isa. xliv. 26. † A symbol of undauntedness.

Hath anyone a cause against me? let him come near to me.
Behold, the Lord Jahveh shall help me: who shall condemn me?
Behold, they all shall wax old as a garment; the moth shall eat them up!
Who among you feareth Jahveh
And hearkeneth to the word of *his servant?*
He that walketh in darkness and hath no light,
Let him trust in the name of Jahveh,
And stay upon his god!"*

The distinction which the prophet constantly makes here, was borrowed from the reality, as we have already been reminded. There existed, in fact, two sorts of Israelites, Israelites in name, and in reality—in the same way that, especially in the final chapters of the book named after Isaiah, the "servants of Jahveh" (in the plural) are contrasted with those who had deserted or forgotten their god.† But it was precisely of this distinction that a new difficulty was born. According to the Israelitish conception of the divine justice, the lot in life of the individual man corresponded with his attitude towards Jahveh: was this also the case with "the servant of Jahveh?" was his condition different from that of the unfaithful? Daily experience taught the contrary: he too had been carried away into exile, and as deeply humbled as they who were in rebellion against Jahveh. How were these sufferings of "Jahveh's servant" to be explained? *He suffers as a part of Israel; he bears the sins of his nation.* Had the prophet confined himself to the utterance of this truth, we should then have to admit that he has grasped and represented the reality more purely than his predecessor Ezekiel,‡ but otherwise we should have no inducement to dwell longer upon this view of his. But he goes further: to him the "servant's" sufferings are more than a sad

---

* Isa. l. 4-10; comp. chap. xlviii. 16; lxi. 1-3.
† Isa. liv. 17; lvi. 6; lxiii. 17; lxv. 8, 9, 13-15; lxvi. 14.
‡ See above pp. 109, seq.

necessity or a burden laid upon him by Jahveh. It is part of his task to bear those sufferings; they are not his least powerful means of benefiting his whole nation—and, as we shall shortly find, the heathen also. This idea, which is just indicated here and there,* is developed expressly in the famous description of the suffering "servant of Jahveh," which the Christian church from the earliest times has seen fully confirmed and fulfilled in the person of its founder. The reader will remember that pathetically beautiful description:—

"Despised and forsaken of men,
 A man of sorrows and acquainted with grief,
 Like unto one from whom a man covereth his face,
 Despised, and esteemed not by us.
  But—it was our griefs that he bare,
 Our sorrows that he carried—
 Yet we did esteem him stricken,
 Smitten of God and afflicted.
 But he was wounded for our transgressions,
 Bruised for our iniquities:
 The chastisement which would give us peace, was upon him,
 And with his stripes we were healed.
 All we like sheep had gone astray
 And had turned every one to his own way,
 But Jahveh laid upon him the iniquity of us all!"†

In all this the increasing depth of religious thought is unmistakable. The Babylonish Isaiah might, with most of his contemporaries, have retained in its simplicity the traditional conception of Israel's election by Jahveh; to the doubts engendered by Israel's degradation he might have replied by referring to the future and the dominion which his nation would then have over its present oppressors. We do, in fact, find this latter notion in his writings: his description of Israel's

---

* Isa. xlix. 4, 7, and in the verses just quoted, Isa. l. 5, 6, 10.
† Isa. liii. 3-6 ; the whole pericope runs from chap. lii. 13 to liii. 12.

approaching glory is even richer and more highly coloured than that of any one of his predecessors.* But side by side with this stand the ideas which we have just quoted. In the limited conception of "Israel" which comes to light in many of the utterances relating to "the servant of Jahveh," the election of that people loses to a certain degree its arbitrary character, and receives an ethical colouring, even if it does not become a moral act. And again, the explanation of the suffering of the pious by the connection in which they stand to the whole nation, is both a real advance in theodicy and an important step onwards in the path to a more spiritual conception of the relation between Jahveh and his people.

The truth of all this becomes still more obvious, when we fix our attention upon *the task of Jahveh's servant*. Here and there in the last chapters of the book of Isaiah—as we remarked just now—is uttered the expectation with which we are already acquainted, viz., that the heathen shall one day serve Israel. This expectation is religious and political at the same time: the nations shall go up to Jerusalem both to pray to Jahveh and to pay homage to Israel. Moreover, this conversion is regarded, in the utterances referred to, as a miracle: Jahveh will call these nations to himself and cause them to go up to his house; full of awe and fear they will repair to his holy mount.† Now from these ideas the sketch of the labours of "Jahveh's servant" among the heathen is easily to be distinguished. Does not his influence upon them exhibit a moral character? The nations witness his preaching and his sufferings, are deeply impressed by them, turn to Jahveh and recognize the close relation between him and his servant, whose glorification is thereby completed. These are the thoughts which are expressed in a few passages already given above,‡ and which we also meet with elsewhere in the second Isaiah. "Behold"—says Jahveh—

---

* See i. a. Isa. xlix. 22, 23 ; liv. 3 ; lv. 5 ; lvi. 6-8 ; lix. 16-20 ; lx.; lxvi. 12, seq † See the passages cited in the preceding note.

‡ See Isa. xlix. 1, 6, 7 ; above, p. 132.

"Behold my servant, whom I uphold,
Mine elect, in whom my soul delighteth:
I lay my spirit upon him,
He shall proclaim right to the nations."*

"He shall not fail nor be discouraged,
*Till he have set right in the earth
And the inhabitants of the coast wait for his instruction.*"†

"I, Jahveh, have called thee in righteousness,
And will hold thine hand,
And will keep thee and place thee for a covenant of the people,
For a light of the Gentiles."‡

"Behold, my servant shall be prosperous,
Shall be exalted, become high and illustrious.
As many have been astonished at him—
So marred, lower than human, was his visage
And his form meaner than those of the sons of men,—
So shall he cause *many nations* to spring up,
And *kings* shall shut their mouths for him;
For that which had not been told them shall they see,
And observe that which they had not heard."§

"Free from the trouble of his soul he shall behold till he be satisfied;
By his knowledge shall my righteous servant bring many to righteousness,
And he shall bear their iniquities.
Therefore will I give him a portion among the great,
And he shall divide the spoil with the strong;
Because he hath given his life unto death,

---

* Isa. xlii. 1, "right" (mishfât), in the estimation of the prophet, is inseparable from religion.
† L. c., verse 4; for "instruction" there stands in the Hebrew "thorah."
‡ Ver. 6. § Isa. lii. 13-15.

> And is numbered with the godless,
> Whereas he bare the sins of many
> And made intercession for the godless."*

It is evident that we have here not a dogma, with sharp outlines and bounds, but an idea which forces itself upon the prophet, a surmise, as it were, as to the destiny of Jahveh's servant and the meaning of his fortunes, which occurred to his mind in consequence of what he saw and experienced. If those other utterances, in which the earlier, politico-religious conception of Israel's glorification stands in the foreground, be from the same author, then it is still more obvious that the expectations concerning "Jahveh's servant" are nothing more than the rudiments of a more moral view of Jahveh's relation to Israel and to the heathen: then they have not yet pushed out the traditional ideas, but serve to complement them. This would also be the case, if the traditional predictions referred to had to be attributed to other prophets: the new ideas about "Jahveh's servant" are merely indicated and are not developed any farther. It cannot surprise us, even, that they are not taken up and worked out by later prophets and poets: they are mere hints which could easily remain unnoticed. But this does not deprive these ideas of their unmistakable importance. They point, as it were, beyond the borders of the Israelitish religion, and form the transition to a universalism which is the more worthy of our notice, since it was not added from the outside, but must be regarded as the fruit of Israel's own religious development.

How interesting soever they may be to us, the new ideas and hints of the second Isaiah naturally made but little impression upon his contemporaries. A deeply agitated period, such as that at which he lived, could lead him and a few kindred minds to a deeper conception of religious truth, but it was unfitted to advance the masses. Their attention was wholly absorbed by the weighty events of which they were spectators. They would listen

---

* Isa. liii. 11, 12.

gladly to the voice of the prophets, when the latter showed them in those events the foretokens of the approaching deliverance. This, therefore, as we have already mentioned,* forms the principal contents of the prophecies which have been preserved to us. Even now, in reading them, we feel the enthusiasm which they breathe: how they must have echoed in the hearts of those whom they concerned so closely! The taunting song on the king of Babylon, with which the unknown author of one of those prophecies concludes,† is eminently adapted to give us an idea of the feeling which prevailed at that time among the exiles. The decisive blow has yet to be struck, and more than one obstacle has still to be removed, but their imagination outstrips all these difficulties, and revels in the humiliation of the tyrant who has robbed them of their country and their independence, and in the certainty that—

> "Jahveh will have mercy on Jacob,
> And will again choose Israel
> And set them in their own land:
> Then shall strangers join them
> And cleave to the house of Jacob."‡

To understand rightly how so bold an expectation found favour with many, if not with all, we must call one more circumstance to mind. There was little or no similarity of religious ideas and practices between the Israelitish Jahveh-worshippers and the people in whose midst they were placed. The image-worship§ and astrology‖ of which they were witnesses, may have had a seductive power over a few, but the great majority of the Israelites, and at any rate the upright worshippers of Jahveh, must have felt altogether strange to them. Thus they must have been the more struck at learning that the Persians professed another religion, and one which had much more resemblance to the convictions and the rites of the Israelites than

---

* Above, pp. 121, seq. † Isa. xiv. 4-23. ‡ Isa. xiv. 1.
§ Above, p. 125, n. ".   ‖ Isa. xlvii. 12, 13.

had the Babylonish. At first the exiles will not have formed at all a correct notion of this fact, but the very rumour of it must have made a deep impression on them. Hereafter we shall have occasion to revert to the Persian religion and its relation to Mosaism.* For the moment we will confine ourselves to stating what will surely be universally admitted—that the similarity existed, and was apparent enough to be noticed by the Israelites, even from a distance. What could be more natural than that this should strengthen their confidence in Cyrus and the Persians ? From this point of view, the manner in which the Babylonish Isaiah speaks of that king is remarkable. His faith in Jahveh's universal direction of events is sufficient to account for his conviction that Cyrus will lend himself to carry out Jahveh's designs: so Jeremiah† had already called Nebuchadnezzar "Jahveh's servant," because he was the instrument for fulfilling the judgment upon the unfaithful Judæans. But Isaiah goes somewhat further, when he speaks thus of the Persian monarch:

"Jahveh saith of Cyrus, 'my shepherd'
And 'he shall perform all my pleasure,
By saying to Jerusalem, Be rebuilt!
And to the temple, Be founded!'"

"Thus saith Jahveh to *his anointed*, to Cyrus,
Whom I hold by his right hand,
To cast down nations before his face
And to loose the girdles of kings,‡
To open doors before his face
And to keep gates not shut:
'I will go before thy face
And make hills level;
Gates of brass will I break in pieces
And cut in sunder bars of iron;

---

* See below, Chap. IX. † Jer. xxv. 9; xliii. 10. ‡ Comp. 1 Kings xx. 11 b.

And I will give thee treasures that lie in darkness
And hidden riches,
That thou mayest know that I am Jahveh,
Which call thee by thy name, the God of Israel.
For the sake of Jacob my servant
And Israel mine elect,
I called thee by thy name,
I spake unto thee, while thou didst not know me.'"*

If the prophet admits, in these last words, that Cyrus is not a Jahveh-worshipper, he connects this "anointed of Jahveh" with his sender so intimately, that he describes him elsewhere† as one "who calleth upon Jahveh's name." He would not have expressed himself so strongly, had he looked upon Cyrus as an ordinary worshipper of false gods. Of the real relation between his religion and Jahvism he too will not have been able to form a clear conception. But what was told about it was enough to make the prophet hope everything good of Cyrus, and was eminently suited to give his predictions weight with his fellow exiles.

Did the Israelites await their deliverance passively? Did they, as much as lay in their power, assist Cyrus, when he had once begun the conflict with the Chaldean monarchy, or at least give him tokens of their hope in the successful issue of his exertions? We have already observed‡ that we must leave these questions unanswered. But whatever we imagine the state of affairs to have been previously, after Cyrus had taken Babylon he must have involuntarily turned his attention to the Jews. Flavius Josephus dishes us up a very improbable story,§ which is not based upon tradition, but must be regarded as a free composition of the Jewish historian. According to this story, Cyrus became acquainted with Isaiah's prophecies, which were written 140 years before the desolation of Jerusalem, and

---

* Isa. xliv. 28; xlv. 1-4.   † Isa. xli. 25; above p. 124.   ‡ Above p. 120.
§ *Jewish Ant.* xi. 1, sec. 1, 2. Comp. *Hk. O.* ii. 101-103.

210 years before the taking of Babylon; he found that his own name was foretold in them and that at the same time it was announced that he would promote Israel's return and the rebuilding of the temple; this made a deep impression upon him and convinced him that "the Most High, who had made him (Cyrus) king over the whole earth, was the same who was adored by the people of Israel;" so he hastened to perform the duty with which he was charged. All this is evidently invented by Josephus, who, as we also know from other parts of his writings, ascribed Isa. xl. seq. to Hezekiah's contemporary, and, searching for an explanation of Cyrus' favourable disposition, thought he had found it in the astonishment excited by the wonderful predictions in those chapters. In one respect he may have guessed the state of the case correctly. It is far from improbable that Cyrus was aware of the fact that the Jews had fixed their hopes upon him, and that the taking of Babylon was announced by their seers some time beforehand. In that case, this was an additional reason for him to be favourably disposed towards them. An additional reason: for he must have been inclined to regard them favourably, independently of this. Like the Jews themselves, he too must have been struck with the resemblance between the Israelitish and the Persian religions. But, above all, policy drove him to satisfy their desire to return to their native land. Palestine was a border-district of the great empire which he was erecting. It was to the interest of the stability of that new erection, that a people should settle there who felt themselves indebted and bound to the ruling Persian nation, and who would side with it in a war with Egypt, or in the event of a rebellion on the part of the recently subjugated nations. This demand of policy could not be better satisfied than by revoking the sentence passed by Nebuchadnezzar upon the Jewish nation. Of course it is taken for granted here that the exiles, or at all events many of them, were anxious to see their native soil again. We shall soon find that this supposition is correct.

"Jahveh the god of heaven hath given me all the kingdoms of the earth, and he hath charged me to build him an house at Jerusalem in Judah. Who then among you belongs to his people, his god be with him, and let him go up to Jerusalem in Judah and build the house of Jahveh the god of Israel; he is the god who dwelleth in Jerusalem. Now as for the Israelites that remain, let in all places each of them be supported by the people of such a place, with silver and gold and goods and beasts, beside the freewill offerings for the house of the god that dwelleth at Jerusalem." In these words a younger Jewish historian* clothes the edict promulgated by Cyrus in the first year of his reign over Babylon (538 B.C.). His statement that the Persian king acknowledged Jahveh as "the god of heaven" in this manner, thanked him for all his victories and declared himself ready to carry out his commands, is very improbable in itself and is not confirmed by other sources: the whole proclamation has obviously a Jewish tint and thus is not authentic. But it is historically certain not only that Cyrus permitted the return of the exiles, but also that he greatly promoted the rebuilding of the temple at Jerusalem, by, among other things, restoring the holy vessels which Nebuchadnezzar had stolen.† A large number of Israelites at once declared themselves ready to begin the journey to Judæa. According to a statement made twice in the Old Testament,‡ there were 42,360 of them who set out. If, as may be said to be probable, this was the number of the heads of families, it was an army of more than 200,000 Israelitish men, women and children, that left Babylonia. If these figures be thought too high, we are at liberty to subtract something from them;§ in spite of this it remains a caravan of considerable size. At its head stood Zerubbabel the son of Shealtiel, a descendant of David, as *hattirsatha*, *i. e.* governor,‖ and Joshua the son of

---

* Ezra i. 2-4. † Ezra vi. 1-5; i. 7-11.
‡ Ezra ii. 64; Neh. vii. 66. § Comp. Note I. at the end of this chapter.
‖ Zerubbabel bears this title in Ezra ii. 63; Neh. vii. 65, 70; and Nehemiah in Neh. viii. 10; x. i.

Jozadak, grandson of Seraiah, who in 586 B. C. served as high priest in the temple at Jerusalem, and was killed by order of Nebuchadnezzar in the same year.*

The reader no doubt expects that we shall now at once accompany the returning exiles on their journey to their own land. But weighty reasons induce us first to remain for a time with the Jews who stay behind in Babylonia. They fill an important place in the history of Israel's religion. This sounds strange, for it is universally admitted that accounts of them are altogether wanting. But we stand on firm ground, when we ascribe to them this important part. Our researches shall themselves furnish proof of this.

What we remarked before on the isolation of the prophet Ezekiel† will be remembered. Unless I be mistaken, those remarks are fully confirmed by our study of the second Isaiah and his contemporaries. In his writings we seek in vain for that thoroughly priestly conception of Israel's destiny and future of which Ezekiel is the representative. We discover at most a few points of contact with it. This is the case, *e.g.*, in a passage on the keeping of the Sabbath, concerning which, moreover, there is still room to doubt whether it must not rather be ascribed to a younger prophet in Judæa than to the Babylonish Isaiah.‡ First, the practice of judgment and justice is insisted upon generally, and the man who devotes himself to this is called blessed.§ But immediately afterwards "the keeping of the Sabbath from polluting it," together with "the restraining of the hand from doing any evil," is named as the characteristic of the righteous,‖ while a glad future is predicted for the strangers who join Israel, and for the eunuchs, if they keep Jahveh's covenant and again take care, in particular, that they do not pollute the Sabbath.¶ The high esti-

---

* 2 Kings xxv. 18; Jer. lii. 24; 1 Chr. vi. 14, 15.   † Above, pp. 105, 118, seq.
‡ Isa. lvi. 1-7.   § Vers. 1, 2 a.   ‖ Ver. 2 b.
¶ Vers. 3-7.

mation of the sabbath which pervades this passage, reminds one of Ezekiel's declarations to the same effect.* But opposed to this one point of agreement, which moreover is notably weakened by the doubtful origin of the prophecy, there are at any rate weighty points of difference. While Ezekiel shows that he attaches great importance to the descent of the priests from Zadok, the later prophet expects that Jahveh will also "take for Levitical priests"† of the Israelites who shall be brought to Jerusalem from all parts of the world by the heathen: he probably means that the other tribes shall also be admitted to the priesthood, but in no case does he, like his predecessor, limit the power of holding that dignity to a single family of Levi. Concerning fasting, too, the younger prophet has his peculiar notions. To the question put by some Israelites:

"Wherefore have we fasted, and thou (Jahveh) didst not see it,
And afflicted ourselves with abstinence, and thou observest it not?"‡

Jahveh answers, that such fasting as that with which they are content cannot be acceptable to him. They not only combine with it attention to their affairs and care for their daily work, but they are guilty of quarrelling and other sins.§ "Is not"—asks Jahveh of them—

"Is not this the fasting that I chose:
To loose the chains of wickedness,
To undo the bands of the yoke,
To let the oppressed go free,
And to take off every yoke?
Is it not to break thy bread for the hungry,
To bring the wandering poor into thy house,
When thou seest a naked man, to clothe him,
And not to hide thyself from thine own kin?"‖

---

* Ezek. xx. 12, 20, 21; xxii. 8, 26; xxiii. 28, &c.   † Isa. lxvi. 21.
‡ Isa. lviii. 3a.   § Vers. 3b-5.   ‖ Vers. 6, 7.

This is genuinely prophetic language, to which a man such as Ezekiel could not have objected, it is true, but which he would not have written down just in this way of his own accord.

It is certain, therefore, that the priestly spirit was not the predominant one among the exiles at the time of their release, and that their prophets in particular moved in another direction. There is even, speaking generally, a tolerably sharp contrast to be observed between the last twenty-seven chapters of the book of Isaiah and the prophecies of Ezekiel. But it is equally certain that the priestly conception of the religion soon had numerous and worthy defenders among the exiles who remained in Babylonia—as if Ezekiel revived among them, not as an individual, but in an entire school, which embraced his principles and took up and carried on his work. It is this remarkable fact which must now be elucidated.

Let us begin by clearing away a—very natural—prejudice with regard to the Jews who stopped behind in Babylonia. At first we cannot be inclined to judge favourably of them. The mere fact that they stayed behind seems to testify against them. The journey to Judæa and the settlement there, in a very thinly populated land, where everything had to be built up from the very ground, were undoubtedly connected with great difficulties, which had the more weight in proportion as the hope of extraordinary and miraculous help from Jahveh, with which they had at first flattered themselves, was contradicted by experience and weakened every day. It would hardly be possible to withhold from those who did not embark upon these troubles, the praise that they made a *wise* choice. But so much the darker a shadow seems then to fall upon their interest in Jahveh and his service. What could they who were not among those " whose spirit God had raised to go up to build Jahveh's temple at Jerusalem"*—what could they be but indifferent and fainthearted, of whom it was to be feared that, forsaken by their more

* Ezra i. 5.

zealous brethren, they would soon become as the nations and the families of the earth, serving wood and stone?*

Perhaps there were some among them whom such a verdict would not have wronged. But there decidedly remained behind not a few who stood much higher than we should have suspected. What kept them back from sharing in the great work to which Cyrus called them, we do not know, but it is easy for us to suppose motives which justified their staying. Even could we not do so, we should yet have to yield to facts. The facts are these: the deputation of Babylonish Jews to the temple at Jerusalem, about the year 520 B.C., mentioned by the prophet Zechariah;† the fervent love of such a man as Nehemiah for his nation and Jahvism;‡ and lastly and above all the character of Ezra and the intrinsic worth of the second colony, which—in the year 458 B.C.—entered upon the journey to Jerusalem under his leadership.§ We shall afterwards revert to this subject and illustrate it more fully. These facts are mentioned here provisionally as so many proofs that interest in the Jahveh-worship was not wanting in those who stayed behind, but on the contrary was very lively. It is true, we have no right to judge of all the rest by these few persons, but much less to regard them merely as exceptions to the rule, and to place those of whom we know nothing—but also nothing bad—far lower than those whose deeds are known to us and bear testimony in their favour.

Interest in the religion of their fathers was therefore far from extinct among the Jews who remained. But how do we know that it was precisely the *priestly* conception which found supporters among them and was further developed? Provisionally we are disposed to gather this from what we are told about Ezra and his colony. We may already assert without fear of contradiction—and it shall be expressly proved in the next chapter—that a tendency which was priestly and legal at the same time, predominated among them. Ezra and his adherents would not be its only defenders. There is not the slightest ground

---

* Ezek. xx. 32.   † Zech. vi. 9-15.   ‡ Neh. i. 1—ii. 8.   § Ezra vii. seq.

for drawing so sharp a line of demarcation between them and the rest of the Babylonish Jews. In the absence of any proof to the contrary, we rather assume that, as they went out from Babylonia, so also they represented the predominant feeling among the Jews there.

Upon closer consideration, details present themselves in Ezra's accounts, which confirm this provisional conclusion. But before we point them out, we will strike into a side-path which will bring us nearer to the end at which we are aiming. We will take the Pentateuch—with the book of Joshua, so closely related to it—into our hands, and notice the phenomena which occur there. It will soon be evident that this examination furnishes important results.

Our present Pentateuch contains a great number of *priestly elements*, i.e. documents of legislative and historical tenor, which were written in a priestly spirit and in the priestly interest, and therefore probably by priests, as they treat of what directly concerns them and belongs to the sphere of their labours. Which these documents are, can really be gathered from what has already been said of the Pentateuch in this history.* Take away the prophetic historical narratives and the few laws included in them, especially the Book of the Covenant;† then remove the work of the Deuteronomist, in the first place his legislation, and also the documents of an exhortatory tendency which were added to it subsequently, and the deuteronomic redaction of the older prophetic historical narrative, and all that remains in the Pentateuch and Joshua is priestly in origin and tendency. But we shall undoubtedly gain in clearness, if, instead of resting content with this indication, we lay the priestly elements themselves before the reader.

As we have already said, they are partly laws and partly narratives. This double character of the priestly legislation does not surprise us in the least. It entirely agrees with the

* Comp. Vol. I. p. 104, sq.; above p. 15, sq., and elsewhere.
† Exod. xxi.-xxiii.

practice followed by the other lawgivers. The Book of the Covenant was preserved to us as an integral part of a history of the patriarchal and Mosaic times. The Deuteronomist not only put his laws into an historical frame, but also linked them afterwards to the prophetic historical narrative, and then worked up in his own spirit the accounts relating to Joshua as well. The legislation of the priests conforms to these examples. Its historical elements, as was to be expected, are easy to distinguish from the prophetic (and deuteronomic). They are characterized by the spirit in which they are written, and by peculiar expressions. They are to be found throughout the whole of the Pentateuch and in Joshua, so that the priestly lawgiver appears to have handled history from the creation of the world to the division of Canaan among the Israelitish tribes.

But let us confine ourselves first to *the laws*, which occupy the most space, and thus no doubt are of more consequence in the estimation of the author—or authors—of the priestly elements than the historical narratives. To these laws, then, belong: the ordinance as to the feast of the passover, which is inserted in the account of Israel's exodus from Egypt;* the precepts concerning the tabernacle and the consecration of the priests,† from which the long description of the execution of these precepts‡ is inseparable; all the regulations which together form the book of Leviticus; and, finally, several chapters of Numbers, containing both laws in the strict sense§ and semi-historical documents relating to the numbering and division of Israel,|| the legislative tendency of which, however, is so obvious that they must decidedly be placed here.

* Exod. xii. 1-28, 43-50. † Exod. xxv. 1—xxxi. 17.
‡ Exod. xxxv.-xl.
§ Num. iii., iv.; v., vi.; viii. 23-26; ix. 1-14; x. 1-9; xv., xviii.; xix.; xxviii.-xxx.; xxxiv., xxxv.
|| Num. i., ii.; vii.; viii. 1-22; ix. 15-23; xxvi.; xxvii. 1-11; xxxi.; xxxvi. The line dividing this group from the previous one (note §) cannot be drawn without some arbitrariness.

All these laws are mutually related and breathe one spirit, yet they are not from one hand or one time. This is evident both from the difference of expression, and from the mutual antagonism of some of the laws. Thus they originated in succession, probably in the same circles. The younger regulations appear to be additions, whether it be to complete and explain the older ones, or to provide for the wants which did not become visible till after the older documents had been written. Great difficulties—we need scarcely say—are connected with the chronological arrangement of the priestly laws in their entirety. The least hazardous method seems to be to divide them into *three groups*, of which

the first embraces some laws concerning clean and unclean things, the priests and religious worship, which are now included in Leviticus chap. xviii.-xxiii., xxv., xxvi., but in an elaborated form and linked with a few younger regulations;

the second is formed by a complete system of priestly ordinances, the author of which was acquainted with and adopted the first group; to this group belong in great part the laws in Exodus chap. xii., xxv.-xxxi., in Leviticus chap. i.-xvii., xxiv., xxvii., and most of the priestly documents in Numbers, both the purely legislative and the semi-historical.* From this *corpus* of the legislation of the priests must now, finally, be distinguished

the third group, which includes the later additions: they are usually closely united with the older documents, in the three centre books of the Pentateuch, and cannot be separated from them without difficulty.

Let the following suffice, provisionally, to vindicate and explain this distribution. The Book of the Covenant, as well as the Deuteronomic legislation in its original form, is concluded by an exhortatory discourse, which sets forth the consequences both of the observance and the transgression of the preceding laws.† Now we also find a similar discourse—otherwise very

---

* Comp. above, p. 149, n. § and ||. † Exod. xxiii. 20-33 ; Deut. xxviii.

peculiar in language and style—in Leviticus, in chap. xxvi. It does *not* belong to the priestly legislation in its entirety, as may be inferred from its very position—not at the end, but before Lev. xxvii. and the laws in Numbers. It must rather be regarded as the concluding discourse of another, likewise priestly, legislation, which, according to the thoroughly unequivocal subscription, Lev. xxvi. 46, was instituted *on mount Sinai*, and thereby plainly distinguishes itself again from the legislation to which most of the ordinances of the present Pentateuch belong, which were promulgated not on the mountain, but *in the desert of Sinai*.* Now it is surely very improbable that of that other legislation the exhortatory discourse, Lev. xxvi., alone was included in the Pentateuch; it is much more credible, at all events, that other documents also, and especially laws, were borrowed from it. Now in the chapters immediately preceding (xviii.-xxiii., xxv.) we find exactly what we seek: a number of ordinances which exhibit some agreement in expression with Lev. xxvi., and, conversely, differ altogether from the rest of the priestly laws in language and style. One of these ordinances, relating to the year of the sabbath and of the jubilee, is actually expressly stated to have been delivered *on mount Sinai*.† It would have been perceived long before this, therefore, that the laws which were referred above to the first group, must be distinguished from the rest of the priestly legislation, were it not that the peculiar expressions of those other laws occurred from time to time in this our first group also. This seems to upset again the distinction which otherwise is very obvious. Yet it ought to be retained, with this understanding, however, that the laws of that first group be considered to have been adopted and worked up by the author of our second group. This hypothesis accounts satisfactorily for all the phenomena which occur here. Of course, it presupposes that the first group is the oldest of the three—for which reason we placed it first.‡

* Comp. Note II. at the end of this chapter.   † Lev. xxv. 1.
‡ Comp. Note II. at the end of this chapter.

We need not enlarge here upon the second and third groups of priestly laws. We shall revert to them hereafter.* The necessity of keeping these two groups apart, or, in other words, of distinguishing the later additions from the real *corpus* of the legislation, is not admitted by many, and, in fact, is not apparent at once. A reason the more for not dwelling upon it longer here, in this provisional survey.

We now turn from the laws to the *historical* documents of priestly origin. It seems superfluous to enumerate them all here. Presently, in this very chapter, an opportunity will occur of making known their contents. Let it suffice to remind the reader that, to begin with, the first narrative of the creation,† and, further, all the documents related to it in Genesis and in the following books, as far as and including Joshua, are of priestly origin. There is, upon the whole, so much in them that is peculiar, that they can be separated with tolerable certainty from the remaining prophetic historical narratives. The latest writers upon this subject are unanimous upon all the main points. In this also they are at one, that the priestly narratives are the most intimately related to the second group of laws mentioned above. Without hesitation, therefore, we attribute them to the author of that second group. Perhaps some of the historical documents must also be regarded as later additions, and would then stand upon a level with our third group of laws. For our present purpose this further division is of less moment.

We now have to connect the results of these investigations with the Jews in Babylonia and their labours in the domain of religion. The reader will suspect already that, in my opinion, we have them to thank for the committal to writing of the priestly laws and narratives. This is indeed the case. *The laws of the first and second groups and the historical narratives belonging to them were written down in Babylonia, between the years* 538 *and* 458 B.C. Let it be considered,

* In Chapter IX. and its Note I. † Gen. i. 1—ii. 3.

in the first place, that when Ezekiel, in the year 572 B.C., wrote his description of the new Israelitish state (chap. xl.-xlviii.), no written regulations for religious worship, no complete priestly legislation, yet existed, and the laws of our second group, especially, had not yet been made;*

in the second place, that no evident trace of these laws, or of the spirit which they breathe, is to be found in the prophecies which saw light towards the end of the captivity, about 538 B.C.;†

and lastly, that in the year 458 B.C. Ezra could start for Jerusalem "with the law of his god in his hand,"‡ to introduce that law some years afterwards into Judæa, where it had hitherto been unknown.§ This "law" is none other than the priestly legislation—as will be expressly shown hereafter.∥ Ezra, who had already won for himself in Babylonia the title of "ready scribe of the law of Moses,"¶ must thus be considered to have brought thence what originated there.

If we put these reflections together, we arrive at the following idea of the course of the priestly legislation. Ezekiel, in uttering his wishes as to the future, made a beginning of the committal to writing of the priestly tradition. The priests in Babylonia went on in his footsteps. A first essay in priestly legislation—remains of which have been preserved to us in Lev. xviii.-xxvi.—was followed by others, until at last a complete system arose, contained in an historical frame. Possessed of this system, the priestly exiles, and among them Ezra in particular, could consider themselves entitled and called upon to come forward as teachers in Judæa, and to put in practice the ordinances which hitherto had been exclusively of theoretical interest to them.

The objections which can be made to this conclusion on the score of probability, are easily removed. At the first glance,

---

* See above, pp. 114-117. † See above, pp. 144-146. ‡ Ezra vii. 14, 25.
§ Neh. viii. 15-18. ∥ See below, Chapter VIII.
¶ Ezra vii. 6, 11, 12, 21; Neh. viii. 1, comp. Ezra vii. 10.

no doubt, so great an activity on the part of the priests of Jahveh in the land of exile is singular. Had not sacrifice been confined to the temple at Jerusalem, in accordance with the deuteronomic law, since Josiah's reformation? how then could the priest prosecute his work in a foreign country and actually, in a certain sense, take the lead there? Let us consider, first of all, that the priest's task embraced more than the mere offering of sacrifices. To his office belonged, besides this, a share in the administration of justice and the giving of "instruction" (*thorah*), *e.g.*, concerning clean and unclean. It lay in the nature of the case that this last gradually acquired greater significance in that foreign, unclean land, where the real worship was at a standstill. Thus the priest remained in office and in honour. We are not surprised, therefore, to find that, upon the return of the exiles, Joshua the priest, next to the descendant of David, assumes the lead of the expedition. But after the departure of the first colony, according to the hypothesis advanced above, the zeal and influence of the priests in Babylonia increased: is not that very singular? By no means. Let the reader observe, in the second place, the peculiar position of the Jews who stayed behind. They themselves did not regard it as final. In as much as they were Jews, not only by birth, but also by religion, they must always have had their eyes fixed upon the holy land and have looked forward to a restoration of the Israelitish state. Even after the year 538 B.C. that restoration was still of the future: what Zerubbabel and Joshua effected was nothing more than a beginning—a poor beginning even, as we shall see hereafter. Thus there were no reasons for the priests of Jahveh to lay down their task. If, as was involved in the nature of the case, the prophets, the second Isaiah and those of his mind, joined the first expedition to Judæa, then it was most natural that those who stayed behind should look upon the priests as their leaders, and that the latter should feel the importance of their office even more than they had done before. From the very fact that they were unable to perform a good deal of the practice of that office, they must have felt called upon to collect and commit to writing the rules which hitherto had been orally handed down. That which reached their ears concerning the state of affairs in Judæa may have augmented this zeal. There is, indeed, nothing strange in their taking this interest in distant matters; on the contrary, it is extremely natural from a psychological point of view, as was shown before with regard to Ezekiel.* In addition to this, in the third place, the need of settled religious institutions, which showed itself among the Jews in Babylonia, must have served to encourage the priests to go on in the path upon which they had of their own accord entered. After his arrival in Judæa, Ezra endeavours to gain influence by reading out the law; soon after his time began the meetings of the Jews on the sabbath, at which this public reading was the chief feature.† It is no hazardous supposition that these practices existed in Babylonia, and were not invented by Ezra, but were brought by him to Palestine. The want of the temple and of the opportunities which it gave for common worship must have made itself felt in the strange land more deeply than ever, especially after the completion of the sanctuary at Jerusalem. In those regular meetings, for which the day of rest was so well suited, a proper substitute was sought and found. They were so urgently needed to supply the existing and generally acknowledged wants, that they must have sprung up of themselves as it were: nothing can surprise us less than that history is unable to name the man who introduced them. Now, assuming that the priests were consulted, and, moreover, already had inducement to commit their ideas and ordinances to writing, must not the opportunity of communicating them to the people which was offered by the sabbath-meetings have incited them to go on in the road which they had taken? Is it not evident, from the increased necessity for religious instruction, speaking quite generally,

---

* See above, pp. 117, seq.   † See again below, Chapter VIII

that the time had arrived for writing down what hitherto had been delivered verbally? A number of "teachers" undertook the journey to Judæa with Ezra the priest and scribe :* may we not infer from this fact, after all the foregoing, that we have formed a correct idea of the condition of the Jews in Babylonia and of the movement which took place there in the domain of religion?

There is one more detail which may not be passed over here in silence. The Jews' growing knowledge of the Persian religion could not well fail to have influence upon them. We shall revert to this in connection with other points: to estimate the influence of that religion upon Jahvism, we must be acquainted with facts which will not come to light till further on in our investigations. Here we will confine ourselves to observing, what is scarcely open to contradiction, that the contact with the Persian religion must have led the Jews to study their own religion and to define it more exactly than had been done hitherto. In the Persians they learnt to know for the first time a people which, as far as the development of its religion was concerned, could be compared in some measure to themselves; which moreover was possessed of a religious legislation regulating even to the minutest points its whole life and worship. Independently of what they could borrow from such a system, to complete their own usages, it must have induced them to take count of what they possessed and to draw up an inventory of it as it were. The wish not to be in any respect behind the Persians, to whom they could consider themselves in many respects superior, was truly not unnatural. Who will not admit that the activity which we ascribe to the Jewish priests in Babylonia tended to meet that wish, and thus again from this point of view may safely be acknowledged as historical?

The whole of this survey still lacks something of great importance. I have twice referred to Ezra and put forward my

* Ezra viii. 16.

conception of his labours in Judæa. Far too little has been said upon this subject, however, and, in consequence, the whole is wanting in perspicuity and perhaps even seems more or less arbitrary. Let the reader, therefore, suspend his judgment, until he sees Ezra appear upon the scene and witnesses his doings, in the next chapter. He will then be in a position to judge whether our conception of Ezra's preparation for the task which he undertook and carried out is to be considered admissible.

The preceding investigation can now at once be supplemented in another way. The result which we have obtained is, that the system of priestly legislation which was indicated as the second group (p. 150), together with the narratives that belong to it, was written down in Babylonia before Ezra's journey to Judæa. It will be best to speak of the particular ordinances and rules included in that system, when we narrate its introduction into Judæa. But the system as a whole, and especially the historical suppositions upon which it rests, can be set forth here. Nay, this alone is the proper place to describe them. In sketching the situation of the Jews in Babylonia, it is necessary to answer the questions, what notions did the priests who were settled there hold as to the course of religious development? and what was the ideal which they formed? If they are to be found anywhere, we shall find the answers to these questions in the historical and legislative writing which one of those priests composed. With this end in view, then, we will make ourselves acquainted with the contents of that writing.*

Scarcely, however, have we begun to do so, before we arrive at the conviction that we cannot regard the author of *the Book of Origins*—as, in imitation of others, we will call the system of priestly legislation already mentioned—merely as a representative of the order to which he belonged. It is true, he is a *priest*, and as such is deeply attached to the Jahveh-worship, its ceremonies and the privileges of the priesthood. Hence it

* Compare with the following Note III. at the end of this chapter.

is that he regulates public worship expressly and exhaustively, and draws up several rules in the interest of the priests. Any other priest in his place would have done the same. But besides this, there is something which is peculiar to him personally. He is a friend of order, regularity, and symmetry. It is a necessity to him, to reduce everything to number and measure. He is fond of distinguishing between different periods and demonstrating a regular gradation in them. One might call him a statistician. But now we must at once add to this, that the historical reality has but little value in his eyes. He sacrifices it without hesitation to his need for a minute and tangible representation of the past. In doing so, therefore, he gives rein to his imagination and is more a poet than an historian. Yet his imagination is anything but poetical in the ordinary sense of the word. His descriptions display unmistakable talent, but still they are monotonous and sometimes even dry, namely when they are given in the form of authentic documents or records, although in truth nothing could be less so in reality. Examples of all that I am saying will present themselves to us directly in abundance. It will surely be generally admitted that in them the writer proves himself to be a man of peculiar, sharply defined characteristics. We certainly should not be justified in putting down his work, in so far as it is the expression of this individuality, to the whole priesthood, and this we wish to avoid. But on the other hand, can it be by accident that we meet with a man such as this among the priests? Is there not an unmistakable connection between the office which he fills and the interpretation and notion of things which we have just sketched? At the least it can hardly escape our attention, that in this he so often coincides with the priest Ezekiel, who, in fact, deserves to be called his predecessor in more than one respect.

The author of the Book of Origins was not the first in Israel to narrate history, from the creation of the world to the settlement of the people in Canaan. The course which he had to follow, therefore, had been pointed out to him by his predecessors, and especially by the author of the second creation-narrative* and the accounts connected with it.† But the latter's interpretation and conception of events could not possibly satisfy him entirely. Not only did he miss a great deal in his narratives and the laws that they contained—*c. g.* the whole of the regulations as to public worship and the rights and duties of the priests, which the Deuteronomist did not give completely either—but he found in them things that were at variance, or only partially agreed, either with his views of the past or his wishes for the future. He therefore went his own way. He only included in his work the priestly laws which form our first group (p. 150).

"In the beginning Elohîm created the heaven and the earth." This is the simple and sublime commencement of this work.‡ That first act of creation produced a chaos (Hebrew, *tohu vabohu*), over which the spirit of Elohîm hovered.§ But this chaos was soon to be reduced to order. In six days were created in succession: light; the firmament; the sea, the dry land, herbs and trees; the sun, moon and stars; fishes and birds; four-footed beasts and creeping things, and finally man.‖ The regular climax is obvious. Man is created as male and female, in the image and likeness of Elohîm; then dominion is given him over the earth and sea and their inhabitants, and the fruit of herbs and trees is ceded to him for his food.¶ At the close of the whole description, it becomes evident why the work of creation is divided over six days: the seventh day Elohîm devotes to rest, and therefore blesses it and hallows it for the future also.** Thus at the very beginning of things one of the principal Mosaic institutions is prepared.

---

* Gen. ii. 4, seq.
† Which these accounts are, the reader can infer from the 2nd chapter of this work (Vol. I. p. 104, seq.), where the prophetic notion of the course of history is given in its main features.
‡ Gen. i. 1.   § Verse 2.   ‖ Verses 3-27.
¶ Verses 28-30.   ** Gen. ii. 1-3.

Now begins the first period of the history of mankind. The writer gives nothing more of it than a genealogical list, which from Adam down to and including Noah contains *ten* names.* They are borrowed from older records,† but the writer is able to give the year of the birth and the age of each of the ten patriarchs. With the exception of Enoch—concerning whom tradition said that he had lived 365 years, precisely as many years as the solar year has days; in fact, Enoch was *originally* the year—with the exception of Enoch, all these men attained a very great age, reaching to close upon 1000 years. Noah forms an exception to the rule that their eldest sons were born before they themselves had reached the age of 200 years,‡ for he was 500 years old when Shem came into the world :§ this the writer does in order to let Methuselah die in the year of the deluge, but according to his notion certainly before that catastrophe.‖ It is already apparent, and it will be confirmed as we go on, that we have here before us no history or legend, but an ingenious system, built up from a few mythic names.

Again, following in the footsteps of one of his predecessors,¶ the author now describes to us the deluge. He makes Noah's residence in the ark last exactly 365 days, *i.e.* a solar year; he is able also to fix the exact length of the shorter periods which together form the year.** After the deluge, Elohim makes a covenant with Noah and his family.†† He blesses them, as he had formerly blessed the first human beings,‡‡ but

---

* Gen. v. excepting ver. 29. When this verse was introduced, "a son" was substituted in verse 28 for "Noah." † Gen. iv. 17, 18, 25.

‡ See verses 3, 6, 9, 12, 15, 18, 21, 25, 28. § Verse 32.

‖ Methuselah is born in the year of the creation 687, and lives 969 years (verse 27); thus he dies in the year of the creation 1656, in which year the deluge also falls.

¶ Whose account Gen. viii. 21, 22, was present in the mind of the second Isaiah, chap. liv. 9.

** In Gen. vi.-viii. his account is fused with that of the predecessor into one whole. The dates fixed in chap. vii. 11, 17, 24; viii. 4, 13, 14, are from his hand. One (lunar) year [= 355 days] + 10 days = 365 days elapse between vii. 11 and viii. 14. †† Gen. ix. 1-16. ‡‡ Gen. i. 28-32.

besides the fruit of trees and herbs, he also gives them the flesh of animals to eat, and at the same time most strictly forbids the eating of blood*—another preparation for Mosaism, which emphatically maintains this prohibition.†

Noah's descendants are now enumerated, and first $70 = 7 \times 10$ greater and lesser nations which sprang from his three sons, Shem, Ham and Japheth;‡ after this come Shem's offspring, *ten* in number, down to and including Abraham.§ Their genealogy is the companion picture to that of the patriarchs before the flood, only it is somewhat more concise; their ages are considerably less, do not exceed 600 years, and approach more and more to the ordinary length of the human life.

Our writer looks upon Abraham's journey to Canaan as an ordinary migration,‖ at variance with the older prophetic author, who accounts for it by an express command from Jahveh.¶ On the other hand, he lays all stress upon Elohîm's covenant with Abraham, an important epoch in his historical system. Elohîm makes himself known to Abraham as *El Shaddai;* circumcision is the token of the agreement made between them.** Thus we are again brought a step nearer to Mosaism. It is also worthy of remark, that as yet, according to our author, *no sacrifices* are offered to Elohîm.

The fortunes of the patriarchs are disposed of with comparative brevity.†† The main features of the legend are retained, but all details are omitted, and consequently the historical picture lacks life and motion. Thus, according to the priestly writer, Esau and Jacob remain united as brothers till after Isaac's death, when the former quits the land and settles on

---

* Gen. ix. 4. † Lev. iii. 17; vii. 26, 27; xvii. 12-14.
‡ Gen. x. 1-7, 13-32. § Gen. xi. 10, seq. ‖ Gen. xi. 27-32; xii. 4b, 5.
¶ Gen. xii. 1-3. ** Gen. xvii.
†† With tolerable unanimity the most recent writers upon this subject ascribe to him Gen. xix. 29; xxi. 1b, 5; xxiii; xxv. 7-20, 26b; xxvi. 6, 34, 35; xxvii. 4b, —xxviii. 9; xxxi. 17b, 18; xxxiii. 18, 19; xxxv. 6a, 9-16, 23-29; xxxvi.; xxxvii. 1, 2a; xlvi. 5b—27; xlvii. 7-11, 27, 28; xlviii. 3-6; xlix. 1a, 28b-33; l. 12, 13, 22.

mount Seir, while Jacob continues to live in Canaan.* The author is exhaustive and circumstantial only in the narrative of the negociations between Abraham and the Hittites for the purchase of a burying place for Sarah,† probably because upon the lawful possession of that burying-place he bases a certain right of the Israelites to the possession of Canaan; and further in his chronological statements.‡ It would seem that only a portion of his account of the migration of Jacob and his family to Egypt has been preserved to us;§ probably, however, he also only included the main features of the older narratives in his review. On the other hand, we possess his very brief information as to the oppression in Egypt,‖ and his return of the precise length of the sojourn there, 430 years, exactly twice as many years as had elapsed between Abraham's migration and the settlement in Goshen.¶

Before we describe the writer's conception of Moses and his labours, we must make a general observation with regard to his chronology. It is only recently** that attention has been paid to the remarkable fact that, according to his genealogies and the dates which accompany them, 2666 years, *i.e.*, two-thirds of 4000 years, had elapsed at the exodus of Israel from Egypt since the creation of the world. There is no question of accident here, for, as we have already pointed out in one or two instances, the author's figures show evident signs of thought and calculation. Most probably, therefore—like so many other old writers, *e.g.*, Berosus the Babylonian and Manetho the Egyptian—he had a chronological system of his own, which reckoned the duration of the earth at 4000 years, and made the exodus from Egypt open the last third of that cycle. Some of the subdivisions of the 2666 years had already been fixed

---

* Gen. xxxvi. 6, 7; xxxvii. 1.   † Gen. xxiii.
‡ See Gen. xii. 4b; xvi. 16; xxi. 5; xxv. 7, 17, 26; xxxii. 28; xlvii. 9.
§ See the passages in n. ‡.   ‖ Exod. i. 13, 14; ii. 23b-25.
¶ Exod. xii. 40; comp. Vol. I. p. 162, seq.
** By Th. Nöldeke. *Untersuchungen zur Kritik des A. T.*, p. 110, sqq.

by others, more or less exactly, before his time;* the rest he determined himself in such a way, that collectively they made up the number mentioned. Does not the use of such a system furnish conclusive proof that the author belongs to the *later* historians, and that his accounts can by no means be regarded as reproductions of popular tradition?

To return to Moses. Of his earliest adventures and his residence in Midian our writer makes no mention. He sketches the first revelation which occurs to him in Exodus chap. vi. Here Elohim makes himself known as *Jahveh*, with the positive assertion that Abraham, Isaac, and Jacob had addressed him not as Jahveh, but as *El Shaddai*.† Thus again a new period opens in the history of God's manifestations: a new covenant, after the deliverance out of Egypt, and the settlement in Canaan are announced.‡ The narrative of that deliverance, which in the present Pentateuch is combined into one whole with the older accounts, we can pass over in silence. As is done in those earlier narratives, our author too makes the death of the Egyptian first-born of man and beast Jahveh's last judgment upon Pharaoh's obstinacy. But the way in which he connects the first paschal sacrifice and the institution both of the feast of unleavened bread and of the passover with this sentence, is peculiar.§ His precepts in this respect are exhaustive and minute; he evidently moves here upon his own ground, as he had also done before in his rules for the circumcision in Genesis xvii., with which chapter the paschal law entirely agrees in style and language.—But as yet he has not approached the promulgation of the laws. After describing the deliverance, he brings Moses and the people to Sinai, the holy mountain, which for a long time had been regarded as the scene of the lawgiving. In this, therefore, he remains true to tradition.

* Comp. Gen. xv. 13 with Exod. xii. 40, and further above p. 160, the remark upon Enoch.

† Exod. vi. 2, 3. The author of Exod. iii. 1, seq. likewise places the announcement of the name of Jahveh in the Mosaic time. ‡ Exod. vi. 4-8.

§ Exod. xii. 1-23, 28, 37 (?), 40-51 are from his hand.

But in his account of the covenant made there with Israel, he diverges from the older prophetic writers as much as he sustains in it his priestly character.

Our author's account of the delivery of the law is as follows. Immediately after the arrival at Sinai, Moses receives from Jahveh very exhaustive rules concerning the building of the tent of assembly or the tabernacle, the dress of the priests and their consecration to their office.* In accordance with these commands, the tabernacle is now built, and Aaron and his sons are consecrated to serve as priests.† The further manifestations of Jahveh take place in the tabernacle; they are communicated either to Moses alone, or to Moses and Aaron, and refer to sacrifices, cleanness, the priesthood, feasts, and other kindred subjects.‡ About this time, in the beginning of the second year after the exodus, the whole of Israel is numbered,§ a plan of encampment based upon that numbering is introduced,‖ and the tribe of Levi is set apart in its entirety—not for the priesthood, but—for the service of the sanctuary.¶ Shortly afterwards the Israelites break up their camp and take their departure for Canaan.** But according to our author also the unwillingness of the people to penetrate into Canaan after the spies have been sent out, results in Israel being condemned to wander in the wilderness for forty years.†† He gives us a few historical details and laws belonging to this period.‡‡ The settlement in the region beyond the Jordan and the death of Moses takes place at its end.§§

It will be observed that in this copious and important part of his work, the writer really lays before us two different things: a description of Israel in Moses' time, and laws which

---

* Exod. xxv. 1—xxxi. 17. † Exod. xxxv. seq.; Lev. viii.-x.
‡ These regulations are to be found in the book of Leviticus. § Num. i.
‖ Num. ii. ¶ Num. iii. 5, seq.; viii. 5, seq. ** Num. x. 11-28.
†† His narrative is fused in Num. xiii. xiv. into one whole with the older accounts. ‡‡ Num. xv. xvi. (in part); xvii.-xix.
§§ 1. a. Num. xxvi.-xxxi. xxxii. (in part); xxxiii (almost all); xxxiv.-xxxvi.; Deut. xxxii. 48-51; xxxiv. 1-3 and 5, 7-9 (in part) originate from our author.

are intended to be in force in Israel in later times as well. There is an intimate connection between these two elements: to the picture of Israel's condition there also belongs the fact that the people received the several ordinances from Moses, while the sketch of that condition at the same time furnishes a rule for what is to be done in the future. But let us make an attempt here to keep these two elements apart. The Mosaic laws, which were also applicable to the future, we will reserve for the next chapter, which treats of their introduction by Ezra. Here is the place to sketch the author's delineation of the past. It is well adapted to show us his standpoint, and moreover it throws a strong light upon his relation to the older prophetic narratives, which he pre-supposes and at the same time modifies on main points.

The Israelites are numbered by Moses twice, in the second and the fortieth years after the Exodus,* both times with the exception of the Levites, who, on account of their being destined for the sacred service, are not included in the fighting-men. How authentic soever they may be in appearance, the lists which give us the results of these numberings are merely the compositions of the priestly author. The figure 600,000 for the collective fighting-men, had already been given in older writings.† Divided among the twelve tribes, it gave an average of 50,000 combatants for each tribe. Now the two lists are drawn up so that six tribes always remain above this number, and six below it. But not the same tribes in each list: Simeon and Naphtali, which in Num. i. contain 59,300 and 53,400, are reduced in Num. xxvi. to 22,200 and 45,400, while, conversely, Asher and Manasseh are raised from 41,500 and 32,200 to 53,400 and 52,700. It is clear that all this is fictitious. Should anyone be still unconvinced by the proportion of these figures to 50,000, let him reflect that while the total sum of the fighting-men during the forty years remains nearly the same,

---

* Num. i. xxvi. † See the passages quoted in Vol. I. p. 124, seq., 172.

Simeon *falls* from 59,000 to 22,000, and Manasseh *rises* from 32,000 to 52,000, and yet, in the historical accounts of the same author, the two tribes share the same fortunes. The writer's aim was simply and solely to place before his readers a clear and pointed view of Mosaic Israel; for this purpose he deemed returns of the numerical strength of the separate tribes indispensable.*

He now divides the (about) 600,000 combatants into four groups, headed by the tribes Judah, Reuben, Ephraim, and Dan. The first group encamps towards the east, the second towards the south, the third towards the west, and the fourth towards the north. They are so composed that they do not differ from each other too much, and each of the four remains below 200,000, and above 100,000, in number. The Israelites march in the same order. All this is as unhistorical as the foregoing. In the Sinaitic desert such an encampment is as inconceivable as such an order of march.

But in this description the writer has a definite end in view. *In the centre* of the encampment thus formed he places the tabernacle, and round this the tribe of *Levi*. We shall perceive more clearly what this means, if we first mark in what respects this description of his differs from the earlier one.

The prophetic narrators, too, are acquainted with a "tent of assembly," in which the ark of Jahveh was deposited at the resting-places. But this tent was evidently small and primitive.† And as the ark went before the Israelites when they were on the march,‡ therefore the tent was pitched outside the camp.§ Now in this the priestly historian makes, in the first place, this alteration, that for the small, insignificant tent he substitutes a tolerably large and splendid tabernacle. The latter is built after the model of the temple of Solomon, and

---

* Comp. Nöldeke, l. c., p. 116, sq. † Comp. Exod. xxxiii. 7.
‡ Num. x. 33.
§ Exod. xxxiii. 7; Num. xi. 16, 26; xii. 4; Deut. xxxi. 14, 15.

therefore consists of a holy of holies, a sanctuary, and a court.*
The holy of holies contains the ark; but whereas the latter, in
Solomon's temple, was placed under the cherubim, and thus was
overshadowed by their wings,† here the cherubim are attached
to the lid of the ark ‡—a modification which was absolutely
necessary, if the ark was to be constantly moving about, and
yet to be always covered by the cherubim.§ The holy of holies
is divided from the holy place—not, as in the temple, by
folding doors,|| but—by a veil, which hides the ark from the
sight of the people, nay, of the priests also;¶ only once a year
the High-priest enters the holy of holies.** How the sacred
vessels are placed and the tabernacle itself is arranged and
put together, can be read in the minute description of our
author.†† It will then be observed that he no longer makes
the ark go before the Israelites,‡‡ but expressly points out how
it must be covered over with the greatest care, and carried by
the Levites in the centre of the marching host.§§ In fact—and
this is the second important departure from tradition which
the author allows himself—the whole tabernacle is placed in
the centre of the camp.|||| Could the writer express more
plainly his conviction as to the sanctity and the central importance of "the tent of assembly" and the ark which was
kept in it? He makes known by this account, much better
than by exhortation and warning, how he wishes the Israelites
to regard the sanctuary and public worship.

It scarcely needs mention that this tabernacle, according to
the author, is *the only place of sacrifice*. The Deuteronomist,
part of whose aim it was to elevate the temple of Solomon to
this rank, had yet admitted that unity of worship did not exist

---

* Exod. xxvi.; xxvii. 9, seq.
† 1 Kings vi. 23-28; viii. 6, 7. Comp. Vol. I. p. 258.   ‡ Exod. xxv. 18, seq.
§ Comp. Vol. I. p. 234, 257, seq. || 1 Kings vi. 21, 31-35; viii. 8.
¶ Exod. xxvi. 31, seq. and elsewhere.   ** Lev. xvi.; comp. Exod. xxx. 10, &c.
†† Exod. xxv. seq.   ‡‡ As in Num. x. 33.
§§ Exod. xxv. 10-22; xl. 20, 21; Num. iv. 5, 6, 15.
|||| Num. ii. 2, and the whole chapter.

during the journey in the desert.* Our writer goes a step further and makes Moses ordain and introduce it at Sinai.† Of still greater consequence, however, is another divergence in which he indulges. The reader will remember what we have said about the priestly tribe of Levi, both its actual condition and the deuteronomic precepts relating to its exclusive qualification for the sacrificial service and all the other priestly duties.‡ The Deuteronomist had already ascribed the choosing of the Levites to Moses,§ and the priestly lawgiver retains this idea, but at the same time modifies it on more than one point. He places the selection earlier, not after Aaron's death and at one of the last stations of the journey in the wilderness,‖ but in the second year after the exodus and at Sinai.¶ He further draws a very sharp line of demarcation between Aaron and his sons (descendants), as the only lawful priests, and the Levites in general as qualified exclusively for subordinate duties in and about the sanctuary.** In reality this distinction had arisen immediately after Josiah's reformation, when the priests of the high places were admitted into the temple at Jerusalem, but not to offer sacrifices.†† Ezekiel had sanctioned this distinction for the future by recognizing "the sons of Zadok"—as the families of priests who had served in the temple of Solomon from the very first were called—as the only lawful priests and by assigning inferior positions to all the rest of the Levites.‡‡ Our priestly author goes to work in a much more thorough manner. According to him, the difference between priests and Levites was original, was based upon the extraction of each, and had been acknowledged by Moses from the very beginning and emphatically maintained by Jahveh in the desert upon the occasion of Korah's rebellion.§§ The fact that all this is entirely

---

* Deut. xii. 8, 9. † Lev. xvii.
‡ Vol. I. p. 337, seq.; above, p. 26, seq.   § Deut. x. 8, 9; xviii. 1-8.
‖ As the Deuteronomist does, chap. x. 6-9.   ¶ Num. iii. 5, seq.; viii. 5, seq.
** Exod. xxviii. xxix.; Num. xviii. 3, 7, and elsewhere.
†† 2 Kings xxiii. 9.   ‡‡ Above p. 116.
§§ Comp. Num. xvi. xvii. An older narrative of the rebellion of Dathan and Abiram includes an account of our author relating to Korah's claims to the priestly office and their rejection, to which, i. a., belong Num. xvi. 6-11, 16-22, 35.

unhistorical does not trouble our writer. He wishes to perpetuate, but at the same time to confirm, what had come into existence by degrees more than a century before and was already regarded in his days as reasonable, but had hitherto possessed no legal standing. Was he the first who derived that precedence of the priests from their descent from Aaron, or had others already done this before him? We are unable to decide this, but we consider it very probable that the honour of the discovery is due to him. This much is certain, that this—so to speak, genealogical—settlement of the dispute between the priests of Jerusalem and those of the high places may be said to have been a great success: of course "the Levites" were not very pleased with the rank assigned to them,* but, as far as we know, they did not oppose the exclusive fitness of the "sons of Aaron."—And finally the author diverges from his predecessors also in this, that he elevates the High-priest—first Aaron, and afterwards his eldest son Eleazar—far above the rest of the priests. This too was something new. Before the exile the High-priest was looked upon as the first among his equals. Now he gives him, in contradistinction to all the rest, an official dress to be worn by himself alone,† whereby he acquires, among other things, the exclusive right of consulting Jahveh by means of the "urim and thummim,"‡ and is both allowed privileges and charged with duties which do not exist for the other priests.§

If we put all this together, we can say that in his description of the Mosaic time the author puts forward a thoroughly hierarchical system. The tribe which is dedicated to the service of the sanctuary, stands with the sanctuary itself in the centre of the Israelitish state. We notice a regular gradation among those who belong to this tribe. The High-priest is the visible head of the whole. In conformity with this, Aaron the

---

* See below Chapter VIII. on this point.
† Exod. xxviii. 2-38; Num. xx. 26, 28.   ‡ Comp. Vol. I. p. 96-100.
§ Lev. xxi.-xxii. Comp. again Chapter VIII.

first High-priest is placed as much as possible in the foreground;* if he, as could not well be otherwise, remains subordinate to Moses, his son Eleazar stands higher in reality than Moses's successor, Joshua.†

There are still a few traits to be added to the sketch of this system. We can pass over in silence the mode in which the writer divides the service of the sanctuary among the three Levitical families :‡ his decrees in this respect, however precise they may be in appearance, are worth no more as history than the rest; they serve simply to give greater perspicuity and the necessary finish to the whole conception; moreover they are mutually antagonistic.§ But, on the other hand, it deserves mention

(1.) that the author alleges as a motive for the setting apart of the whole of the Levites for the service of the tabernacle, the idea that Jahveh has accepted them as substitutes for the first-born of the Israelites who were spared by him at the exodus from Egypt, and thus became his property.‖ Jahveh's right to the first-born was acknowledged from the very earliest times, and was connected with the exodus and thus historically explained, long before the days of the writer of the Book of Origins.¶ But our writer is the first who includes the election of the Levites in the sphere of these ideas. To do this, he must assume that there were about as many Levites as Israelitish first-born : according to his account, the number of the former does, in fact, amount to 22,000, and that of the latter to 22,273, so that only 273 Israelites remain who have to ransom themselves for five shekels a head.** In writing this, the author forgets that then only one Israelite in 42 must have been a first-born son! His account has already given exegesists

---

* Comp. Num. xiii. 26 ; xiv. 2, 5, 26, (and on the contrary xiii. 27 ; xiv. 11, 39); xvi. 3, 18, 20, &c.) xx. 1-13 ; xxxiii. 1.
† Num. xxvii. 18-23 ; xxxiv. 17; Josh. xiv. 1 ; xxi. 1.
‡ Num. iii. 15-39 ; iv. § Further details in Nöldeke, l. c. pp. 118, sq.
‖ Num. iii. 11-13, and elsewhere. ¶ Vol. I. p. 239, seq. ** Num. iii. 39, 40-51.

much trouble to no purpose. We must consider that here too he gives way to his desire to reduce everything to figures, but in doing so does not trouble himself at all about the truth or even the probability of his returns;

(2) that liberal provision is made for the incomes of the priests and Levites.* We shall enter hereafter into the details of what the writer allows them. But the fact that his precepts are very much in favour of the priests compared with those of Deuteronomy,† belongs to the sketch of his historical system;

(3) that, in conflict with history and with the Deuteronomic legislation, the priests and Levites have particular cities set apart for them, together with the adjacent pastures for their flocks and herds. These cities are 48 in number and are distributed over the territories of all the tribes.‡ The author also tells us of the execution of this precept,§ when each tribe gives up four cities to the Levites or priests, with the exception that Naphtali gives three and Judah and Simeon nine between them. In spite of this the whole affair is unhistorical. Joshua cannot possibly have exacted four cities for this purpose from each tribe, down to the very smallest. He cannot possibly have allotted to the descendants of Aaron, who at that time were still very few in number, *thirteen* cities, and these in the territories of the tribes of Judah, Simeon, Benjamin, not near the place where the sanctuary then stood (Shiloh), but, on the contrary, in the vicinity of Jerusalem, the later temple-city. In a land such as Canaan, the commandment relating to the pastures round about those cities‖ could not possibly have been carried out. And besides this, as we have already pointed out, there is not a single trace of such cities for priests and Levites in trustworthy historical accounts. They are a product of the imagination of our priestly writer: their equal distribution over the twelve tribes and the regular form of the pastures which belong to them stand upon a par with Ezekiel's proposal to

---

* Num. xviii. and the parallel passages in Leviticus and Numbers.
† Above, p. 26.   ‡ Num. xxxv. 1-8.   § Josh. xxi.   ‖ Num. xxxv. 4, 5.

divide the land of Canaan among the twelve tribes by drawing a number of parallel lines.*

Thus it is already evident that the writer is not inconsistent with himself, when he handles the settlement of the Israelites in Canaan. To the conquest of the land, it would seem, he only referred in passing.† He dwells so much the longer upon the division of Canaan among the tribes. According to him, it took place *by lot,* in the presence of twelve men, one from each tribe, with Eleazar and Joshua at their head.‡ This, again, is an utterly unhistorical hypothesis, and it condemns itself, for, on the one hand, the territory must be assigned to each tribe according to its numerical strength,§ while, on the other, its territory must be assigned by lot. But it is a necessity to the author to put everything in a systematic form, while, moreover, he is glad to confer an important duty both upon Eleazar‖ and upon the representatives of the twelve tribes.¶ He is also consistent with himself in this, that he gives us in full the boundaries of the territory of each tribe and the names of the cities that were situated in it.** He no doubt borrows these returns from older records, but includes them in his work in order that it may show an official character, as it were, to the very end, and lay before us the fulfilment of Jahveh's promises, not merely in a general way, but as proved by authentic documents.

Have we perchance dwelt too long upon the *Book of Origins,* and given up too much space in this History to the review of its contents? In truth, were we engaged now in studying Israel's earliest fortunes, the patriarchal and Mosaic times,

---

* Ezek. xlviii.

† We find clear traces of his hand only in Josh. iv. 15-17, 19; v. 10-12.

‡ Num. xxxiv. 13-29; comp. xxxiii. 54; also Josh. xiv. 1, 2; xv. 1, &c; xviii. 10.

§ Num. xxxiii. 54; comp. upon the whole subject Vol. I. p. 131, seq.

‖ See above, p. 170, n. †.

¶ Comp. Num. ii.; vii.; xiii. 3-16 (utterly unhistorical, according to Vol. I. p. 137, seq.).

** Josh. xiii.-xx., in great part borrowed from the Book of Origins.

such great fulness could not well be justified. But we are now examining the *Book of Origins* from another point of view, not as a witness to the past, but *as an historical fact*. It lies there before us as an irrefragable proof that the prophetic conception of Israel's early history and of the Mosaic legislation no longer fully satisfied the priest in Babylonia; that in him the necessity arose and the power was present to recreate the past, as it were, and to hold up as he thought a truer picture of that past to his contemporaries. Even in itself this attempt is interesting, but its significance is increased beyond this both by the result which it has accomplished, and by the presage which it contains. The author of the Book of Origins succeeded in his undertaking: the conception of the past which he advocated, gradually became a part of the consciousness of the Jewish nation, and has remained the traditional account down to the present day; we all begin by picturing Israel to ourselves as he has drawn it; it is only with difficulty that historical criticism has freed itself from the prestige which he exercised over his contemporaries and posterity.* Such a success may be of no value as evidence for the historical truth of the picture which he designed, yet it must avail as proof of the power of his mind. And therefore I spoke, in the second place, of the presage which the Book of Origins contains. The priesthood which produces such a book is capable of great things. It is ready to pass to practical ground and there to assume the command. He who is able so to recreate the past, certainly possesses the power to reform the future. The Book of Origins is an achievement and the prophecy of other achievements.

* Comp. my remarks upon the Chronicler in Chapter X.

NOTES.

I.—*See pp.* 99, *n.* *; 143, *n.* §.

The returns of the number of Judæans who were carried away and of those who went back to their native land, considered both separately and together, present difficulties which have not yet been removed. Although I myself am not in a position to clear up everything, I think it my duty to make the reader acquainted with the real state of the case and to make an attempt at a solution.

We will begin by studying the returns themselves. In doing this let us remember that the Israelites only included and counted the *men* in their genealogies (comp. *e.g.*, Exod. xxx. 11-16; Num. i.; xxvi.; whenever this rule was broken there were special reasons for so doing, *e.g.*, Num. iii. 39-51, and even then the women were not included). This will also be the case with the figures relating to those who were carried away and to those who came back : and also with Jer. lii. 29, 30, although in this passage "souls" are mentioned; for it is said of Jacob that he and his were seventy "souls," in which number the women, with the exception of Dinah, are not included (Gen. xlvi. 26, 27). Therefore, in order to get at the full number, we must always multiply our returns by four or five.

The first transportation took place in the year 597 B.C. How many it affected we learn from 2 Kings xxiv. 14-16, on which verses compare Thenius and Keil. In the passage quoted only the exiles from *Jerusalem* are enumerated, but it does not appear that inhabitants of the country were carried to Babylonia besides these. The total amounts (verse 14) to 10,000, which are subsequently divided into three groups : 7000 men of means, 1000 craftsmen and smiths (?) and (therefore 2000) courtiers, princes, and men of high rank. Of course this is entirely a round number, the accuracy of which cannot be guaranteed. It merely proves that a tolerably large multitude was carried away from Jerusalem.

According to the Masorethic text the number of those carried away with Jehoiachin is given once more in the Old Testament, in Jer. lii. 28. That passage speaks of Nebuchadnezzar's seventh year, *i.e.*, of the same year which in 2 Kings xxiv. 12, is called the eighth, for in calculating the years of Nebuchadnezzar's reign, the author of Jer. lii. 28-30 is always one year behind the author of Kings (comp. Jer. lii. 29, with 2 Kings xxv. 8; Jer. lii. 12). The number given is 3023, and thus it does not at all agree with 2 Kings xxiv. 14-16. This is already a first reason for doubting whether Jer. lii. 28 really refers to the exile of 597 B.C. But another consideration is of greater weight. Verses 28 and 29 evidently form an antithesis, and the *Judæans* of verse 28 are opposed to the captives from *Jerusalem* of verse 29. This antithesis does not receive its due until for *seven* in verse 28 we read *seventeen*, and assume that this verse refers to the inhabitants of Judæa who were sent to Babylon during the siege of the capital, while in verse 29 follow the citizens of Jerusalem who were banished after the fall of their city. This opinion, which is defended by Ewald and others (*Hk. O.* ii. 214, n. 8), is recommended by the fact that in Jer. lii. we do expect to find information about the number of those who were carried away in 586 B.C., but not about the exiles who left their native land eleven years before. Thus Jer. lii. loses its place among the witnesses to the first exile.

The second transportation took place after the reduction of Jerusalem in 586 B.C. The writer of 2 Kings xxv. confines himself to stating that "the rest of the people that were left in the city, and the fugitives that fell away to the king of Babylon and the rest of the craftsmen [so read for "multitude;" comp. Graf, *Jeremia*, p. 626] were carried away by Nebuzaradan," (verse 11; Jer. lii. 15)—without giving any figures. Now Jer. lii. 28, 29, fills in this omission by naming 3023 Judæans and 832 captives from Jerusalem. These figures have an appearance of accuracy and are also guaranteed by the total given at the end of verse 30.

There now followed a third transportation, five years after the one just mentioned, and therefore in the year 581 B.C. Josephus' account of it is handled in *Hk. O.* 284, sq. Dr. H. Oort's conjecture respecting the connection between this transportation and the murder of Gedaliah, to which we referred above, p. 55, n. *, is very attractive. The number of those carried off amounts to 745—according to Jer. lii. 30, the only place in the Old Testament in which this fact is mentioned.

If we put all this evidence together and examine it in connection with the further accounts by the authors in whose writings it occurs, we arrive at the conclusion that *a very large number of Judæans remained behind in their own country*. It is true, 2 Kings xxv. 12 (Jer. lii. 15) states that in 586 B.C. Nebuzaradan "left of the poor of the land to be vine-dressers and husbandmen," or, as Jer. xxxix. 10 expresses it, "of the poor of the people, which had nothing," so that even the vineyards and fields had to be *given* to them. But it is most obvious that we must not understand this literally, but rather with great reserve. That which Jer. xl. seq. tells us of those who remained behind, gives us the impression that they formed no despicable remnant, or at all events soon increased to a considerable number through the return of the fugitives from the surrounding districts. This is confirmed by Jer. lii. 30, the fresh exile in the year 581 B.C.; and further by Ezek. xxxiii. 23-29, (above p. 98); and finally by the undeniable fact that the Babylonians did not send any colonists to Judæa, which they would have had to do, if the land had been almost depopulated. Nor must we lose sight of the fact that the writer of 2 Kings speaks of those who remained after the *first* exile as "the poor of the land" (2 Kings xxiv. 14)—and this although that remnant was numerous and powerful enough a few years later to resist Nebuchadnezzar for two years: this is truly a proof that we may not take this writer at his word.

During the Babylonish exile, therefore, *many* Judæans remained in their former dwelling-places, and these we have also to notice in the history of Israelitish literature. Compare *Hk. O.* ii. 150, n. 8; 339, sqq.; iii. 357, sq. In spite of this we could say above, p. 55, that "the Israelitish nation had ceased to exist in its native land." Not only had those who remained in Judæa much to suffer from the neighbouring tribes, and especially from the Edomites, who appropriated a good portion of the territory of the tribe of Judah (comp. *Hk. O.* ii. 152, sq., 341, n. 4), but they also lacked organization and leaders. The aristocracy, in more than one sense, had been carried off to Babylonia. Those who were left formed a part of the population of a Chaldean province, but they were no longer a people and no longer represented a nationality. When a fresh nucleus was formed in Judæa, they were able—as we shall see directly —to join it and greatly increase it. But left to themselves they had no alternative but to become gradually absorbed by the foreign intruders and to cease to exist as Israelites.

We will now pass to the accounts relating to the return of the exiles from Babylonia. In Ezra ii. we possess a list of "the children of the province (Judæa) that went up out of the captivity, of those which had been carried away, whom Nebuchadnezzar had carried away unto Babylon, and came again unto Jerusalem and Judah, every one unto his city" (verse 1). After this heading follow the names of the men who stood at the head of those who returned, Zerubbabel, Joshua and ten others (verse 2a); then there comes another heading: "the number of the men of the people of Israel" (verse 2b), with which compare the commencement of verses 36, 40-43, 55. The same list occurs again in Neh. vii. 6, seq., in the memoirs of Nehemiah himself, who relates that he found it while searching for the means of increasing Jerusalem's population: so much is certain therefore, that this list was in existence about the year 440 B.C., and was provided with the same heading as it bears now. We find a third copy of the same list in the Greek book of Esdras (III Ezra), chap. v. 7, seq. —of course a translation of the Hebrew original, but from a text which differs a good deal from that in Ezra ii. and Neh. vii. and which moreover, at any rate here and there, deserves the preference. The three texts give the same total: 42,360 Israelites. Ezra ii. 2b; Neh. vii. 7b lead us to believe that these were the grown-up men; but in III Ezra v. 41, it is stated that all who had attained the age of 12 are included; this is probably a conjecture of the Greek author to which we can attach no value. Now it is remarkable that this total does *not* agree with the preceding figures of which it ought to be the sum; in Ezra ii. these figures amount to 29,818; in Neh. vii. to 31,089; in III Ezra v. to 30,143. There can be no question here of a mistake in the total, in which the three texts agree. The separate numbers are not nearly so well guaranteed, and actually differ in the three copies. But it would be a very strange coincidence, had they been corrupted in the three texts in such a manner that in each case they fell short of the total—and this by about 12,000. This presents a difficulty which as yet we are unable to solve.

We have now to remark further that the exiles did not all return, that even very many remained behind, the latter being apparently quite equal in number to those who had set out under Zerubbabel. This appears from Ezra vii. viii.: 1496 Jews began the journey to their own country with Ezra (chap. viii. 3-14), not counting the priests, the descendants of David (verse 2) and the Levites (verses 15-20); III Ezra viii. 28-40 gives 1690 instead of the 1496. But even then many Jews remain behind in Babylonia, as the sequel of the history will teach us. Compare provisionally Graetz, *Gesch. der Juden*, iii. 283, sq.; iv. 302, sqq.

Now how are these returns of the Jews who went back and of those who remained in Babylonia to be reconciled with the accounts of the number of those who were carried away into exile? How can the figures given by the former be so much higher than those given by the latter?

The simplest way would certainly be to suppose that those who came back also included descendants of the ten tribes, so that they only partially corresponded with those carried off by Nebuchadnezzar, and could easily be more numerous than the latter. But this supposition is prevented by Ezra i. 5 (only Judah, Benjamin and Levi); ii. 1 (the exiles carried away to Babylon by Nebuchadnezzar), &c. It is true, the inhabitants of Judæa look upon themselves as the representatives of the whole of Israel, and are thus prone to make use of the number twelve (Ezra ii. 2; vi. 17), but as the returned exiles settle within the borders of the kingdom of Judah, nay, at first in the immediate neighbourhood of Jerusalem (comp. Bertheau, *Esra, Nehemia u. Ester*, p. 34, sq.), so also they belong to the two tribes which had remained faithful to David and his house.

There is more foundation for the opinion that the returns of the number of those carried away are incomplete. This is even beyond all doubt, as we have already shown. 2 Kings xxiv. 14-16 is especially open to this interpretation. Should we not be going too far, however, in assuming, with Herzfeld (*Gesch. d. V. J. von der Zerstörung des ersten Tempels*, &c. i. 116, 447, 452), that the exiles of the year 586 B.C. were from 300,000 to 400,000 in number? Is not so high a figure too much in conflict with the evidence preserved to us in the Old Testament?

We must also take into consideration the increase of the Israelites in the land of their captivity. Their condition, upon the whole, was very tolerable, so that their number assuredly increased during the fifty or sixty years of their sojourn in Babylonia. But this growth too has its limits; it somewhat lessens the difficulty, it is true, but it does not remove it.

On the other hand, we can hardly believe either that subsequently to 586 B.C. many of those who had remained behind in Judæa went voluntarily to Babylonia (Stricker, *Gesch. van het Joodsche volk*, 1862, p. 5), or that the transportation of 581 B.C. (Jer. lii. 30) was followed by other transportations (Graf, *Jeremia*,

p. 630, sq.). We find no trace anywhere of either the one or the other. Would such a voluntary migration have been permitted by the Babylonish authorities? Must it not have been preceded by an allotment of territory, somewhere in Mesopotamia? Were the men who remained in Judæa, however numerous they may have been, powerful enough to resist the Chaldeans, or even to awaken their fears, and so to occasion repeated transportations?

All the attempts hitherto mentioned to make the accounts relating to the exiles agree with those relating to the return, start from the latter and pre-suppose their absolute authenticity. But still suspicion, or at all events doubt, has been thrown also upon these. Professor E. Reuss (Schenkel's *Bibel-Lexikon*, ii. 245) writes somewhat to this effect: "The number given in Ezra ii. 64, sq.; Neh. vii. 66, sq., is quite out of proportion to the number of those carried away. We shall have to assume, either that the list of those who had returned (Ezra ii. and Neh. vii.) also contains the names of those who came back subsequently, or that it refers to a later period, or that during the exile the number of the Israelites had very greatly increased—which is not probable,—or finally, that the said list gives us the result of a census in which the component parts of the nation, as far as their origin was concerned, were not accurately distinguished, so that other Israelites, who had joined the families which had returned from Judah and Levi, were included in it. In any case the arrangement of the list is very peculiar and surprising. Side by side with a number of very numerous, but otherwise entirely unknown families, among which are some that contain more than 2000 persons, we find a series of much smaller groups, comprising the inhabitants of separate, well-known places. We have here a riddle of which criticism will probably be able to give no more than a doubtful solution."—It seems to me that these reflections of Reuss have been already satisfactorily answered in part by Bertheau, in his commentary upon Ezra ii. The names of the families which we meet with in Ezra ii. 3-19, and do not indeed read without surprise, occur also in other places—in Ezra viii.; Neh. viii.-x., &c.—and thus do not present any insurmountable difficulty. Besides this, Neh. vii. 1-5 forbids us to carry our doubts too far. Moreover, before venturing to draw a definite conclusion, we ought to possess a better knowledge of the organization of the new colony than we are now able to employ. Yet Reuss puts forward a conjecture which is worthy of all consideration. Why should we not assume that the original list of those who returned was amplified after the lapse of some years, and that then the Judæans who had remained in their own country, for so far as they had joined the former, were added to it? There was opportunity enough for such an addition in the interval between 538 and about 440 B.C.—when Nehemiah found the list. That the original inhabitants were included among those who came back, and not, conversely, the latter among the former, lies in the nature of the case: the leadership of the Jewish state rested with the men who had returned; they took the lead in every domain. This hypothesis also explains why we hear nothing of the Judæans who were already on the spot: they became assimilated by the new comers, and so negatived at the same time. And finally, it is recommended by the fact that it agrees with Neh. x. 28—a passage to which we shall return in Chapter VIII. If, upon the occasion of Ezra's reformation, some Judæans who had remained behind joined those who had returned—they are indicated in the passage referred to by the words " all they that had separated themselves from the peoples of the lands unto the law of God"—what can be more natural than the hypothesis that others had done the same thing before?

Perhaps in the want of agreement between the total and the preceding figures, to which we have referred, a trace has also survived of a redaction which the original list has undergone. At any rate this antagonism affords proof that the whole document, however it may have been done and whoever may have done it, has suffered, so that it cannot be called presumptuous to remove the difficulties in our way by conjectures such as these.

If by this means the total of those who returned is reduced and that of the exiles, on the contrary, increased, then the chief difficulty has been cleared away. In the absence of historical records we must be content with a hypothetical solution, and therefore we can rest satisfied for the present with this attempt.

II.—*See p.* 151, *n.* * *and* ‡.

Among the hitherto most disputed—but not on that account the most disputable—positions from which we start in this History, belongs the more recent origin, during the exile or the period after the exile, of the priestly (ritual) laws of the Pentateuch and of the narratives connected with or related to them. We have already advanced evidence in justification of this opinion. Thus in Vol. I. p. 96, seq., attention was drawn to the regulations as to the urîm and thummîm; on pp. 124, seq., 175, seq., to the numberings of the people in the desert; on p. 162, seq., to the chronology in Exod. xii. 40, and other allied passages; on pp. 233, seq., 257, seq., to the precepts respecting the ark of the testimony; above, p. 26, to the laws regulating the incomes of priests and Levites; on pp. 87, seq., to the ordinances concerning the feast of the passover; on pp. 95, seq., to the laws relating to clean and unclean things—all for the purpose of showing that priority to the Book of the Covenant and Deuteronomy is attributed to the priestly or ritual laws incorrectly, and that it is equally incorrect to regard the priestly narratives as older than the prophetic. In Chapters VII., VIII. and IX., too, some of the principal arguments in favour of the exile or post-exile origin are touched upon and others are worked out more fully. But even when all this is put together, the proposition mentioned above is still far from thoroughly proved. That which is wanting here cannot be entirely supplied in the Notes to Chapters VII.-IX., unless the latter are to transgress all bounds and swell into a volume. On the other hand, it still seemed advisable not to omit all explanation and further evidence. Therefore in this and the following Note, and also in Note II. to Chapter VIII. and Note I. to Chapter IX., some of the chief points will be further elucidated and confirmed, preference being given to such as seemed to admit of a curtailed and more popular treatment. In the *Theologisch Tijdschrift* for 1870 (pp. 391, sqq., 487, sqq.) the whole of this important subject is handled, with especial reference to the opinions which differ from mine.

In this Note the combination of Lev. xviii.-xxiii., xxv. and xxvi. in one group and their separation from the rest of the ritual laws will be vindicated.

It is universally admitted by critics that the book of Leviticus, from chap. xviii., according to some even from chap. xvii., as far as and including chap. xxvi., contains divergences from the idiom and style of the laws which precede in chap. i.-xvi. and follow in chap. xxvii. But opinions differ as to the way in which these divergences are to be explained. According to one view, these chapters contain *later additions* to the real kernel of the laws of Leviticus, *i. e.* to "the Book of Origins" (above p. 157) or the so-called "Grundschrift." Others, on the contrary, find in these chapters *older laws*, adopted and partly modified by the author of the Book of Origins. There are also some who hold the said chapters to be *partly younger* and *partly older* than those which precede and follow them. In the abstract these opinions are of equal value: one accounts as well as the other for the divergences which we observe in reading Lev. (xvii.), xviii.-xxiii., xxv. and xxvi. Of course, however, only one of these opinions can be correct.

Let us begin by examining the first opinion, that of Knobel (*Exod. u. Levit.* pp. 494, sqq.). He refers the larger portion of Leviticus to the "Grundschrift." But with this have been linked—by the "Ergänzer," the Jahvist—some documents which he borrowed from the "Kriegsbuch," namely: Lev. xvii.-xx., xxiii. 2 (partly), 3, 18-19 (partly), 39-44; xxiv. 10-23; xxv. 18-22; xxvi. The general considerations against the system of which this opinion is a subdivision, I have set forth in the *Godg. Bijdr.* of 1862, pp. 369-83. The supposition that Lev. xxvi. belongs to the "Kriegsbuch," *i.e.*, was written in the reign of Jehoshaphat, is entirely irreconcilable with the contents of that discourse—as will appear shortly. But the following considerations in particular plead against Knobel's opinions upon these chapters:

a. He makes Lev. xix. 5-8 (Kriegsbuch) younger than Lev. vii. 15-18; xxii. 29, 30 (Grundschrift). The converse is true. The older, general regulation that thank-offerings must be eaten on the day upon which they are offered, or the next day (Lev. xix.), is adopted in Lev. vii., but at the same time is made stricter, so that one sort of thank-offering, the praise-offering, may not even remain till the next day. If this had been held to be prohibited when Lev. xix was written, the author of this chapter would have been *forced* to forbid it; but he does not do so; thus he precedes chronologically the author of Lev. vii. 15-18, (and the parallel passage, Lev. xxii. 29, 30).

b. Lev. xix. 21, 22 give one—although they did not give Knobel—the impression that they are a later addition, a priestly limitation of the exemption decreed in verse 20. But it is an addition quite after the spirit and the style of the Book of Origins, which must therefore be younger than Lev. xix. in its original form.

c. Knobel (pp. 550, sqq.) is correct in holding Lev. xxiii. 39-44 to be an addition to the calendar of feasts upon which Lev. xxiii. is founded. But the precept concerning the day of atonement, verses 26-32, is introduced in exactly the same manner—with "but"—and therefore the same verdict must probably be passed upon it. Now this precept belongs to the Book of Origins (comp. Exod. xxx. 10; Lev. xvi.; Numb. xxix. 7-11; Lev. xxv. 9), with the idiom of which the beginning with "but" entirely agrees (comp. xxxi. 13; xii. 15; Num. xxxi. 23, &c.). Therefore the author of that book adopted and extended the original of Lev. xxiii.

d. It has not escaped Knobel's notice that Lev. xxiv. 10-23 is singularly placed and breaks the continuity (p. 556). But this is also true of Lev. xxiv. 1-9 : chap. xxv. should immediately follow chap. xxiii. The two pericopes, however, Lev. xxiv. 1-9 and verses 10-23, are quite in the style of the Book of Origins, or rather of the later additions to that book (of which more in Chapter IX), as Knobel himself admits with regard to the first (p. 552). Thus it again appears that the writer of that book is the interpolator and therefore must be placed later than the author of Lev. xviii. seq.

Upon the strength of these and other difficulties, which will come under our notice directly, Knobel's opinion must be rejected. But the supposition which I named above in the third place, is also inadmissible. It is to be found, among other places, in Nöldeke, *Untersuchungen*, &c., pp. 62, sqq. He judges very correctly of Lev. xviii.-xx, as we shall see presently. But he holds (pp. 65, sq.) Lev. xxvi. 3-45 to have been inserted afterwards, for the purpose of emphatically enjoining the observance of the preceding laws. The chief argument for this opinion is the later origin of Lev. xxvi.— which, however, would prove nothing, should it appear that the "Grundschrift," the Book of Origins, is still younger. Nöldeke himself admits that Lev. xxvi. agrees somewhat in idiom with Lev. xviii.-xx. (comp. Knobel, p. 573), and wishes to explain this by the fact of the author having read those preceding chapters, because there is also a difference and Lev. xxvi. contains so much that is peculiar to itself. But is it not much more reasonable to conclude from this agreement that they were written by one author, and to explain the difference by the surely undeniable fact that Lev. xviii.-xx. gives us *laws*, whereas Lev. xxvi. is a *castigatory discourse*?

The opinion of Graf (*Die gesch. Bücher des A. T.* pp. 75-83), which I have made my own above at pp. 151, sq., is much more admissible than these two. Let the following remarks serve to recommend it.

I. It is certainly a strange phenomenon that a document such as Lev. xxvi. 3-45 should occur in the midst of the priestly legislation. The analogy of Exod. xxiii. 20-33 ; Deut. xxviii. at once renders it very probable that this discourse formerly stood at the end of a collection of laws, such as the Book of the Covenant or the Deut. law; and this the more, because verso 14 clearly refers to those preceding ordinances. This probability is also considerably increased by the subscription in Lev. xxvi. 46. We are not surprised to find such a subscription at the end of the next chapter, Lev. xxvii. 34: in dividing the Pentateuch into five books it was likely that such a line of demarcation would be drawn (comp. Num. xxxvi. 13). Had Lev. xxvi. 46 the same form as Lev. vii. 37, 38 ; xi. 46, 47; xiii. 59; xiv. 55-57—even then this subscription would lead to no conclusion whatever. But it is evidently intended to close a certain whole, not to indicate the end of one particular law, or of one group of laws upon the same subject.

II. Besides this, the same subscription mentions "mount Sinai" (above, p. 151). I have no doubt that in this a trace has been preserved of a legislation which chronologically precedes the Book of Origins, although I must admit that the evidentiary value of this phenomenon is open to dispute. Upon the fusion and working up of the various collections of laws, such traces of their separate existence are usually obliterated, so that the little which remains of them can be interpreted in more than one way. The question stands thus. According to the order in which the various portions now follow each other, the description of the tabernacle, &c., Exod. xxv.-xxxi., was delivered to Moses *on mount Sinai* ; comp. xxiv. 18; xxv. 1; xxxi. 18; xxxii. 1, seq. In the mean time it appears from Exod. xxv. 9, 40; xxvi. 30; xxvii. 8 (comp. Num. viii. 4), that, *according to the author of the description*, Moses was no longer upon the mountain when it was given to him—although, on the other hand, the subdivisions of this description are elsewhere (in younger additions to the Book of Origins ?) said to have been delivered *on mount Sinai*, Num. iii. 1 (comp. Exod. xxviii. sq.); xxviii. 6 (comp. Exod. xxix. 38-42). However this may be, after the tabernacle is finished (Exod. xxxv.-xl.), Jahveh speaks to Moses *out of the tent of assembly*, Lev. i. 1; Num. i. 1; or—what comes to the same thing and is merely less definite—*in the wilderness of Sinai*, Num. iii. 14; ix. 1. There are exceptions, however, to this rule, which otherwise entirely agrees with what we should expect. The first exception is Lev. vii. 38: "(the law of sacrifices) which Jahveh commanded Moses *on mount Sinai*." This conflicts with Lev. i. 1, and is most probably an old clerical error for *in the wilderness of Sinai*, which words now stand, quite superfluously and even incongruously, at the end of verse 38, but no doubt were originally written as another reading next to "on mount Sinai" (comp. Nöldeke, l. c., p. 61). The second and third are Lev. xxv. 1; xxvi. 46, which I hold to be real exceptions, and regard as proofs of these chapters having been borrowed from elsewhere. The fourth is Lev. xxvii. 34, which note we have already (sub. I.) brought into connection with the division of the Thorah into five books; thus it is of very late date, and has evidently been worded like Lev. xxvi. 46 on purpose; it does not explain the origin of Lev. xxvii.

III. When we have once seen that Lev. xxvi. 3-45 forms the closing discourse of a separate legislation, we involuntarily search for the remains of that legislation in the book of Leviticus. No one would look for them in chap. i.-xvi. But from chap. xvii. onwards phenomena occur which evidently point to the use of sources, to loans from other records. In chap. xvii. however, the departures from the style and language of the Book of Origins are still very insignificant. They become much more important in the eighteenth and following chapters. We will hear what Nöldeke says of them. "Die Schwierigkeit" —he writes with reference to the relation of chap. xviii.-xx. to the "Grundschrift"—"scheint mir immer noch am leichtesten auf die Weise zu lösen, dass wir (vgl. Ewald, *Gesch.* i. 31, 140) die Benutzung einer *älteren schriftlichen Gesetzsammlung* durch den Verfasser der Grundschrift annehmen. Er behielt die Ausdrücke derselben zum Theil bei, änderte sie aber auch nach Bedürfniss ab, und führte Manches nach seiner eignen Weise weiter aus. — — — Ueberhaupt scheint nun die Grundschrift diese Gesetzsammlung gelegentlich schon früher benutzt zu haben. [Nöldeke refers to Exod. xii. 43-49], wie auch weiter unter mehrfache Berührungen zwischen beiden ein ähnliches Verhältniss ergeben, z. B. in Lev. 21 ff. ; 26: 1, 2 sind sicher ganz aus derselben Quelle als Lev. 18-20."—All this is perfectly correct, and essentially agrees with the result obtained by Graf, l. c. It is naturally the strongest possible confirmation of the conclusion drawn from Lev. xxvi. 3-45 and 46.

IV. With regard to the details there is still much doubt. There is room for divergent opinions especially with respect to the traces of the older, priestly legislation in Lev. xxi.-xxiii. and xxv. (upon chap. xxiv. see above). It seems to me that Lev. xxi., xxii. have been very much worked up by the author of the Book of Origins, although much that is characteristic has survived in them. In chap. xxiii. we have already noticed, in verses 26-32, 39-43, the hand of the same author. Chap. xxv. certainly belonged originally to the legislation of which Lev. xxvi. 3-45 is the concluding discourse: this is evident both from chap. xxv. 1 ("on mount Sinai") and from chap. xxvi. 34, 35, 43, which verses render it probable that that legislation insisted upon the keeping of the sabbath-year, as is actually done in chap. xxv. 2-7. On the other hand, however, chap. xxv. has been entirely worked up, as is evident from verse 9 (which mentions the great day of atonement) and verses 32-34 (which mention the Levite-cities and their pastures). Graf believes that in chap. xviii. 2-5 he discovers *the introduction to the whole of the older legislation*, but he himself refers to verses 24-30, which might lead to the conclusion that the first-mentioned verses are an introduction to chap. xviii. alone. In any case these two passages (chap. xviii. 2-5, 24-30), and also chap. xx. 22-26, teach us how easily the author of those laws falls into a tone of exhortation, and thus how very much cause there is for ascribing Lev. xxvi. 3-45 to him.

If the foregoing has justified the opinion advanced above (pp. 151, sq.) as to the relation between Lev. xviii. seq. and the Book of Origins, the question, *when* must we consider that older legislation to have been written, still remains to be answered.

Not before the Babylonish exile. Lev. xxvi. is the work of an author to whom not only the settlement in Canaan and the erection of high places and sun-images are things of the past verse 30), but who also knows that the sabbath-year has not been observed (verses 34, 35, 43) and consequently can look upon the compulsory rest of the land, during the exile of the people, as a punishment for this neglect. The preceding laws in Lev. xviii. seq. also set us down in the post-deuteronomic times. This is true of *all* priestly laws, as will become continually more apparent in the sequel, but especially of those which occur in Lev. xviii. seq. and cannot be considered to have been worked up by the author of the Book of Origins. Thus, *e. g.*, the calendar of feasts in Lev. xxiii., even if we remove the later additions, is more recent than Deut. xvi. 1-17; the law relating to the sabbath-year in Lev. xxv. 2-7, is younger than Deut. xv. 1-11; that relating to the year of jubilee in Lev. xxv. 8, seq. (even before the redaction in which we now possess it), younger than Deut. xv. 12-18, &c. The comparison of Lev. xviii., xx. with Deut. xxvii. leads to the same result; comp. Graf, l. c., pp. 76, sq.

On the other hand, it has already been proved that Lev. xviii. seq. *are older than the Book of Origins, i.e.* than the year 457 B.C. (above pp. 153, sq. and Chapter VIII.).

Graf, l. c., pp. 81-83, has attempted to give a more exact chronology. He draws attention to the very remarkable similarity in language, style and thought between Lev. xviii. seq., especially Lev. xxvi., and the prophet *Ezekiel*, and, upon this ground, holds the latter to be the author of that priestly legislation. Bertheau agrees with him (*Jahrb. für D. Theol.* xi. 150, sqq.). In the meantime Graf's main argument is not conclusive: the similarity exists, but it can also be accounted for by imitation (comp. Nöldeke, l. c., pp. 67-71), nay, it requires this explanation, if it be found that differences also exist. Now this is actually the case. I do not mean here differences of expression, but of *facts*. In the same way that Ezekiel differs in many details from the laws of the Book of Origins (comp. above, pp. 114, sq.), so he does not entirely agree with the ordinances in Lev. xviii. seq. Some points of difference fall away before the hypothesis that those ordinances were worked up by the author of the Book of Origins. Thus, *e. g.*, the difference between Ezek. xli. 23 (the most holy place separated from the holy place with doors, as in the temple of Solomon, 1 Kings vi. 31, 32) and Lev. xxi. 23 (where the curtain is mentioned, comp. above, p. 167). The priesthood of Aaron and his sons might also be attributed to the redaction of Lev. xxi., xxii. (comp. above, pp. 169 and 116, sq.), in the same manner as the day of atonement, Lev. xxiii. 26-32; xxv. 9—with which Ezekiel was not acquainted, chap. xlv. 18-20—has been interpolated into chap. xxiii., xxv. But it does not seem to me to be possible to account in this way for these points of difference:

a. Lev. xxi. 5 does not quite agree with Ezek. xliv. 20;

b. the distinction between the duties of the priests and the high-priest, Lev. xxi. 1-9 and verses 10-15, does not occur at all in Ezekiel;

c. compared with Lev. xxi. 7, 13, 14, Ezek. xliv. 22 appears to be an older regulation, which was afterwards somewhat relaxed for the priests and made more stringent for the high-priest;

d. Ezek. xlv. 21-24 not only prescribes other sacrifices than Lev. xxiii., but also passes over in complete silence the sheaf of the first-fruits and the feast of Pentecost (Lev. xxiii. 10, seq.).

How can this difference be accounted for upon the hypothesis that Ezekiel was the author of Lev. xxi. seq.? It is especially in conflict with Graf's opinion (p. 83) that Ezek. xl.-xlviii. gives us the prophet's *later* notions; the precepts contained there are much rather anterior to those of Lev. xxi. seq. And besides this there is another objection to Graf's opinion. The custom of putting the laws into *Moses'* mouth may be considered to have been already established in Ezekiel's time. Probably the prophet himself would have followed this custom without hesitation in the case in point. But it does not appear that he did so. And from the fact that in chap. xl.-xlviii. he makes Jahveh himself proclaim the organization of the new theocracy, it follows that he did not observe that custom, rather than the reverse. Is it not, upon the whole, more probable that Ezekiel's school made use of Moses' name, than that he himself, the prophet, took refuge in that mode of representation?

I believe, therefore, that I must place even the older priestly legislation, in Lev. xviii. seq., after Ezekiel, and ascribe it to a priest who went on working in Ezekiel's spirit. So far as I can see, there is but one objection of any weight which can be advanced against this conclusion. Ezekiel speaks in chap. xlvi. 17 of "the year of release" as the year in which a field reverts to its lawful owner. This seems to be a reference—the only one in the whole of the Old Testament—to the law of the year of jubilee, Lev. xxv. 8-55, in which the same word occurs (verse 10), and therefore it appears to be a proof that Ezekiel was acquainted with that law and with the collection of laws of which it formed a part. I should indeed admit this conclusion, were it not that so many other phenomena lead to precisely the opposite one with regard to the relation between these two writings. I must now point out (1) that Ezekiel xlvi. 16-24 contains two appendices which do not really stand quite in their proper places, and, if they were added by the writer at all, were at any rate added subsequently. Comp. *Hk. O.* ii. 296, n. 1 ; (2) that "release" also occurs elsewhere, particularly in Jer. xxxiv. 8, 15, 17, and that therefore "the year of release" need not be precisely the year of jubilee; (3) that, even were this so, it would not prove that the prophet made use of Lev. xxv. He may have had in view either a postulate which was current in his time in priestly circles, or another regulation relating to the same subject that is handled in Lev. xxv. Comp. above, pp. 96, sq. where I have already drawn attention to the probability that disconnected priestly ordinances or thorahs were in circulation before the exile, even though a system of priestly legislation was wanting at that time —nay, even in Ezekiel's days.

III.—*See p.* 157, *n.* *.

The priestly elements—laws and narratives—of the Pentateuch and the book of Joshua were indicated above (p. 157) by the name—adopted from Ewald—of the "*Book of Origins.*" Now this book comes under discussion both in Chapter VII. and in Chapters VIII. and IX., and this in such a manner that in the former attention is directed more towards its historical contents, and in the two latter chiefly towards the laws which it contains. In conformity with this division of the subject, this note is devoted to *the representation of historical facts and persons* in the Book of Origins. It must serve especially to bring to light the relation of this representation to that of other narratives included in the Pentateuch, and to uphold, as briefly as possible, the verdict pronounced upon this subject above (pp. 157-173).

In the work which we have already quoted of K. H. Graf, *Die geschichtlichen Bücher des A.T.* (Leipzig, 1866), and especially in the first treatise (pp. 1-113), proof is given that the priestly or ritual laws belonging to the B. of O.—as it shall henceforward be written for shortness' sake—are younger than Deuteronomy and, *a fortiori*, than the Book of the Covenant (Exod. xxi.-xxiii.). But Graf, in the work referred to, detaches those *laws* from the *narratives*, which were usually attributed to the same author. He acknowledges a relationship between the two, but accounts for it by the hypothesis that the narrator was imitated—*e.g.*, in Gen. xvii—by the much younger lawgiver. His conclusion is this, that the B. of O. of Ewald and others is not a whole, but that the oldest, historical elements of the Pentateuch and Joshua, as well as the youngest legislative portions of the Pentateuch, have been added to it. As was to be expected, this result—which the author himself does not put forward without hesitation (pp. 92, sq.)—has not found favour: the priestly historical portions and the priestly laws are connected much too closely to be thus torn apart and even separated by an interval of many centuries. Nöldeke, namely, in his *Untersuchungen*, &c., pp. 1-144, has clearly shown the unity of the priestly historiography and legislation, and thus at the same time has confirmed the current opinion as to the extent of the B. of O. I am not surprised that even Graf himself has admitted this objection to be well grounded. In his paper entitled *Die sogenannte Grundschrift des Pentateuchs* (in the *Archiv* of Merx [1869], i. 466-77), the last which we had from his hand, he acknowledges his mistake on this point. But now, instead of holding with Nöldeke, that the priestly laws are as old as the narratives of the B. of O. are usually considered to be, he holds, conversely, that those narratives are as recent as the ritual legislation. A re-examination of the Pentateuch, as early as the year 1866, led me to the same conclusion. Now is this result upheld by the careful study of the priestly narratives?

I do not hesitate to reply in the affirmative. In the paper just referred to (p. 468), Graf writes : " Was der Anerkennung dass die ' Grundschrift' [=B. of O.] den jüngsten Bestandtheil

des Pentateuchs bildet, im Wege steht, ist nur—*die Gewöhnung.*"
This is perfectly true. When one has once freed oneself from the power of tradition—which is very great even in the domain of criticism—one discovers on all sides most convincing evidence in favour of the proposition that the narratives of the B. of O. give a later representation of facts and persons than that which is given by the prophetic narrators, the so-called Jahvist and his predecessors.

Let us begin by making sure that the field of our investigation is free. It would be conceivable, namely, that there were conclusive reasons for placing the priestly narratives so early as is usually done. In that case we should have to give way and to acquiesce in that chronology, even though it did not seem to us to be supported by the contents of those narratives. But such *proofs of the higher antiquity of the priestly narratives do not exist*. The evidence which it is customary to adduce in its favour proves nothing, or even pleads for the opposite opinion. For

(1.) it is now pretty generally admitted that the Jahvist or prophetic narrator in Genesis—Numbers, who was formerly regarded as the "Ergänzer" or supplementer of the B. of O., worked independently. See the evidence which, in my opinion, raises this above all suspicion, in *Hk. O.* i. 105-112;

(2.) The Deuteronomist is *not* acquainted with the narratives of the B. of O. Whereas he makes constant use, especially in Deut. i.-iv., of older accounts, and particularly of the Jahvistic narratives, his statements nowhere clearly betray the characteristic priestly conception of events. See this demonstrated by Dr. W. H. Kosters, *de historie-beschouwing van den Deuteronomist met de berichten in Genesis—Numeri vergeleken* (Leyden, 1868);

(3.) the traces of acquaintance with the narratives of the B. of O. which it is thought can be discerned in the pre-exile writings, are few in number and anything but conclusive. Where similarity really exists, it often remains doubtful on which side the priority lies. Men point, *e.g.*, to Am. iv. 11 compared with Gen. xix. 29; to Jer. iii. 16; xxiii. 3 (the combination of "to be fruitful and multiply," as in Gen. i. 28 and elsewhere); iv. 23; Isa. xxxiv. 11 compared with Gen. i. 2; and further to a number of expressions which Ezekiel has in common with the B. of O., comp. Zunz, *die gottesd. Vorträge der Juden*, pp. 160, seq.; Nöldeke, l. c., p. 69. Surely no one will base a conclusion upon the first mentioned passages. And with regard to Ezekiel, what can be more natural than that his language should have many points of resemblance to that of the author of the B. of O., who lived, as he did, in Mesopotamia, and can be considered to belong to his school? Let us conclude with one more quotation, which is more conclusive than a long dissertation. Dr. H. Gelbe, who in his *Beitrag zur Einl. in das A. T.* gives the results of his comparison of the Pentateuch with the rest of the books of the Old Testament, sums up (p. 112), before giving a tabular view of the parallel passages, as follows: "Besonders ist hierbei darauf zu achten, dass die *nicht der Grundschrift angehörigen* Theile des Pentateuchs sehr hohes Alter zeigen, da auf einzelnes bei ihnen schon von den ältesten Profeten Rücksicht genommen wird." The author who writes this does not himself doubt the high antiquity of the "Grundschrift." We who are not convinced of it, are confirmed in our opinion by his conclusion.

We can now examine the narratives themselves. All agree in acknowledging their *priestly* character, and consider that this is already clearly expressed in Genesis, *e.g.*, chap. ii. 1-3; ix. 4; xvii., and in a number of other passages. Does not this in itself afford a first proof of the later origin of those narratives? Does not the prime of prophecy precede, *omnium consensu*, that of the priestly tendency among the Israelites? Is it then to be considered probable that the Jahveh-priests preceded the prophets, or, as Nöldeke, for example, assumes, laboured contemporaneously with them, in the domain of literature?

A second and still stronger proof is furnished by the conception of history which the B. of O., taken as a whole, expresses. Let the reader glance once more at the review given on pp. 157 to 173. Is such a historiography to be expected from a writer belonging to the period when Israelitish literature was in its prime, to the 8th or 7th century B.C.? Much rather does the B. of O. unite in itself all the characteristics of the later historiography. Comp. Vol. I. p. 175. The precise and yet unhistorical chronology; the statistical method, which yet represents the truth but apparently; the regular climax and systematic course—everything is just as we should expect to find it in an author who no longer draws upon living tradition, but depends entirely upon learned research and combinations which to our eyes seem arbitrary, but in his own estimation were quite legitimate. It is indeed very strange that a scholar like Nöldeke, who (pp. 108, seq.) has judged so accurately of the style of the B. of O., should, in spite of this, place the author in the 9th century B.C.

When we descend more into details and compare the narratives in the B. of O. with the prophetic (jahvistic) accounts which correspond to them, we obtain exactly the same result. We have already drawn this comparison here and there in our survey (pp. 162, 166, sq., &c.). But in addition to this let us now consider the following parallel passages.

a. The two narratives of the creation, Gen. i. 1, seq. and ii. 4, seq. It is unnecessary to show again that they are mutually antagonistic, and utterly irreconcilable. But is it not equally clear that the standpoint of the second narrator, the Jahvist, betrays a higher antiquity than that of the B. of O.? His conception of the creation is childishly simple; his representation of Jahveh-Elohim strongly anthropomorphistic. Gen. i., on the contrary, bears witness to a broad view of things, to much reflection, and to a strong desire to arrange and systematize; moreover Elohim is not represented here so much in the likeness of man as, *e. g.*, in Gen. ii. 7, 8, 19.

b. It has long been remarked that the two genealogies in Gen. iv. 17, seq., and Gen. v. are variations on one theme, or, in other words, that both are built up out of the same names. If they be placed side by side, can there be any real doubt of the priority of the jahvistic list? Surely very few would now uphold the figures in Gen. v. But if they do not represent the truth and cannot be attributed to misunderstanding, what else can they be but later fiction?

c. Gen. ix. 1-17 corresponds to Gen. viii. 20-22. It is obvious that the former pericope is a priestly extension, and at the same time a purification, of the latter. Noah's sacrifice is omitted, because in the system of the B. of O. the pre-Mosaic periods are distinguished from the Mosaic and post-Mosaic time, among other things, in this, that their pious men, in the absence of a place of sacrifice appointed and a law of sacrifice promulgated by Elohîm, offer no gifts to the deity. So, too, the very anthropomorphistic expression in Gen. viii. 21 is left out. The promise in verse 22 is adopted in chap. ix. 11, but at the same time is enlarged into the description of a *covenant* which is made by Elohîm with the men and beasts saved, and of which the rainbow becomes the token (verses 8-17). The commandments in verses 4-6, and also the permission to eat meat in verse 3 and the promises in verses 1, 2, 7, are connected with this covenant. Now compare with this, on the one hand, Gen. i. 28, seq., and on the other hand Gen. xvii. and the accounts of the B. of O. relating to the covenant between Jahveh and Israel. Everything is planned according to a fixed design, all is artistic and well considered.

d. It is generally admitted that the representation of patriarchal history in the B. of O. differs from that given by the prophetic writers. Whereas the latter make mention of a quarrel between the shepherds of Abraham and those of Lot, of Ishmael's expulsion from his father's house, of Jacob's flight before Esau; all these particulars are wanting in the B. of O., and everything goes on regularly and amicably. See

Gen. xiii. 6, 11b, 12a; xxv. 9, seq.: xxxvi. 6, seq.; xxxvii. 1. Here simplicity is on the side of the priestly writer; the prophetic accounts seem to be more embellished than his. Precisely for this reason the latter have usually been looked upon as the younger. But the converse is the case. The simplicity of the B. of O. is not the simplicity of nature, but of art; it is the uniformity obtained by the omission of that which is concrete and individual—those constant characteristics of living legend. The amicable parting which takes place exactly in the same way between Abraham and Lot, Ishmael and Isaac, Esau and Jacob, is—I had almost said the respectable residue of the animated and striking older narratives, which the author thought he could insert in his picture of pre-Mosaic history. If the figures of Lot, Ishmael and Esau had once existed in the imagination of the Israelites as they are drawn in the B. of O., it is altogether inexplicable how they were afterwards transformed into the men of more or less marked individuality sketched for us by the Jahvist. On the other hand, the simplification which we ascribe to the author of the B. of O., is in harmony with analogy. He treated the narratives of his predecessors in about the same way as the Chronicler treated those of Samuel and Kings: saving the difference which results from the nature of the case, the David and Solomon of the Chronicler stand to those of tradition as the patriarchal figures of the B. of O. stand to those of the Jahvist.

The comparison between the priestly and the prophetic documents in Gen. xii.-l. can be pursued further, always with the same result. Among others, the difference between the revelations of El-Shaddai to Abraham (Gen. xvii.) and Jacob (Gen. xxxv. 9-16)—both as sober as they are solemn—and the theophanies or angelophanies in Gen. xv., xviii., sq. is instructive. We have already pointed to the minute, artificial and unhistorical chronology of the B. of O., in treating of this period. Let the reader also observe

e. Gen xix. 29 compared with Gen. xviii.1-xix. 28. It is

still the same contrast. But it is even more obvious here than elsewhere that the priestly narrator is not the older historian, but presupposes the older accounts and gives a summary of their contents in a few words; no other interpretation accounts for the manner in which the B. of O., in the verse which we have quoted, makes mention of Lot's deliverance.

f. We have drawn attention above (pp. 169, sq.) to the place which the B. of O. assigns to *Aaron*. Aaron also appears out of the Pentateuch, and this as, next to Moses, the liberator of Israel out of the Egyptian bondage; see Mic. vi. 4; 1 Sam. xii. 6, 8; Josh. xxiv. 15. We do not find him mentioned anywhere in pre-exile documents as high-priest and tribe-father of the lawful priesthood. But neither do the prophetic narratives of the Pentateuch depict him in this character. There too he is Moses' helper (Exod. iv. 14, 27-30; v. 1, 4, 20, &c.; xvii. 10; xviii. 12; xix. 24; xxiv. 1, 9, 14; xxxii; xxxiv. 30, 31). In Num. xii. he appears as a prophet (verses 2, 6); this narrative is diametrically opposed to the notion that he was high-priest, and Exod. xxxii. was written at a time when that dignity had not yet been attributed to him. Deut. x. 6, on the contrary, speaks of the priestly office which he filled and which passed at his death to Eleazar. The author of that account assumed without doubt that upon solemn occasions Aaron, by virtue of his intimate relation to Moses, offered up the sacrifices for the whole people, and consulted the oracle. But he is still so ignorant of any *exclusive fitness* of Aaron and his sons, that immediately afterwards he causes *the whole tribe of Levi* to be set apart for the priestly service (Deut. x. 8, 9). This conception is of earlier date than Ezekiel, who pre-supposes it (above p. 116), just as the representation given in the B. of O. is later than that of this prophet.

g. We have already pointed out that the B. of O., quite unhistorically, refers Caleb to the tribe of Judah (Num. xiii. 6; xxxiv. 19), and thereby distinguishes itself unfavourably from its prophetic predecessors, who either admit or at any rate do not deny Caleb's descent from Kenaz (above p. 172, n. ¶ ; Vol. I. p. 137). A similar remark must be made with reference to Joshua. It is true, complete unanimity has not yet been attained with respect to the composition of the narrative, Num. xiii. xiv. (comp. Knobel ; Kosters, pp. 38-56 ; H. Oort in *Theol. Tijdschrift*, iii. 256, seq. ; Nöldeke, pp. 75, seq. ; de Wette's *Einl.* i. 289, sq.). But this much is certain, that Joshua is counted among the spies sent to Canaan for the first time in the B. of O., and, in connection with this, is separated with Caleb from the other spies, and deemed worthy to enter Canaan. This not only conflicts with passages such as Exod. xxiv. 13 ; xxxii. 17 ; Num. xi. 28 (Joshua the servant of Moses), explained by Exod. xxxiii. 11 (where he is indicated by the same title, and besides this is called a "young man" or "boy"), but is also evidently a later notion, derived from a combination of the older accounts and by way of deduction from them. Deut. i. 19-46 (see especially verses 37, 38) and Josh. xiv. 6-15 (see especially verse 6), are of earlier date than the B. of O., and may have assisted to give rise to the notion—which otherwise the authors of those accounts do *not* share—that Joshua had been one of the spies, and thus had been faithful with Caleb.

Compare together also Num. xxvii. 12-23 (Joshua ordained Moses' successor by Eleazar) and Deut. xxxi. 3, 7, 14, 23 (Joshua designated as Moses' successor). The first account, from the B. of O., was evidently unknown to the Deuteronomist (comp. Kosters, pp. 85, seq.), and moreover is decidedly younger than his time : the part which it ascribes to Eleazar is characteristic evidence in favour of the priestly author.

The remarks advanced here in support of the later origin of the B. of O. may be dismissed with the argument which Schrader (De Wette's *Einl.* i. 266, n. f.) employs against Graf: "wogegen indess schon die kritische Analyse ihr Veto einlegt." One of the results of that analysis, namely, is (p. 313 n. *a*) that "die prophetischen Abschnitte Rücksicht nehmen auf die Schrift des annalistischen Erzählers" (= the B. of O.). But the reader must pardon me for preferring not to attempt to remove this difficulty. More weight must in justice be allowed to evidence such as that which we have put forward above, than to the arguments which Schrader seems to think decisive. It is often impossible to decide with certainty even whether two given pericopes can have arisen independently of each other. And, supposing that their mutual dependence must be allowed, the question of priority still remains unsettled and is frequently beyond settlement. Unless I be entirely mistaken, " die kritische Analyse" will have to yield to the considerations which are advanced on pp. 157-173 and in this note, and not the reverse.

CHAPTER VIII.

The Establishment of the Hierarchy and the Introduction of the Law.

UNDER the leadership of Zerubbabel and Joshua, the Jewish exiles, a numerous company, full of glad anticipations, began the journey to their native land. No farther description is given us of their march, but it certainly was not free from troubles and privations. They succeeded, however, in overcoming all difficulties. Upon their arrival in Judæa, the various families settled down in their former dwelling-places.*

Before we proceed farther, we will glance at the composition of the new colony. From the list of those who returned† we find, in the first place, that, irrespectively of the staff of the temple, they belonged to the tribes of Judah and Benjamin: the towns and villages whose former inhabitants went back, were all situated in the territory of these two tribes.‡ The continued use of the sacred number twelve,§ therefore, proves—not that "the children of the exile" belonged to all the twelve tribes, but—that they considered themselves the lawful representatives of all Israel. In the second place, our attention is attracted by the returns concerning the staff of the temple. Separate mention is made of: the priests,‖ the Levites,¶ the singers,** the porters,†† the Nethînîm ("those given," *i.e.* temple-slaves)‡‡ and the children of Solomon's servants,§§ *i.e.* the Canaanites whom Solomon had made his slaves and who had thus been in-

---

* Ezra ii. 70. The question whether Sheshbazzar (Ezra i. 8, 11 ; v. 14, 16) must be distinguished from Zerubbabel is passed over here, as it is not connected with the history of the religion.
† Ezra ii ; Neh. vii. Comp. above pp. 177, sq.
‡ Ezra ii. 21-35 ; Neh. vii. 26-39.   § Ezra ii. 2 ; vi. 17.
‖ Ezra ii. 36-39 ; vii. 39-42.   ¶ Ezra ii. 40 ; Neh. vii. 43.
** Ezra ii. 41 ; Neh. vii. 44.   †† Ezra ii. 42 ; Neh. vii. 45.
‡‡ Ezra ii. 43-54 ; Neh. vii. 46-56.   §§ Ezra ii. 55-58 ; Neh. vii. 57-60.

corporated into Israel.* If we add the number of all these upper and lower temple-servants together, we obtain a total of more than 5000; thus they formed nearly an eighth of the entire colony, perhaps even about a sixth, if the returns of the numerical strength of the single families be more worthy of credit than the figure which is given as the total amount.† Though this proportion is remarkable in itself; yet there is more that calls for our notice. The Levites, the singers, &c., are distinguished here from *the priests*—and this for the first time. Among the returning exiles, therefore, there were persons who were appointed to serve in the sanctuary, but were not considered fit for the actual priestly functions. If we remember, such under-priests—as one might call them—had existed since Josiah's reformation (621 B. C.).‡ It was very natural that the line of demarcation between them and the priests had not been gradually obliterated, but rather defined more sharply. Ezekiel had ordained, in his description of the restored Israelitish state, that for the future only "the sons of Zadok," *i.e.* the descendants of the priestly families of Jerusalem, should take charge of the service of the altar, and had excluded from the priesthood the rest of the sons of Levi, precisely because they had been foremost in worshipping Jahveh on the high places.§ It is now evident that the reality began to answer these requirements of the prophet. But at the same time another circumstance is now explained. The priests are more than 4000 in number;‖ the Levites only amount to a total of 74, or 341 if we include the singers and porters.¶ This proportion remains an insolvable riddle to anyone who, with the (younger) Mosaic laws, holds the priests or sons of Aaron to be a small subdivision of the tribe of Levi. On the other hand, it is extremely natural, if the Levites be

---

* 1 Kings ix. 20, 21.
† Comp. Ezra ii. 64 ; Neh. vii. 66, and above, pp. 180, sq.
‡ Above p. 13.   § Above, p. 116.
‖ Ezra ii. 36-39 and Neh. vii. 39-42 agree in the number 4289.
¶ Ezra ii. 40-42. According to Neh. vii. 43-45, the total is 360.

regarded as degraded priests : probably they were less numerous than their brethren at Jerusalem from the very first, but at any rate the desire to go up to Jerusalem must have been less strong in them than in the men who had the prospect of occupying the highest rank in the new temple.* And finally it does not escape our notice, that in the list already mentioned of those who returned the singers and porters occur next to the Levites and thus are distinguished from the latter. If this only happened here, we might perhaps suspect a slight inaccuracy of expression, and—in agreement with the Chronicler† and tradition—assume that the whole of the servants of the temple belonged to the tribe of Levi. But the same distinction is made elsewhere.‡ The singers are included among the Levites for the first time in a document of considerably younger date,§ and the porters also still more recently, by the Chronicler.∥ It appears, therefore, from the historical accounts themselves, that it was only by degrees that the whole temple-service was assigned to the tribe of Levi, yet not by removing from their posts the non-Levitical families connected with it, but by including them in the tribe of Levi by means of fictitious genealogies. This happened, e.g., with "the sons of Asaph," singers and musicians, who no doubt were appointed to the temple because they were skilled in music, and had made themselves indispensable there, when the idea arose that an office such as theirs could only be filled by the offspring of Levi: Asaph now became a descendant of Levi,¶ and a contemporary of David.** But we shall revert to this hereafter: that idea did not yet exist at the time with which we are occupied now.

The accounts of the first fortunes of the new colony†† are in-

* Comp. Ezra viii. 15, seq.
† 1 Chr. xxv. xxvi. 1-17, and elsewhere. Comp. 1 Chr. xxiii. 3-5.
‡ Ezra vii. 7, 24 ; x. 23, 24 ; Neh. vii. 1 ; x. 28, 39 ; xii. 47 ; xiii. 5, 10.
§ Neh. xi. 15-18 (=1 Chr. ix. 14-16 ; comp. Hk. O. i. 293, sqq.). After the total of "all the Levites in the holy city" has been given in Neh. xi. 18, the porters are treated separately in ver. 19. ∥ 1 Chr. xxvi. 1-17, &c. ; comp. n. †.
¶ 1 Chr. vi. 39-44. ** 1 Chr. xxv. and elsewhere. †† Ezra iii.-vi.

complete and moreover of later date, so that they must be used with caution. Luckily, however, we can supplement them from the contemporaneous prophecies of Haggai and Zechariah.*

The pivot upon which the history of the returned exiles at first revolves, is *the building of the temple*. In the year of their arrival in Judæa, in the 7th month, they assembled at Jerusalem and there built an altar, upon which sacrifices were offered regularly from that time forward. The feast of tabernacles was also kept.† The redactor of the book of Ezra, to whom we are indebted for this information, adds, that *immediately after this* they began to prepare for the building of the temple: as early as the 2nd month of the 2nd year the foundations of the new house of God were laid, amidst very mixed emotions on the part of those present, among whom there were some who still remembered Solomon's temple, and, mentally comparing it with the building which was now to arise, could not share the joy evinced by younger men.‡ The comparison of the utterances of the prophets Haggai and Zechariah renders it at least doubtful whether such great haste was made with the important work; we should rather infer from their words that it was not until fifteen years later, in the second year of the reign of the Persian king Darius Hystaspis, that the foundations of the temple were laid.§ But however this may be, difficulties soon arose which made it impossible to continue the work. The inhabitants of the former kingdom of the ten tribes came to Zerubbabel and Joshua and requested permission to take part in the building of the temple. It was refused them, and this on the ground of Cyrus' mandate, whereby leave to carry out that work was granted to the returned exiles exclusively.|| As was to be expected, this refusal aroused great animosity. Those who were repulsed "hired counsellors against the Jews, to

---

* In chap. i.-viii. of the book named after him; chap. ix.-xiv. are older. Comp. *Hk. O.* ii. 374, seq. † Ezra iii. 1-6. ‡ Ezra iii. 7-13.

§ Hagg. i. 2, 4, 8, 14; ii. 18; Zech. i. 16; iv. 9, 10; vi. 12, 13. Comp. also Ezra v. 2, 16 (taken by the redactor of the book from an older writing).

|| Ezra iv. 1-3.

frustrate their purpose, all the days of Kores king of Persia until the reign of Darius king of Persia."* What the accusations were which they made against the Jews with such good result, we are not told. But if we may judge from what took place on other occasions,† they succeeded in throwing doubts upon their fidelity to the Persian monarchy, and in awakening the suspicion that they wished to make themselves independent. We are surprised that this complaint was at once believed, but if we knew the circumstances of the case, our surprise no doubt would disappear. It is enough that the prosecution of the work could not be thought of.

The inhabitants of the former kingdom of Ephraim now appear on the stage of history for the first time. Thenceforward they repeatedly come in contact with the Jews, mostly as enemies. To understand rightly the part which they play, it will be necessary for us to study specially their origin and religious standpoint.

It lies in the nature of the case, that after the fall of Samaria (719 B.C.) the extensive territory of the kingdom of the ten tribes was not entirely depopulated by the Assyrians. They confined themselves—as the Chaldeans did subsequently in the kingdom of Judah‡—to carrying off the kernel of the nation as captives. But this and the war which preceded it occasioned so heavy a loss to the population of the land, that it was deemed necessary to send foreign colonists thither. This was done, either at once by Shalmanezer,§ or some years later by Esarhaddon, Sennacherib's successor.‖ It would seem that they were military colonies which the Assyrian king transferred to the cities of Samaria, and to other parts of Syria as well, and that they were under the command in chief of Osnappar,¶ "the

---

* Verses 4, 5.   † Ezra iv. 12, sq., 15, sq., 19, sq.
‡ Comp. above, pp. 98, sq., 174, sq.
§ As is stated in 2 Kings xvii. 24, since the "king of Assyria" mentioned here is no other than Shalmanezer, verses 3, seq. Verses 7-23 were introduced by the last redactor. According to the Assyrian monuments Sargon must take the place of Shalmanezer.   ‖ Thus Ezra iv. 2.   ¶ Ezra iv. 10.

great and renowned," as he is called, of whom, however, we know nothing more. Concerning the foreigners who settled upon Israelitish territory, we are told that they came from Babylon, Cuthah, Ava, Hamath and Sepharvaim;* that at first they served their own gods, but, in order to be freed from the wild beasts which made their land unsafe, they allowed a Jahveh-priest, whom the Assyrian king sent to them, to instruct them in the service of Jahveh;† that thus from that time forward the worship of Jahveh was combined with that of their former gods.‡ It may be assumed as probable that these foreign colonists gradually became fused with the Israelites whom they met with in the land, and that consequently the service of Jahveh spread among them and acquired more and more prominence. But it is equally probable that other Israelites, especially in the more northern districts of Canaan, remained unmixed. This explains the fact that in the time of Zerubbabel and Joshua the colonists referred to continued to regard themselves as non-Israelites, and expressly declared that they had served Jahveh "since the days of Esar-haddon,"§ and therefore not before. We now understand, also, why Zerubbabel and Joshua flatly refused their request to take part in the building of the temple. Had they been Israelites, or had the Israelitish element at least been predominant among them, then, it may be presumed, their admission would not have been thought so objectionable. Certainly the descendants of the ten tribes were received without hesitation, if they were prepared to comply with the laws which were in force in Judæa.‖ The admission of such descendants also helps to explain how it is that, about four centuries later, we find a large portion of northern Palestine peopled by Jews.¶ But the refusal given to the descendants of the Assyrian colonists was quite compatible with this willingness to admit the tribes which were still regarded as their brethren.

* 2 Kings xvii. 24.   † Verses 25-28.   ‡ Verses 29-33.   § Ezra iv. 2.
‖ Comp. below the remarks occasioned by Neh. x. 28.
¶ Comp. 1 Macc. v. 9, 14, 17, seq.

It would have been far from singular if those colonists, after they had been repulsed by the Jews, had gradually become estranged from the service of Jahveh. But this was not the case. It is true, thenceforward a bitter hatred prevailed between them and the inhabitants of Judæa; they also continued their hostilities under Ahasveros (Xerxes)* and Artachshast (Artaxerxes I Longimanus),† upon which occasions they again appeared in their character as foreigners, and even made a very sharp distinction between themselves and the Israelites.‡ But meanwhile they went on worshipping Jahveh. Hence it was that some Jews who—we shall shortly see why—had fled from their native land, were received by them with open arms, and that, when they happened to get a priest of Jerusalem, they actually founded a Jahveh-temple on Gerizîm, and from that time forward gradually purified their Jahvism from foreign elements. Thenceforward they also called themselves "sons of Israel," and even set great store by the purity of their pedigree. The Jews, however, did not acknowledge them even then as their brethren, and called them Cutheans,§ or, after their chief city, Samaritans. To some of the points which we have just touched upon here we shall naturally revert when they present themselves in chronological order. We will now resume the thread of the historical narrative.

The first design, therefore, which the Jews had cherished on their journey to Judæa, turned out to be unattainable for the present. About fifteen years elapsed before they could put their hands to the work in real earnest. In the 2nd year of the reign of Darius Hystaspes, Haggai and Zechariah the son of Iddo made their appearance as prophets. Thanks to their influence, the zeal of the people and its leaders was awakened. Alternately by earnest warnings and glorious promises they set the lazy and indifferent in motion. To many, the scarcity

---

* Ezra iv. 6.   † Ezra iv. 7, 8-23; Neh. ii. 10, 19, &c.
‡ Ezra iv. 9; verse 12; verse 15, and the sequel of the letter given there.
§ Comp. 2 Kings xvii. 24.

of food which prevailed just then was a reason for postponing the work still further. According to Haggai, it was a manifestation of Jahveh's anger, and ought therefore to induce them to make a beginning, the sooner the better.* Zechariah appealed to the fulfilment of the predictions of the former prophets, to dissuade his contemporaries from imitating the sins of their forefathers.† If there were any who were discouraged by the comparison between the Salomonic and the new temple, Haggai consoles them with the promise that the latter shall exceed the former in glory: Jahveh shall set the heathen world in commotion, so that it shall acknowledge his supremacy and come to pay homage to him in his house at Jerusalem.‡ The two prophets address themselves to Zerubbabel and Joshua in particular, to encourage them in their arduous task, and to promise them a successful issue to their exertions.§

The words of these prophets did not fail to take effect. Men began to build and continued to do so even after the governor of Syria had demanded a statement of their intentions.‖ He allowed himself to be induced to let the builders go on until Darius should express his pleasure.¶ The latter decided in favour of the Jews.** The work now made good progress and was finished in the sixth year of the Persian king's reign.†† The later historian who tells us this, adds that the consecration of the temple took place with great solemnity, and was soon followed by the celebration of the passover and the feast of unleavened bread.‡‡ The one is as probable as the other. It costs us some trouble, however, to believe that the author had received definite information as to these two feasts. At all events he is inaccurate in saying, " they set the priests in their orders and the Levites in their divisions for the service of God in Jerusalem, *as it is written in the book of Moses ;*"§§ for this book contains no precepts on this subject. The writer rather

---
* Hagg. i. 2-11.   † Zech. i. 2-8.   ‡ Hagg. ii. 1-9.
§ Hagg. ii. 20-23 ; Zech. iii. ; iv. ; vi. 9-15.   ‖ Ezra v. 3, 4.
¶ Verse 5.   ** Ezra vi. 1-12.   †† Verse 14, 15.   ‡‡ Verses 16-22.
§§ Ezra. vi. 18.

supposes than knows by tradition that the entire organization of public worship agreed with the Mosaic laws. We shall shortly investigate whether this supposition can be allowed.

The prophecies of Haggai and Zechariah awaken our interest for other reasons than their immediate results. Did their appearance perchance give rise among their contemporaries to the expectation that prophecy would play the same important part in the new Jewish state as it had played in ancient Israel, before the exile? That expectation would not have been unnatural. In the strange land the voice of the prophets had not been silenced; when the time of deliverance drew near, they had even made themselves heard with vigour and emphasis: now, only a few years after the return, their addresses again exercised an important influence. . . . . And yet the great difference between the older and the younger prophets could long remain hidden from none but superficial judges. There exists, in fact, a tolerably sharp contrast between the inspired language of the Babylonish Isaiah and the prophecies of his younger contemporaries, Haggai and Zechariah—a contrast as great as that between the high anticipations of the former and the sad reality which forced the latter to speak. Babylon had fallen, Israel's bonds had been broken, but—in a manner so entirely different from that which they had imagined! The edict of Cyrus, however remarkable and gladdening it may have been, was a very natural event; the return to their native land had been marked by nothing out of the common; the Jews remained dependent as before, and were soon to find how heavily the yoke of Persian servitude would press upon them: they even saw themselves disappointed in their reasonable desire to possess a sanctuary of their own. A single sentence of Zechariah's can sketch to us their position better than a long treatise. Sixteen years had elapsed since the settlement of the Jews, when this prophet brought in "the angel of Jahveh" speaking in these words: "O Jahveh of hosts, how long wilt thou not have mercy on Jerusalem and on the cities of Judah, against which thou hast had indignation these threescore and ten years ?"* The deliverance had taken place and—Jahveh's anger had not been averted. Is it a wonder that under such circumstances the prophets' enthusiasm is very small and that their discourses bear witness to a certain languor and weariness ? This does not show itself in the two envoys of Jahveh quite in the same manner. Haggai is characterized by simplicity, but at the same time by a want of elevation. Zechariah is more dependent than he upon his predecessors, to whom he even expressly refers and whose thoughts he appropriates.† Besides this, his visions, eight in number,‡ betray more deliberation and art than true inspiration. In this respect there is great similarity between him and Ezekiel, with whom, too, he has his priestly extraction in common.§ We detract nothing from the high merit of both men, when we say that their studied addresses are rather a feeble echo of the true prophetic discourse than the announcement of a new period in the history of prophecy.

There is yet another point of view from which Zechariah deserves our attention. We spoke just now of the similarity between his visions and those of Ezekiel. This similarity is evident from, among other things, this, that *angels* play an important part in both. That we must look here to foreign influence, is probable in itself, and is distinctly proved by Zechariah's prophecies. We find in him notions which clearly betray their Persian origin, *e.g.*, that of "the seven eyes (according to others, the seven watchers) of Jahveh which walk to and fro through the whole earth ;"‖ the way in which he introduces Satan,¶ also, reminds us of Persian dualism. We shall find an opportunity further on of dwelling upon this at greater length,** but we ought already to note that the Jews proved themselves not disinclined to enrich their theology with

---

* Zech. i. 12, comp. 7. † Comp. *Hk. O.* ii. 378, sq. ‡ See l.c. pp. 376, sq.
§ See l.c. pp. 395, sq. ‖ Zech. iv. 10. ¶ Zech iii.
** See below, Chapter IX.

such elements of the Persian doctrines as they could adopt without being unfaithful to their own principles.

In the year 516 B.C. the temple was finished; in 458 B.C. Ezra came to Jerusalem. The intermediate period of nearly sixty years is a blank to us. All that we are told of it is contained in this one statement: "in the reign of Ahasveros,* in the beginning of his reign, they [the Samaritans] wrote an accusation against the inhabitants of Judah and Jerusalem;"† what follows about the events under Artachshast,‡ most probably relates to the years after Ezra's arrival. The book of *Esther*, which transfers us to the reign of the Ahasveros just mentioned, does not treat of Judæa, and, moreover, cannot be regarded as an historical narrative. One can understand that the fortunes of the returned exiles afforded but little material for historians. Yet their silence causes a void which we lament the more, because, as subsequent history shows, not unimportant changes, of the course of which we would gladly be accurately informed, took place in Judæa during that half century. It is the period of *the rise of the hierarchy*.

Even at the return, the high-priest Joshua, next to Zerubbabel, stood at the head of the people. It was quite in the nature of the case that he should soon take the first place. Zerubbabel was a descendant of David. This served to recommend him to many among the people. But in the eyes of the Persian king, or of the Persian governor "on this side the Euphrates," to whose jurisdiction Judæa also belonged, his extraction easily rendered him a somewhat suspected and dangerous person: what guarantee had they that he would not attempt to place himself upon the throne and render his people independent? Thus it was not unnatural that the government of Judæa was entrusted to men of another family, perhaps even by preference to foreigners.§ Such a governor, whether he

---

* Xerxes I. 485-464 B.C. † Ezra iv. 6.
‡ Artaxerxes I. Longimanus, 464-421 B.C. See Ezra iv. 7-23.
§ Comp. Neh. v. 15.

were an Israelite or a stranger, represented in either case the sovereign power of Persia, to which exclusively he owed his elevation. Meanwhile there remained room for a *national* authority next or opposite to him; nay, its rise must have been desired and promoted by the Persians in their own interest. This position was now taken up as a matter of course by the Jerusalem priesthood, with the high-priest at their head. His dignity descended by inheritance to his eldest son, so that it did not lack the requisite stability. He was moreover the acknowledged representative of the religious individuality and unity of the Jewish people, which had acquired undisputed precedence since the nation had ceased to play a part in politics. Nor should we forget that he found a firm support in the comparatively large number of the priests, Levites, and other officers of the temple, and must have had great influence as their head alone, irrespectively of the might and honour attributed to him by the whole nation. An authority which is indicated by circumstances, as it were, and in the continuance of which, moreover, the whole of a powerful order is directly interested, derives great strength from each of these facts.

Unless I be mistaken, the comparison of the two prophets Haggai and Zechariah with each other proves that we are not wrong in taking the support of the priesthood into account. The former is well disposed towards the priests; he gives them the honour which is their due;* but yet it is Zerubbabel whom he calls the chosen one of Jahveh and almost identifies with the promised saviour of Israel.† Conversely, while Zechariah, the man of priestly descent, assigns a very high place to Zerubbabel,‡ yet he regards Joshua as the real representative of the nation, upon whom, therefore, Satan directs his attack, but who, absolved from all blame, is permitted to hear the promise that "he shall direct Jahveh's house and keep his courts;" with whose person, moreover, the appear-

* Hagg. ii. 11-13.   † Hagg. ii. 21-23.   ‡ Zech. iv. especially vers. 6-10.

ance of "the Branch, Jahveh's servant" is most intimately connected.* Upon Joshua's head he places the costly crown made from the gifts of the Jews who had stayed behind in Babylonia: he thus raises him to a type of the "Branch," who—it says—"shall build the temple of Jahveh, who shall bear the ornament and shall sit and rule upon his throne: *he shall be a priest upon his throne*, and peaceful counsel shall there be between them both (the priest and the ruler)."† Is it not evident from this that the elevation of the high-priest proceeded, although not exclusively, it is true, from those upon whom in the first place his lustre would be reflected?

It would now be of the highest importance to know the form in which the high-priest exercised his power. But our information on this point is very defective. From the silence of Ezra and Nehemiah we infer that in their days—and so much the more in the intermediate period of which we are now treating—there was still no fixed court, such as the Council of the Elders (Gerusia) or the Sanhedrim was in after centuries. We therefore assume that at first the high-priest exercised his authority, which was tolerably unrestricted and nowhere accurately defined, alone, or consulted the priests of the highest rank and the heads of the families.‡ No doubt no step of any importance was taken without their consent. In very weighty matters the decision even rested with the whole community, which was summoned to Jerusalem for that purpose.§ When we reflect that the sphere within which the Jews could do as they liked was tolerably narrow, we are not surprised that great irregularities or even arbitrariness prevailed in all these matters; everything depended upon the personal character of

---

* Zech. iii., especially vs. 7, 8. The appellation Z*'mach*, Branch, which occurs in chap. iii. 8; vi. 12, is borrowed from Isa. ix. 2; Jer. xxiii. 5; xxxiii. 15, and indicates the deliverer of Israel, whose coming the earlier prophets had announced.

† Zech. vi. 9-15.

‡ Nehemiah mentions repeatedly the Jewish "nobles" and "rulers," chap. ii. 16; iv. 14; v. 7; viii. 5, comp. vi. 7; xiii. 17. "The heads of the parent houses" or "families" occur in Neh. vii. 71 (Ezra ii. 68); viii. 13; the "princes" in Neh. ix. 38; xi. 1. § Ezra x. 7, seq.

those who stood at the head of affairs, whether as lieutenant-governors or as high-priests; it was only by degrees that each man's authority was marked out more definitely and that thus the necessity of binding its exercise to set forms made itself felt.

In this state of the case, every particular relating to the men who filled the office of high-priest would be welcome to us. But our curiosity remains unsatisfied. Even with respect to Joshua we are very imperfectly informed. From a fragmentary communication in the book of Nehemiah,* we should almost infer that he laid the foundation for the division of the priests into twenty-four classes. In the list of the exiles who had returned, the whole of the priests are referred to four families and the classes are not mentioned.† When therefore twenty-two divisions of priests are afterwards enumerated as having gone up to Jerusalem with Zerubbabel and Joshua, the conjecture is very obvious that Joshua divided the four families in this way; two more may have been added subsequently, perhaps after the arrival of Ezra and his colony.‡ Of Joshua's successor Joiakim we only learn this, that the said classes of priests still existed in his days.§ His son Eliashib was a contemporary of Nehemiah‖ and will come under our notice again when we study his labours. He was succeeded by Joiada, Jonathan and Jaddua,¶ which last lived to see the fall of the Persian kingdom and the subjection of the Jews to Alexander the Great.**

We should have to confine ourselves to this dry enumeration of mere names, were we not able to draw some conclusions as to the internal condition of the Jewish colony, and of the spirit which animated its leaders, from the more circumstantial accounts relating to Ezra and what befell him at Jerusalem. Without anticipating what will be said presently about Ezra

---

* Chap. xii. 1-7. † Ezra ii. 36-39; Neh. vii. 39-42.
‡ Comp. Ezra viii. 2. § Neh. xii. 12-21.
‖ Neh. iii. 1, 20, sq.; xiii. 4, 7, 28; comp. xii. 10, 22, 23.
¶ Neh. xii. 10, 11. ** Neh. xii. 22.

and Nehemiah, we may assume it to be known here that both these men met in Judæa with much, very much that seemed to them reprehensible. They were especially scandalized at the tolerance to which the numerous marriages of Jews with foreign women bore testimony. Even priests, Levites, singers and porters had been guilty of this evil.* Of this evil? But was alliance in marriage with other tribes then really a sin? was it not merely narrowness of mind and national pride that opposed it? In truth, there was not a little to be said in support of such an approach to the neighbouring tribes. It was in all respects capable of being idealized, and is, in fact, defended and commended from a purely jahvistic standpoint in the book of Ruth. As we shall see shortly, the author of this book and the men of his mind acted in good faith in taking it under their protection against those who vehemently assailed it. But it does not follow from this that it was the manifestation of a praiseworthy universalism from the very first, or even —for it could also be viewed in this light—of the desire to bring the heathen to Jahveh. Probability pleads for another interpretation. We must regard this union with the foreigner as a fruit of indifference, as an actual sign of want of interest in that which distinguished the Jews from the tribes that surrounded them. This is evident not only from the verdict of Ezra and Nehemiah, who knew their contemporaries' motives better than we do, but also from the reception given to their attempts at reformation. Moreover, that indifference is perfectly explicable under the circumstances in which the Jews were placed. As we have already observed, their lot, from the time that they were granted permission to return, was one of uninterrupted disappointment. If we knew their adventures more in detail, we would probably think it still more natural that their zeal for religion gradually slackened. More than ordinary strength of mind was indeed required in those days to continue to believe in Israel's destiny. Is it a wonder that

* Ezra x. 18-24.

many fell short in this and showed less and less concern? The strict isolation from the neighbouring peoples was necessarily the first to suffer. But as the alliances with them became more numerous and more intimate, the purity of Jahvism was also in great danger. So the Jewish nation stood upon an inclined plane. Its exemplars and leaders, the priests and the rest of the temple-servants, may have been faithful in the discharge of their duty; we have no reason to suppose the contrary; but they proved unequal to the difficult task which they had just then to perform. " The people of Israel *and the priests and the Levites* are not separated from the peoples of these lands;"* so runs the account which was brought to Ezra and was contradicted by no one. It was to be feared that the individuality of Israel and of Israel's religion would be gradually effaced; that the great results which had already been obtained in the domain of religion were not being preserved and developed, but, with their inestimable value unrecognized, were being given up and lost. Once again in the course of centuries after the exile, under the Syrian dominion, Israel was exposed to a similar danger. But let us not forget, that now, in the first half of the 5th century B.C., the danger was much more threatening than it was or could be at a later period. As yet the Jews lacked the sure guarantees for the preservation of their religion in its integrity. Many of the writings which were afterwards to occupy a place of honour in their sacred literature were in existence, but they were scattered here and there, and were not yet acknowledged by all; as yet they were without the stamp which they required before they could pass as law and rule the further development of the life of the nation. Yet, in spite of this, the Jewish nation even of those days would have been proof against a persecution for its faith's sake. But would it also be proof against the danger of amalgamating with the neighbouring and kindred tribes, and thus of gradually sinking back to the standpoint upon which it had stood in

---
* Ezra ix. 1.

former times, and above which Edom, Moab and Ammon had not yet been able to raise themselves? The service of the strange gods, which had been so seductive in the exile, did not certainly after the exile all at once lose its attractiveness. Unless we be mistaken, the position of Israel's religion about the middle of the 5th century B.C. was most critical. If no rescue came, the longer existence or at least the future of Jahvism was doubtful.

The rescue was not long in coming. It cannot well have been by chance that precisely at the time when the danger which we have just sketched was rapidly increasing, Jewish men in Babylonia felt themselves roused to go up to Jerusalem and to reinforce the colony in Judæa. Constant intercourse undoubtedly existed between the Jews who had returned and those who had stayed behind.* The wants which made themselves felt in Judæa were not unknown in Babylonia. We already know enough of the Jews settled there to think it most natural that they were deeply moved by the accounts which reached them from their mother country. But instead of involving ourselves in the calculation of their motives, we will let the facts speak for themselves.

It is nothing less than a revolution which we are about to describe. The labours of Ezra and Nehemiah form a turning-point in the history of Israel's religion. And yet, however clear this may be to us, the high importance and the real significance of their work are still not generally acknowledged. Thus it is necessary, not merely to give utterance to our conception of this work, but also to prove its truth: on this subject less even than on any other can the reader be asked to believe any assertion on mere authority. Before we go further, then, let us glance at the accounts furnished us by the Old Testament.

In the seventh year of the reign of Artaxerxes (458 B.C.) Ezra the priest and scribe left Babylonia for Judæa, accom-

---

* Comp. Zech. vi. 9-15; Neh. i. 1, seq.

panied by a band of his fellow-exiles. Touching this journey and Ezra's actions immediately after his arrival, we possess a narrative which is partly from his own hand (Ezra vii.-x.). It breaks off suddenly, so that we are altogether in uncertainty with respect to the events of the years immediately succeeding. It was in the 20th year of the same Persian king (445 B. C.) that *Nehemiah* asked and obtained leave to go to Judæa as governor and rebuild the ruined walls of Jerusalem. He himself tells us how he succeeded in that mission (Nehemiah i.-vii.; xii. 27-43); in doing so he only mentions Ezra once, upon the occasion of the dedication of the walls of Jerusalem (chap. xii. 36). On the other hand, in a succeeding portion of the book called after Nehemiah, the two men, *Ezra* and *Nehemiah*, appear, acting in concert: the event related there, in Nehemiah viii.-x., took place *in the seventh month*,* but the year in which it fell is not given; thus we must place it between 444 B.C., the year after Nehemiah's arrival, and 433 B.C., when he went back to Persia,† and presumably at the beginning of this period. If this presumption be correct, again some years elapsed of which we learn nothing. Of Nehemiah's departure for Persia, too, we are only told in passing. But he visited Judæa once more, probably as early as 432 B.C., and drew up a narrative which we still possess of what happened then (Nehemiah xiii). How long his second visit lasted, it does not show; and it also leaves our curiosity as to other points unsatisfied. Fortunately we can supplement it in some measure from the prophecies of Malachi, who is held with great probability to be a younger contemporary of Nehemiah.

These accounts are not all of the same importance to the history of the Israelitish religion. The restoration of Jerusalem's walls lies almost outside of that history. But all the rest is of so much the greater importance. Let us begin by simply narrating the facts.

---

* Chap. vii. 73; comp. chap. viii. 13; xi. 1.   † Neh. v. 14.

Ezra the priest, "a ready scribe of the law of Moses,"* had —we read†—"prepared his heart to study and keep the law of Jahveh and to teach in Israel statutes and right." He must have been at work in this spirit for some time among his fellow-exiles in Babylonia, when he conceived and matured the plan of going to Jerusalem and there continuing these labours. But to do this, he required the permission of the Persian king and his authority to carry out his plans in Judæa. These were graciously granted to him. Artaxerxes made an edict which, unfortunately, we no longer possess in its original form. The later redaction which has been preserved to us,‡ written in a Jewish spirit, exaggerates the king's gracious orders. But unless it altogether misrepresents the tendency of the original, Ezra got leave to go to Judæa, with those who should join him, and important subsidies were granted him for the journey; he further obtained privileges and exemption from taxes for the temple at Jerusalem and its servants; and finally, he was empowered to test the condition of his nation by "the law of his God, which was in his hand,"§ to organize the administration of justice in accordance with that law,‖ and to take the necessary steps to make it known.¶ It speaks well for the distinction which Ezra enjoyed among the exiles, that so many of them declared themselves ready to go to Judæa under his leading. We are not told how numerous the two priestly families of Gershom and Daniel and the Davidic house of Hattush were;** but 1496 men volunteered besides these.†† If, as we saw above,‡‡ the Levites were badly represented in the first expedition, now it appeared that they were absent altogether. Ezra considered this so great a want that, to provide against it, he submitted to a short delay. A deputation which he sent to a certain Iddo at Casiphia, who must have had great influence there, succeeded beyond expectation: 38 Levites and

---

* Ezra vii. 6 ; compare verses 11, 12, 21 ; Neh. viii. 1 ; xii. 36.
† Ezra vii. 10. ‡ Ezra vii. 11-26. § Verse 14a. ‖ Verse 25a.
¶ Verse 25b. ** Ezra viii. 2. †† Verses 3-14. ‡‡ p. 203.

220 Nethinîm decided to accompany Ezra.* So now the journey could be commenced. A day of fasting was kept at the river Ahava, where they had assembled, and Jahveh's help was implored. "For"—writes Ezra himself, and even here we are struck with the close combination of piety and national pride which marks the whole of his labours—"I was ashamed to ask the king for soldiers and horsemen to help us against enemies on the way; for we spoke to the king, saying, the hand of our God is upon all them for good that seek him, but his power and his wrath are against all them that forsake him."† When the day of prayer was over, the gifts for the temple were entrusted to twelve priests and as many Levites.‡ The journey was successfully completed. Upon their arrival at Jerusalem, they rested for three days. The gold and silver which they had brought with them was then delivered into the treasury of the temple, and a great sacrifice was offered up to Jahveh.§ The governors "on this side the river" were made acquainted with the king's mandate, and "they furthered the people and the house of God."‖

Ezra goes on to tell us what happened next. It was sad news which the princes—of their own accord, or at his instigation?—brought to him: "the people, the priests and the Levites had taken wives for themselves and their sons out of the tribes which they found in Judæa and in the adjacent regions; so the holy nation had mingled themselves with the peoples of the lands; the princes and rulers, far from preventing this evil, had set the example in committing it."¶ This account has a crushing effect upon Ezra. He mourns and humbles himself before all the people. For some time he sits motionless and stunned. About the hour of the evening sacrifice he breaks this silence. He throws himself in his rent garments to the earth and turns in prayer to Jahveh. It is a humble confession of guilt which he pours forth in the name

* Ezra viii. 15-20.   † Verse 22.   ‡ Verses 24-30.   § Verses 31-35.
‖ Verse 36.   ¶ Ezra ix. 1, 2.

of the whole nation. If their fathers had already sinned and thereby drawn down destruction upon their heads, now their children, in spite of the mercy which had been shown to them, had also acted in direct opposition to Jahveh's commandments. He scarcely ventures, after such great sins, to appeal afresh to God's mercy. "O Jahveh, God of Israel,"—so he ends his prayer—"thou art righteous, for we are left as a remnant, as it is this day. Behold, we are before thee in our guilt, for there is no one who, notwithstanding this sin, can stand before thy face!"* Thus did the assembled multitude hear Ezra pray, and his words sank deep into many hearts. One of his hearers, Shechaniah ben Jehiel, acknowledges their transgressions in the name of all, but at the same time expresses his trust that there is yet hope for Israel. "Let us"—he proposes —"let us all make a covenant with our God to put away these wives and their children, according to the counsel of my lord and of those that fear the commandment of our God; and it shall be done according to the law."† Ezra hastens to accept this proposal. He binds the chief of the priests, the Levites and the people by oath to submit to it. Shortly after this a great national assembly is convened at Jerusalem: every one had to be there within three days under pain of the "ban" upon his goods‡ and of being thrust out from the community.§ On the 20th day of the ninth month—which corresponds nearly with our month of December—all the men of Judah and Benjamin were assembled in the open place before the temple, disconcerted at so peremptory a summons at that season of the year, and shivering in the rain which fell in torrents. Ezra stands up and says, "Ye have transgressed, and have taken strange wives and thus have increased the guilt of Israel. And now, make confession to Jahveh the God of your fathers, and do his pleasure, and separate yourselves from the nations of the land and from the strange wives."|| It was scarcely conceivable that this

* Ezra ix. 6-15. † Ezra x. 2, 3. Others translate: "the counsel of the Lord, &c.," but the authorized version must be retained
‡ Comp. Vol. I. 290. sq. § Ezra x. 7, 8 || Ezra x. 10, 11.

vehement demand should be resisted. Yet there were four men —the historian gives us their names*—who dared to speak against it. But they were outvoted by the whole gathering, which willingly submitted, and merely urged that the matter should not be settled then and there, but by their rulers, in conjunction with the elders of the cities.† This request was granted. The enquiry, which occupied two entire months, began on the first day of the tenth month. The writer—not Ezra, but a later author, who made selections from Ezra's records—concludes his narrative with a list of the names of those who put away their wives. Four of them, who belonged to the family of the high-priest, had to sacrifice a ram for their crime.‡ Of the rest we learn no details. But what bitter scenes of woe are hidden behind that laconic ending: "All these had taken strange wives, and some of them sent wives and children away!"§

"*It shall be done according to the law.*" This maxim was put into execution by Ezra without pity, directly after his arrival at Jerusalem. If his zeal needed stimulating, the success of this first attempt was the best encouragement. Therefore we now expect to learn what he did next: so much still remained to be done, and the field was ready. To our great astonishment, however, the narrative of the book named after him breaks off here. It is true, he appears again upon the scene subsequently, but not till the arrival of Nehemiah, and therefore after an interval of 13 years.|| No doubt his own records said what was necessary about this interval. But the Chronicler, who gave the book of Ezra its present form,¶ did

---

* Ezra x. 15. "Only Jonathan the son of Asahel and Jehaziah the son of Tikvah opposed this matter, and Meshullam and Shabbathai the Levite supported them."—*Amended Translation.* † Ezra x. 12-14. ‡ Ezra x. 19.

§ Ezra x. 44. The Hebrew text of this verse is unintelligible and must probably be corrected as shown in the translation given here. Comp. Bertheau on this point. Verses 18-43 name 113 fathers of families in all.

|| See the passages already cited above (p. 219), Neh. xii. 36, and viii.-x.

¶ Comp. *Hk. O.* i. 357, seq.

not think fit to enlighten us upon it. Here therefore a wide field is opened to conjecture. If the sketch of Ezra's later actions in Neh. viii.-x., be correct,* then those 13 years are not merely a gap in our knowledge of Ezra's history, but a period of actual rest or cessation in his work; in that case he did not continue his task under Nehemiah's governorship, but set about it with vigour then for the first time. The manner in which he acts in those chapters admits of no other interpretation. We already know enough of him to venture to assert that this rest was not voluntary, but forced. Its cause may have lain within himself or beyond him: his preparation may have been defective in some respect, or circumstances may have hindered him from carrying out his plans. And why not one as much as the other? We shall soon see that the facts most strongly recommend this supposition.

The first thing we have to do is to form an accurate conception of Nehemiah's mission. Formerly the opinion was pretty general, that the walls of the capital had *not yet* been restored, when (445 B.C.) he arrived there, so that he went to Jerusalem to finish Zerubbabel's task as it were. But this is incorrect. The state of affairs of which he, as cup-bearer at the court of Artaxerxes, received information, had only arisen *shortly before*, as appears from the very words of Nehemiah's own narrative.† What led to the destruction of the walls of Jerusalem and the burning of her gates, we do not know for certain. But the discontent which had already begun to prevail in the more remote provinces of the Persian empire, and in which the Jews may have been involved even against their will, is quite enough to account for such an occurrence.‡ We also know from authentic records—which have been preserved to us in consequence of their having been inserted in the book of Ezra, though in a wrong place§—that precisely in Artaxerxes' reign

---

* Comp. Note I. at the end of this chapter. † Neh. i. 1-3.
‡ Comp. Rutgers, *Het tijdvak der Babyl. ballingschap*, etc. pp. 127, sq.
§ Ezra iv. 7-23

the Assyrian colonists in Samaria came forward with complaints against the Jews, and so hindered the restoration of the walls of their capital. Nothing prevents us from assuming that the war, which became so fatal to Judæa in particular, broke out shortly after Ezra's arrival. In that case it becomes most natural, that when he had but just begun, he found himself doomed to inactivity. The change in Artaxerxes' disposition towards the Jews, of course deprived the powers granted to him of their force. Peace and quiet were indispensable for a reform such as that which he had in view. In troubled times it could not have been difficult for those who disagreed from him to render his efforts unavailing. In short, it is very easy to comprehend that he was obliged to wait for better days, and when we find that he set to work directly after the completion of the walls of Jerusalem, we consider it almost certain that it was political circumstances which had hitherto stood in his way.

It lies beyond our purpose to study specially the vigorous way in which Nehemiah came forward, and the happy issue of his exertions. This can be read in his own narrative.* We must only pay attention for a moment to two points which wil be useful to us hereafter. In the first place, if Nehemiah allotted Ezra also a place in the procession at the solemn dedication of the walls of Jerusalem,† it may be inferred from this that from the very beginning the two men were on good terms with each other. In the second place, it does not escape our notice that Nehemiah, even when he was bent upon the rebuilding of the walls, had to combat the opposition of some of his fellow countrymen, and especially of the Jahveh-prophets of those days.‡ Viewed by themselves, his efforts to raise Israel from the deep abasement into which she had sunk do not account for this opposition. May it not be regarded as a proof that Nehemiah made himself known at once as a

* Neh. i.-vi.   † Neh. xii. 36.   ‡ Neh. vi. 10-14.

by no means neutral man, as the powerful advocate of a definite religious-political tendency? Did his joining Ezra perchance cause some forthwith to mistrust him and to fear injury in the future from the success of his first undertaking?

We will enquire presently what use Ezra himself made of his period of forced repose. First we will investigate how he laboured with Nehemiah's support. A very distinct picture of that work is drawn for us in a section of the book of Nehemiah (chap. viii.-x.), which we have already mentioned.

On the first day of the seventh month a general gathering of the people was held at Jerusalem. Men, women, and children who had arrived at years of discretion, assembled on the open place before the watergate of the temple. A lofty and capacious platform had been erected. Upon this Ezra took his stand with fourteen priests, seven on his right hand and seven on his left. At the request of the people, he had brought—from the temple? —the "book of the law of Moses, which Jahveh had commanded to Israel." He now opens the roll; the whole multitude stands up; Ezra utters a doxology to which the people respond "Amen, Amen," bowing down to the earth and worshipping. The reading begins. Distributed among the people there are some* Levites, whose task it is to repeat and, where necessary, to explain the words read by Ezra. So deep is the impression made by the word of the Law, so violent is the emotion aroused by it, that Nehemiah, Ezra and his assistants have to guard against extravagance,—"This day," they say, "is holy unto Jahveh, mourn not therefore, nor weep, rather go your way, eat the fat, and drink the sweet, and send portions unto them for whom nothing is prepared;" let it be a day of joy and remain so. The people give ear to this exhortation. The next day they all assemble again and the reading of the Law is resumed. They then found that it contained directions as to the keeping of the great feast of ingathering, on the 15th and following days of the 7th month, which had not been observed "since

* Neh. viii. 7 gives 13 names.

the days of Joshua the son of Nun unto that day." They were the precepts in Lev. xxiii. 40-43, concerning the dwelling in booths, and steps were now taken for immediate obedience to them.* The feast was kept with great joy for *eight* consecutive days,† and during this time the reading of the Law was not forgotten.‡ Finally, on the 24th day of the same month, a great day of repentance was kept. The Israelites appear in mourning at their usual place of meeting. A fourth part of the day is again devoted to the reading of the Law. This is followed by a general and solemn confession of sins by the Levites in the name of the people. Praying in a loud voice, they recall how Jahveh had chosen Abraham and delivered Israel out of Egypt; what proofs of his favour the nation had experienced at the exodus, in the desert, and during the settlement in Canaan; how it had not responded to all these benefits and, in spite of Jahveh's repeated warnings, had fallen from bad to worse. The threatened punishment had come and Israel had been carried off into exile. "Yet"—they proceed—"in thy great mercy thou didst not destroy them, nor forsake them, for thou art a gracious and merciful god!" O, let Jahveh then take pity upon his people! Nothing had befallen them but what they themselves had provoked by their obstinacy; they had no right to complain; Jahveh was righteous and had proved himself a faithful god, while they had dealt faithlessly with him. But now their condition was so sad and humiliating! "Behold, we are slaves this day; and the land which thou gavest unto our fathers to enjoy the fruit thereof and the good gifts thereof, behold, in that land we are slaves. If it yieldeth much—it is for the kings whom thou hast set over us because of our sins; they have dominion over our bodies and over our cattle, at their pleasure, and we are in great distress!"§

---

* Neh. viii. 15, 16.

† According to Lev. xxiii. 39, while the Deuteronomic law, chap. xvi. 13-15, fixes the duration of the feast at *seven* days.

‡ Neh. viii. 18, 19. § Neh. ix. 5-37,

Thus spoke the Levites. The people were now disposed to enter into the solemn covenant which had been prepared by their leaders. The record of it, the covenant-deed as it were, is given in Neh. x. Its form awakens suspicion; moreover the introduction seems to be wanting; but in the main it may be regarded as authentic.* In the first place Nehemiah the governor;† then the classes of priests, twenty-two in number;‡ then the representatives of the Levites;§ and finally the heads of the people,|| bound themselves by their signatures to observe the obligations which it imposed. These "nobles"¶ were joined by "the rest of the people, the priests, the Levites, the porters, the singers, the Nethînîm and all they that had separated themselves from the peoples of the lands unto the law of God, their wives, their sons and their daughters, who observed with understanding (*i.e.* had arrived at years of discretion.)"** We may dwell for a moment upon this enumeration. It was said before that on that day "the seed of Israel separated themselves from all the strangers."†† Here, on the contrary, "all they that had separated themselves from the peoples of the land" are *distinguished* from the people and their leaders. How is the one consistent with the other? Presumably in this way, that this latter expression refers to the Israelites who, although not belonging to "the children of the captivity,"‡‡ joined them on this occasion. As we remarked before,§§ if the return of the exiles had not taken place, the Israelitish population which was left in Judæa—in great part belonging to the lower orders—would undoubtedly have become entirely fused with the other tribes which dealt in Judæa. After the return they could either remain united with these tribes or join their brethren who had arrived from abroad. It appears that many of them preferred the latter course.

---

* Comp. Note I. at the end of this chapter. † Neh. x. 1a.
‡ Verse 1b-8.   § Verses 9-13. || Verses 14-27.
¶ Verse 29.   ** Verse 28.   †† Neh. ix. 2.
‡‡ Comp. Ezra iv. 1; vi. 16, 19-21; x. 7, 16.   §§ Above, pp. 98, sq., 177.

Their admittance was naturally subject to the same conditions as those to which the returned exiles had now submitted. If the latter entered into an obligation to make no sort of contract with the stranger, it is evident that the Israelites who had not left their native land, had also to begin with "separating themselves."

We now know *the persons who* bound themselves. But *what* did they undertake to do? What were the actual contents of the agreement which was concluded? Of all who allowed themselves to be admitted, it is said that " they bound themselves by an oath and by cursing, *to walk in God's law, which was given by the hand of Moses, God's servant, and to observe and do all the commandments of Jahveh their lord, and his judgments and statutes.*"* This general formula really includes everything. But it is only natural that the obligations which were most in question at that time, are also named separately. Let the reader take the trouble to turn up and peruse the record itself.† He will find there the express declaration that *marriages with women of foreign extraction* will be no longer allowed, and that *the sabbath* and the *sabbath-year* will be kept most strictly;‡ he will further find the promise that each Israelite will bring *yearly the third part of a shekel* to defray the costs of the sanctuary;§ also the agreement that all, in the order decided by lot, shall *provide the wood* required for the service of the temple;|| and finally the engagement to furnish regularly for the benefit of the priests and Levites all to which the Law gave them a right: *first-fruits, first-born* of men, oxen and sheep, and *tithes of the produce of the field.*¶ It is with respect to the last-named point that the records of the covenant enter most into details.

Here the narrative breaks off. But we have already been sufficiently enlightened for provisional purposes. In fact, the meaning of all this is unmistakable. It is *the introduction of*

---

* Neh. x. 29.   † Neh. x. 29-39.   ‡ Verses 30, 31.
§ Verses 32, 33. || Verse 34.   ¶ Verses 35-39.

the Mosaic law of which the historian makes us witnesses. Josiah, 180 years before, had bound his subjects to the observance of Hilkiah's book of the law,* and now his work is taken up again, but at the same time advanced and completed. The book of the law which is now proclaimed, also includes *the priestly laws*. So their promulgation naturally becomes the chief thing, and is also the most prominent in the mind of the author. The former ordinances, and especially those of the Deuteronomist, merely required to be kept up; the public recognition and adoption of the younger, priestly laws gives the covenant now concluded its distinctive character. We do not hesitate to look upon the introduction of those laws, with the historian, as the real task of Ezra and Nehemiah. All that we know of them, and especially of the former, leads us to such a conception of their labours. Ezra, " the ready scribe in the law of Moses," goes to Jerusalem with " the law of his God in his hand." The Persian king had empowered him to make that law known and to apply it, particularly to the administration of justice. His first act was inflexibly to uphold one of its ordinances. In the national assembly which is held at Jerusalem " in the seventh month," the reading of the Law is the pivot upon which everything turns. It was to hear it that the multitude had come together. One of its precepts, which hitherto had been unknown, is carried into execution with great zeal. Ezra and his helpers weary not in reading it out and explaining it; the people pay them unflagging attention to the very end. On the 24th of the month before mentioned the result of the whole, as it were, is at length attained. In accordance with the wish and the plan of the leaders, an agreement is concluded and sealed, by which the people bind themselves to observe the Mosaic laws. The record itself tells us which laws are meant in preference. They are, in a word, the priestly ordinances. The common sanctuary, religious worship, the priests and the rest of the officers of the temple

---

* 2 Kings xxiii. 1-3 ; comp. above, pp. 12, sqq.

stand in the foreground in the minds of those from whom the record originated. The duty of providing the servants of the sanctuary with victuals, and especially of paying them those taxes which had not yet been allotted to them in the former legislation, not even in Deuteronomy, is inculcated with unusual emphasis. All this is quite unambiguous and leads of itself to the interpretation advanced just now.

I have spoken of the " promulgation" and "introduction" of the Mosaic laws. Our former investigations teach us that these expressions must be understood in the widest sense possible. They were not laws which had long been in existence, and which were now proclaimed afresh and accepted by the people, after having been forgotten for a while. The priestly ordinances were made known and imposed upon the Jewish nation *now for the first time*. As we have already seen, no written ritual legislation yet existed in Ezekiel's time.* But his prophecies show that just in his days the want of precise and definite regulations for religious worship and all that belonged to it, made itself felt. Men also worked on in that direction after his time, in Babylonia. But it does *not* appear that the Jews who settled in Judæa, under Zerubbabel and Joshua, were already in possession of the results of that work. We rather gather the contrary from all that we learn of them. The very absence of all mention of the priestly laws, whether immediately after the arrival of the exiles, or subsequently, but before Ezra's time, is conclusive here. Nor does it escape our attention that the prophet Haggai, when he wishes to make his hearers perceive that their offerings are unclean, because they are offered by unclean persons, refers them—not to the enactments of the written law, but—to *the priests*, and advises them to obtain "*thorah*" (instruction) from them.† Is it not evident from this, that as yet only a priestly *tradition* existed, or at all events that its written redaction was unknown in Judæa? This is also the impression given us by the description of Ezra's person and

* Above, pp. 114-117. † Hag. ii. 11, seq.

labours : armed with the ordinances which had been drawn up in Babylonia, he goes to Judæa, there to carry them from theory into practice. This impression agrees with the tradition respecting Ezra. The latter brings him into intimate connection with Israel's sacred literature, and with the Mosaic laws in particular. A parallel is drawn in the Talmud between him and Moses. Jerome, one of the fathers of the church and a pupil of the Jewish teachers of the fourth century of our era, leaves it to his readers whether they will refer certain dates in Deuteronomy " to Moses the author, or to Ezra the restorer of the Pentateuch." The fabulous statement in the apocryphal 4th book of Ezra— written about the end of the first century of the christian era— that he dictated to his assistants the whole of the books of the Old Testament, which had been lost, points to a similar notion of Ezra's labours.* These witnesses and remembrances are of double value, because they come from those centuries in which Moses was acknowledged in all other respects as the author of the whole legislation.

In connection with all the foregoing, a conjecture now forces itself upon me, upon the approval or rejection of which the verdict on the main case cannot be made to depend, but which still deserves mention, were it only because it may make the result obtained still clearer to us. Immediately after his arrival at Jerusalem, Ezra puts his hand to the work, but after having carried his first measures, he does not continue his task— at least so far as we know, and to judge from the way in which he came forward subsequently. For about thirteen years we hear nothing of him. The immediate cause of this lay in the very unfavourable circumstances of the times, in the confused state of political affairs, in the jealousy of the neighbouring tribes, in the opposition of the Persian governors and their lieutenants. But does it not seem very natural to suppose another cause besides this? However brisk the intercourse between the inhabitants of Judæa and their fellow-tribesmen in

* Comp. on the whole of this subject *Hk. O.* iii. 397, seq.

Babylonia may have been, it was only at Jerusalem that Ezra could acquire a thorough knowledge of the religious condition and requirements of his nation. The book of the law which was "in his hand," cannot have fully met the state of affairs which he found there. Nor could it be introduced without the co-operation of the priesthood, which had now already served for 60 years in Zerubbabel's temple. They no doubt had their own traditions and usages, agreeing in the main, it is true, with those which were written by the priests in Babylonia, but yet with divergences of detail. It was necessary that Ezra should come to an understanding with the priesthood, should take its wishes and interests into account, modify the book of the law in accordance with them, and, in general, frame the measures which were needed for the good result of his undertaking. Nothing could be left to chance. The docility of the popular assembly could be counted upon to a certain degree, but not unless the heads had been enlightened and won over beforehand. Prudence absolutely forbade Ezra to attempt so weighty a matter without the necessary preparation. When we consider all this, does not his temporary inactivity become doubly comprehensible? Is it not most natural that the reformer of Israel's religion did not risk the decisive stroke and carry out his far-seeing plans directly after his arrival from abroad, but some years later? Thus we are inclined to regard the years which elapsed between 458 and 444 B.C. as the period of the finishing off and—at all events provisional—final redaction of the Thorah. The foundations of the book of the law with which Ezra came forward in the popular assembly, were laid in Babylonia. But it was in Judæa, and in the interval just mentioned, that it received the form in which—with the exception of the still later modifications, of which we shall speak below—it was thenceforward current among the Jews as the rule of their faith and life.*

* After the above had been written, I found the same conjecture in a paper by Graf in the *Archiv* of Merx, vol. i. 476.

A closer study of that book of the law is now incumbent upon us. We have already examined the notions which the Jahveh-priests in Babylonia entertained of the past, and especially of the Mosaic times.* But their ordinances for the future deserve to be studied and, at all events in their main features, to be sketched. We will not shun this duty. Nor have we yet disposed even of the introduction of the Mosaic laws: so weighty a matter did not end in the repeated reading, or even in the signing of the deed of the covenant; more than this was needed, if not to complete, at all events to insure for the future, the execution of Ezra's plan. But our consideration of these two subjects cannot but gain, if we first make ourselves acquainted with the accounts relating to Nehemiah, to which we have not thus far devoted our attention. A single glance at the review which we gave of our sources,† will show us which documents have not yet been consulted. We shall soon find that they also throw light upon what we have already said.

For twelve years Nehemiah stood at the head of the Jews as governor of the city for the Persian king (445-433 B.C.). The documents from his memorials which are included in the book of Nehemiah, give us somewhat full accounts only with regard to the beginning of this period. They confine themselves chiefly to his exertions in restoring the walls of Jerusalem; besides this, they lead us to believe that he applied himself to increase the population of the city of the temple, and succeeded.‡ We also know from Neh. viii.-x. that he co-operated with Ezra to introduce the Mosaic law. His later acts, and also the reasons for his return to Persia, are unknown to us. Enough that in 433 B.C. he departed thither, but only soon to visit Judæa a second time, in his former capacity of governor for the king.§ He himself tells us what he found upon his arrival at Jerusalem.|| During his absence—he relates

---

* Above, pp. 157-173. † Above, p. 219. ‡ Comp. Neh. vii. 1-5.
§ Neh. xiii. 6. Nehemiah's absence, according to the most probable interpretation of this verse, lasted one year. || Neh. xiii. 1-31.

—the high-priest Eliashib had caused a chamber of the temple in which the holy vessels, the meat offering, the incense and the tithes were usually deposited, to be arranged as a dwelling for Tobiah the Ammonite, to whom he (Eliashib) was related.* Nehemiah's first work was to purify this chamber and restore it to its former use.† Shortly after this he was informed that the tithes for the Levites and the singers were brought in so irregularly, that these officials had found themselves compelled to leave Jerusalem and to cultivate their own fields.‡ He also put an end to this neglect: the authorities, severely censured by him, supported him; the Levites and the singers returned to the temple; the tithes were paid regularly, and care was taken that they were divided equally.§ "Remember me, O my God, concerning these things"—cries Nehemiah, after telling us this—"and wipe not out my good deeds that I have done to the house of my God and to its guardians."‖ These and similar prayers¶ are not incorrectly cited as proofs of Nehemiah's self-satisfaction. But we have an equal right to infer from them that his reforms were only effected with difficulty, and at the cost of much exertion and energy on his part. In truth, the sequel of his narrative also bears testimony to this, as the following incidents show. He found that the Sabbath-rest was not observed faithfully, and that the foreigners in particular profaned it, by carrying on their business on the seventh day, and led the Jews themselves into transgression. Once more Nehemiah spoke about it to the princes of Judah. His reproachful words** show what great value he attached to the hallowing of the last day of the week. Nor did he hesitate to put his own hands to the work of removing this abuse. To prevent the breaking of the day of rest, the gates of Jerusalem were closed and guarded by Nehemiah's own servants. When, in spite of this, the foreign merchants returned on the Sabbath and encamped without the city, he addressed them, and threat-

---

* Neh. xiii. 4, 5.   † Vers. 7-9.   ‡ Ver. 10.
§ Vers. 11-13.   ‖ Ver. 11.   ¶ Vers. 22b, 29, 31b.   ** Vers. 17, 18.

ened to use force if they did not retire. This frightened them away. But even afterwards the gates of the capital were guarded, and this by the Levites, whom Nehemiah had charged with that duty.* We have not yet reached the end of the list of offences which he had to attack. Contrary to their repeated promises, some Jews had married women of Ashdod, Ammon, and Moab; their children spoke a corrupt dialect, and could not even understand the Jewish language. "I contended with them"—Nehemiah himself tells us—"and cursed them, and smote certain of them, and plucked out their hair." These violent measures were coupled with earnest exhortations. Nehemiah really succeeded in prevailing upon them to put away their strange wives.† Those whom he treated in this way were probably simple, humble folks. He did not succeed so easily in convincing another transgressor of his sin. A son of Joiada and grandson of Eliashib the high-priest, had married a daughter of Sanballat the Horonite, one of the chiefs of the Samaritans, the same with whom Nehemiah had had so much trouble during his first governorship.‡ He still refused to part from his wife and was now compelled to leave the country.§ From another source we know—at least we have good grounds for believing—that this priest's name was Manasseh, that he went to his father-in-law and was compensated by him for the loss of his office and its income: the temple of Jahveh on Gerizîm—which for about three centuries was to be the rival of the sanctuary at Jerusalem—was built for him.‖ But more of this shortly. Nehemiah's exertions were evidently neither easy nor agreeable: Joiada's son did not stand alone, or at all events was protected by his powerful relations. "Remember *them*, O my God,"—writes Nehemiah—"because they have defiled the priestly office and the covenant of the

---

* Neh. xiii. 15-22.   † Vers. 23-27.
‡ Comp. Neh. ii. 10, seq.; iv. 1, seq.; vi. 1, seq.   § Neh. xiii. 28.
‖ Josephus, *Ant.* xi. 7, § 2; 8, § 2-4. But Josephus makes this Manasseh a brother of the high-priest Jaddua and a contemporary of Alexander the Great.

priests and Levites."* Characteristic words, which show us Nehemiah not exactly from his most amiable side. We surely are not mistaken in believing that he would have been satisfied with his triumph, and would not have invoked Jahveh's vengeance upon his opponents, if the victory had cost him less effort.

It will have been perceived already why this narrative of Nehemiah's was inserted here. An important fact, of which no trace was to be found in Neh. viii.-x., is placed in the clearest light by this irrefragable evidence of the very person concerned. *In their attempt at reform, Ezra and Nehemiah—for their aims were entirely the same—met with strong opposition.* Could we doubt this after what has just been given, we should only have to glance at the prophecies of Malachi. He too combats the offences, partly of the people, and partly of the priests. Among the people there are some who "marry the daughters of strange gods," and therefore " shall be cut off by Jahveh out of the tabernacles of Jacob."† Further, many are negligent in the payment of tithes and offerings: not until these gifts flow into the temple, will Jahveh " open the windows of heaven and pour down blessing, so that there shall not be garners enough for it."‡ But the prophet finds much to censure in the priests as well. " Despisers of Jahveh's name" he calls them.§ They offer polluted bread upon the altar and do not scruple to sacrifice blind and lame animals, which they would not dare to offer to their governor.|| With great zest the prophet paints the priest as he should be, and the inestimable privileges intended for him by Jahveh. He borrows his colours from "the blessing of Moses"¶ and from Deuteronomy in general, no doubt in the conviction that the ideal drawn there had once been real and that thus the present was far excelled by the past.** " My covenant with

---

* Neh. xiii. 29. † Mal. ii. 11, 12. ‡ Mal. iii. 7-12.
§ Mal. i. 6. || Mal. i. 7, 8. ¶ Comp. Vol. I. pp. 380, sq.
** Comp. here also Vol. I. pp. 370, sq.

Levi"—he brings in Jahveh saying—" was life and peace, and
I gave them to him that he might fear, and he feared me and
trembled at my name. A true *thorah* was in his mouth, and
deceit was not found on his lips; he walked with me in peace
and uprightness, and brought back many from sin. For the
priest's lips keep knowledge, and men seek *thorah* from his
mouth, for he is the messenger of Jahveh of hosts."* But so
much the more severe on this account are his reproaches:
" But ye are departed out of the way and have caused many to
stumble by the *thorah* ; ye have corrupted the covenant with
the Levites, saith Jahveh of hosts. Therefore I also make you
contemptible and base before all the people, for ye keep not my
ways and regard persons in giving *thorah*."† We are unac-
quainted with the particulars which induced Malachi to speak
thus. But it is evident that many priests abused their influence
and especially their priestly advice (" thorah "), contrary to the
ideas which he endeavours to introduce. Now Malachi was of
kindred mind with Ezra and Nehemiah : he may have differed
from them in a few details,‡ but it is quite in their spirit that he
concludes his admonitions with the exhortation to " remember
the law of Moses, Jahveh's servant, commanded unto him by
Jahveh on Horeb for all Israel, with the statutes and judgments."§

So long as we allow ourselves to be guided in our estimation
of the character and aims of this opposition exclusively by the
verdict passed upon it by Ezra, Nehemiah, and, with them,
Malachi, we cannot but think very unfavourably of it. They
look upon their antagonists as recalcitrants and foes to the
worship of Jahveh. It does not occur to them that perhaps
their resistance is prompted by less ignoble motives. Now it
is indeed possible that many of their opponents were not
wronged by such a verdict. But was it applicable to all without distinction ? Were the " prophetess Noadiah and the rest

---

* Mal. ii. 5-7.   † Mal. ii. 8, 9.   ‡ Comp. *Hk. O.* ii. 404, n. 11.
§ Mal. iv. 4.

of the prophets," who resisted Nehemiah in his first governorship, nothing more than cunning impostors, and could they allege no single valid, or at least apparent reason for their opposition? This in itself is almost incredible. But we have only to reflect for a moment, to convince ourselves that it was otherwise. Probability is even in favour of the supposition that many noble and upright men ranged themselves among the opponents of Ezra and Nehemiah from full conviction. This was intimated before in a few words,* but now it must be developed more fully, and this can be done, for now we know both the aim and the means of the two reformers.

First of all, let us not forget that the mode in which they prosecuted their plans gave rise to well-founded suspicions and must have prejudiced many against them. We just now heard from Nehemiah's own lips how he attacked the marriages with strange women; we remember that both upon his arrival at Jerusalem and subsequently at the conclusion of the covenant, Ezra displayed a zeal which savours of precipitation. The whole of the work of the two reformers betrays a violent character. This must have displeased many: probably they would not have proved incapable of conviction, but they involuntarily resisted measures which were carried out thus without exemption or delay. It is true, the number of those who were won over by this zeal was much larger: upon the whole, Ezra and Nehemiah promoted their cause by their precipitation more than they damaged it. But this does not remove the fact that from the very first their line of action excited opposition, and this principally among the more cultivated and discreet of their contemporaries.

But the nature of the cause, no less than its form, furnished grounds for reasonable doubts. All will agree that the reformation of Ezra and Nehemiah was a restriction of the liberty hitherto enjoyed. It imposed a heavy burden upon the laity, loaded them with a number of new duties and also exacted

* Above, p. 216.

material sacrifices from them. It was undoubtedly for the interests of the priests and of the temple-servants in general. But at the same time it minutely defined their duties and deprived them of a portion of the authority which they had previously exercised: as soon as the law was promulgated, the priest ceased to be the sole interpreter of priestly tradition; the written word could be appealed to against him just as well as for him. It was but natural that some priests cared less for the material advantages which they had gained than for the power which they had lost. We must go still further, however. Restriction of liberty is a misfortune in itself. But it is supportable, and even in a certain sense a blessing, when it is only liberty to do wrong which is restricted. But it was not so in this case. Ezra and Nehemiah assailed as much the independence of the religious life of the Israelites, which found utterance in prophecy, as the more tolerant judgment upon the heathen, to which many inclined; their reformation was, in other words, *anti-prophetic* and *anti-universalistic*. This double character and the corresponding opposition deserve to be set forth somewhat more fully.

History teaches us that the reformation of Ezra and Nehemiah nearly coincides in date with the disappearance of prophecy in Israel. Can this be pure accident? Rather is it evident at once that the prophets required a different atmosphere from that which was produced by the measures of these two men. The prophet is the man of inspiration and enthusiasm; his sphere can in no way be measured out and circumscribed; he is driven to act and speak by what he sees; the anxious calculation of the consequences of his actions or words is unknown to him. Thus there is no room for him in such a society as Ezra and Nehemiah tried to establish. He is "the man of the spirit,"* and therefore a child of freedom. He must be able to speak as his heart prompts him, upon every subject which seems to him to concern religion, against

---

* Hos. ix. 7.

all who endanger the spiritual worship of Jahveh. We have no difficulty in discovering in the writings of the prophets before the exile, more than one saying, which, spoken in Ezra's days, would have been considered high treason. Isaiah would have called the "fear of Jahveh" which Ezra introduced, "taught by the precept of men."* And Jeremiah also might have repeated to him Jahveh's words: "I did not treat with your fathers, when I led them out of the land of Egypt, nor give them commandments concerning burnt offerings and sacrifices. But this I commanded them, saying, Obey my voice, and I will be your god and ye shall be my people, and walk ye in all the ways that I shall command you, that it may go well with you."† Now let it not be thought from this that Ezra and Nehemiah repressed the prophetic preaching by force, or at all events were ready to do so as soon as it appeared, so that it disappeared solely or chiefly through these violent measures or the fear of them. The truth is rather, as is evident from the mere fact that these two men came forward in this manner, that the time of free productiveness was past in Israel and had changed of itself, as it were, into a period devoted to the collection and preservation of the treasures already produced. Their reformation and the cessation of prophecy are not related as cause and effect, but are the two sides of one and the same phenomenon. The prophet makes room for the scribe, or rather becomes himself the scribe, as, it is not incorrectly believed, can be shown, e. g., in Malachi's prophecies. But it was only natural that there were some who deplored this and saw in it a reason for opposing the new tendency in religious matters; it was even most natural that the prophetic order of those days was ill-disposed towards Ezra and looked upon his companion Nehemiah with evil eyes.‡ Supposing it to be true that some members of that order disgraced their name, conspired with the foreigner and took refuge in deceit—still their prophetic instinct, the spirit that animated them as a class, very justly

---

* Isa. xxix. 13. † Jer. vii. 22, 23. ‡ Above, p. 225.

rebelled against the efforts of the priest and scribe from Babylonia. Nay, even had they all been unworthy representatives of the title they bore, *prophecy* would still have had grounds for protesting against the new state of affairs which Ezra and Nehemiah were attempting to create.

We must make similar remarks upon the attitude towards the heathen which the two reformers, by virtue of their fundamental principle, both assumed themselves and imperatively prescribed for all others. Let us begin by admitting that the wall of separation which they built between Israel and the heathen was absolutely indispensable at that time: take away their measures, and you would see the small Jewish nation lose itself among its neighbours and vanish without leaving a trace behind. But this did not prevent such a separation from appearing most questionable, not only to the indifferent, but also to many who otherwise were well-disposed. Even before the exile, the Israelitish "wise" men had sought out the points of contact with foreign lands, and, in their own domain, had opposed national particularism.* After the return from Babylonia, their tendency also found advocates, who even developed some literary activity.† Their views must gradually have found acceptance with some whom we cannot exactly count among the "wise." Among the sacred writings of the Jews, two have been preserved to us which are regarded with high probability as products of this period, and in which the freer and more charitable views as to the heathen plainly declare themselves. They are the books of *Ruth* and *Jonah*.

Upon calling to mind the contents of these writings, it is easy to make out their tendency. Ruth, *the Moabitish woman*, is drawn as the model of a true and affectionate daughter, and in conclusion turns out to have become the ancestress of the great king David, by her marriage with Boaz. "Whither thou goest, I will go, and where thou lodgest, I will lodge; thy

* Comp. Vol. I. pp. 333, 387, sq.; above, pp. 45, sq.
† Comp. *Hk. O.* iii. 101, sqq., 172.

people is my people, and thy god my god; where thou diest will I die, and there will I be buried."* So she spoke to her mother-in-law Naomi, as it were in the name of all the foreign women who had become closely related to Israel by their marriages with Israelitish husbands. The blessing which falls to her lot is the guarantee of Jahveh's approval of such alliances. The book of Ruth is written with great descriptive skill and clearness, and no doubt it took effect. It will have made the deeper impression, in that the real point of the story, David's descent from the marriage of one of his ancestors with a Moabitish woman, is undoubtedly taken from popular tradition, and is even probably historical.† Plainly the author did not belong to those of Ezra's and Nehemiah's way of thinking. He and all who joined him must have condemned—not from irreligion, but from an upright love of Jahvism—their general measures, which were carried out without distinction, and struck the innocent with the guilty.

From another point of view it will appear that the author of the book of Jonah has done the same. He really handles one, more special question. Objections were made against the credit of the prophecies, upon the strength of the undeniable fact that some of the threats against the heathen had not been fulfilled. The author admits this fact, but considers himself in a position to explain it satisfactorily: in such instances Jahveh's intentions are modified, on account both of the penitence shown by the heathen and of Jahveh's mercy, which extends to all his creatures. The main idea of the book is expressed in the words: "Thou, O Jahveh, art a merciful and gracious God, slow to anger and of great kindness, *and repentest thee of the evil*" (announced or threatened by thee).‡ From the answer

---

* Ruth i. 16, 17.

† Comp. with the foregoing Geiger, *Urschrift und Uebersetzungen*, p. 49-52. In my opinion, the statement (1 Sam. xxii. 3, 4) that David, when fleeing before Saul, placed the members of his family in safety among the Moabites, pleads in favour of the authenticity of the main fact. In David's time and long afterwards marriages with Moabitish and other foreign women were by no means rare; comp. Vol. I. pp. 182, sq. ‡ Jon. iv. 2.

which Jahveh gives to Jonah, when the latter shows his grief at the fate of the gourd which had shaded him, it is evident that the author means that these virtues of Jahveh also manifest themselves in his dispensations regarding the heathen world. "Thou"—says Jahveh to his prophet—"thou hast pity on the gourd, for which thou hast not laboured, neither madest it to grow, which was the child of one night and has perished after one night: and should I not have compassion on Nineveh, that great city, wherein are more than one hundred and twenty thousand persons that cannot discern between their right hand and their left hand, and much cattle?"* The whole of this writing—which, interpreted historically, so justly gives offence—breathes a spirit of benevolence and universal humanity which is very attractive. Can the author of such a narrative as this—can all those who agreed with him, have been perfectly satisfied with the attempts of Ezra and Nehemiah, which were based upon the recognition of a real and permanent difference between Israel and the heathen, and ended in the implacable enforcement of the bounds which in the book of Jonah are overstepped time after time?†

These remarks upon the opposition to Ezra and Nehemiah would be entirely misconstrued, if they were taken for a picture of the whole of the party which confronted them. The great majority of their opponents undoubtedly stood much lower. We pointed this out before,‡ but we may repeat it here. Yet our previous study was not on this account superfluous. If Ezra and Nehemiah had only had the indifferent against them, victory would have cost them but little trouble. The strength of the opposition lay in the principles which were advocated from full conviction by a few, and accepted as a watchword by all. We have now seen what these principles were, and surely do not hesitate to recognize their comparative truth. By their

* Jon. iv. 10, 11.
† How other details in the book of Jonah, besides those named above, also betray the same tendency, is shown in *Hk. O.* ii. 412-14. ‡ p. 216.

light we will now study the reformation of Ezra and Nehemiah somewhat more closely, and try to form a well-grounded judgment of its character and significance.

Let us begin by assigning to this reformation its proper place in the history of the Israelitish religion. It does not stand alone; nor is it without antecedents. The name "reformation," by which we indicate it, we also give to other attempts to better Israel's religious condition; first of all to *Hezekiah's* measures towards centralizing public worship in the temple at Jerusalem,* but especially to the great revolution brought about by *Josiah*.† The reformation of Ezra and Nehemiah agrees with the latter also in this, that it starts from *a book of the law* and aims at the introduction of the ordinances contained in it.

There are other links as well between the work of Ezra and Nehemiah and the past. The end which they had in view had already been pointed out before their time. Their practice had been preceded by theory. *Ezekiel* and *the author of " the Book of Origins "* were their fore-runners. With them they had the priestly tendency in common.

Thus the reformation of Ezra and Nehemiah by no means lacked due preparation. But this does not diminish the fact that it has a right to the name by which we call it, that it aimed at an *essential change* in the religious condition of the Jews and accomplished it—although, of course, but gradually. We shall see best wherein that change consisted, if we try to express in a few antitheses the character of the period which it closes and of the epoch which it opens. There *the spirit* prevails, here *the letter;* there *the free word,* here *the written word.* The *prophet* represents the time before the reformation; after Ezra his place is taken by *the Scribe*.

Antitheses such as these so easily lead to misunderstanding, that I should consider myself bound to warn my readers against it at once and with all earnestness, did not the preced-

---

* Vol. I. pp. 80-82; above, pp. 1, sq. † Above, pp. 9, sq.

ing investigation* plainly show my meaning. We know already that a great wrong would be done to Ezra and Nehemiah, were we to impute to them the intention of forcibly suppressing, or at least very much curtailing, the freedom hitherto enjoyed. They were not *at war* with their time. They did not attempt to *force* upon their people something which was hostile to their wishes and requirements. They did not impose silence upon the prophet, nor forge chains for every man who should dare in the future to speak his mind freely. Independently of them, prophetic inspiration had gradually grown weaker; the number of the prophets was decreasing; their individuality was on the wane; their discourses showed evident signs of exhaustion and decay. All this was connected with the character of the post-exile times. As we have already remarked, the conception of Jahveh had by degrees become more elevated, the distance between him and the Israelite greater; the religious sentiment had no longer that intimacy and confidence which is involved by the relation of the prophet to his sender; the belief that Amos expressed in the words: "Surely the Lord Jahveh does nothing without revealing his counsel to his servants the prophets"†—this belief had been gradually weakened and at last extinguished.‡ It was not strange, therefore, that they looked for other means of providing for the want of the times. Or rather, it was no longer necessary for them to seek the means; the road had been pointed out and levelled for them. The vigorous, but irregular work of the prophets—who now, moreover, began to refuse their services—was to be replaced by the unambiguous commandment of the Law, regularly instituted and strictly administered. The people had a right to know what they ought to believe. They wanted something tangible. If this want were satisfied, men could hope for better results than had been obtained hitherto. The end which the prophets had had in view, but had not reached,

---

* See especially p. 240, sq. † Am. iii. 7.
‡ Comp. Vol. I. p. 56, and above, pp. 111, sq., 127, sq.

would now be pursued by another road. The time seemed to have arrived for establishing and arranging.

Looked at in this way, the reformation of Ezra and Nehemiah is not *opposed* to the existing state of affairs—least of all as darkness is opposed to light. They merely went a few steps further than the Deuteronomist had gone 180 years before them. Nay, it may be said that he had already aimed at that which they succeeded in introducing. The Deuteronomist had already shown that he perceived that it was not enough to exhort the people to fidelity to Jahveh; that besides this it was necessary to indicate the forms in which Jahvism was to manifest itself. He had also expressly acknowledged the duty of the Israelites to submit to the decision and the thorah of the Levitical priests.* It was even part of his intention to make the deuteronomic law respected as an unchangeable rule, when it had once been promulgated: "What thing soever I command you, thou shalt observe and do it; thou shalt not add thereto, nor diminish from it."† Ezra and Nehemiah could go on building upon this foundation; they had merely to develop and realize the ideas given and uttered here. As far as the Deuteronomic law was concerned, this last project had never got beyond a rudimentary state. Josiah had left the stage of history far too soon, and had been replaced by kings who did not follow in his footsteps. The Levitical priests, upon whose co-operation the Deuteronomist had reckoned, had not been disloyal to Jahvism, it is true, but still had distinguished themselves much more by their patriotism than by their religious zeal. In the middle of the fifth century B.C. the Deuteronomist's plan could now be again taken in hand, and, with the requisite modifications, could be carried out in such a manner that its success seemed to be beyond doubt. There was no longer a king, who from the fact that his co-operation was at all times uncertain could endanger the whole undertaking. His power was divided between the Persian governor, who left the Jews alone in the

---

* Comp. above, p. 31. † Deut. xii. 32, comp. iv. 2.

management of their internal affairs, and the high-priest and the nobles, from whom no opposition was to be feared. The priestly thorah, which in Josiah's days still existed only as oral tradition and the maintenance of which was at that time dependent upon the zeal and interest of the priests, was now committed to writing and thus much better guaranteed than before. Hence Ezra and Nehemiah were able, on the one hand, to take up what had been purposed and attempted before their time, but also, on the other hand, to avoid the rocks upon which their predecessor had suffered shipwreck.

The remarks we have just made show us at the same time the relation in which the reformation of Ezra and Nehemiah stood to the priesthood. Perhaps it has surprised some, that we have not laid more stress upon the *priestly* character of the undertaking of these two men. Were they not the priestly ordinances which were promulgated through their influence; the temple and its servants which were first in their thoughts and whose spiritual and material interests they laboured to promote with unflagging zeal? This is all perfectly true, and yet it would be wrong to regard the reformation as the work or as a victory of the priesthood. It took place in their spirit and to their interest; it even was effected *through the priests*, chiefly through Ezra, but also through other men of priestly descent. Still it cannot be looked upon as a triumph or as the exaltation of *the priesthood*, as such. It was not the priesthood that was raised to supreme power, but *the Law*. He therefore who most identified himself with the Law, could count upon permanently holding the first rank. In other words, *the Scribe* stood higher in Ezra's state than the priest, or was at all events destined to overshadow him. We may not anticipate our subsequent investigations. But it will not surprise us, should it appear hereafter that religion progresses in the direction, not of the temple, but of the synagogue; not of the extension and strengthening of the hierarchy, but of an increasingly higher estimation of the knowledge of the Scriptures.

ESTABLISHMENT OF THE HIERARCHY. 249

Religion "progressing"—but did not Israel, by submitting to the Law, condemn herself to absolute stagnation? Many imagine so, but incorrectly. The sequel of our history will furnish proof of this as well. Let it suffice for the present to warn against the error; the truth will soon be apparent.

The outcome of the whole of this enquiry can be summed up in a few words. A new period in the history of Israel's religion begins with Ezra and Nehemiah. That which had long been in preparation comes into existence under their influence: *Judaism* is founded. The characteristic of this phase in the development of the religion of the Israelites lies in this, that it starts from the revealed will of Jahveh, the Law, acknowledges it as the rule of its faith and life, and refers everything to it.

From the nature of the case, the two reformers could not do more than *found* Judaism. The ideal which was before their eyes was not capable of being realized in a day. But they laid the foundations, and laid them in such a way that, as history teaches us, men could build on regularly after their design. He who at first was indisposed to join, was forced to submit; he who persisted in his obstinacy, was compelled to quit the land. Probably the grandson of Eliashib was not the only one who sought and found an asylum among the Samaritans.* The attachment to the Jahveh-worship which already existed among that people in the days of Zerubbabel and Joshua,† had not diminished since that time. The fugitives were therefore received with open arms, and contributed their share towards insuring the sole power for Jahvism. By degrees the Samaritans became no less zealous Jahveh-worshippers than the Jews themselves. But it did not come to a fusion of the two nations. A constant rivalry and hostility rather prevailed between them. The more the Samaritans identified themselves with Jahvism, the more also did the conviction gain ground among them that they were descended,

---

* Above, pp. 236, sq.   † Above, pp. 205, sq.

not in part, but all without distinction, from the former inhabitants of the land, the Ephraimites. But in spite of this they remained distinct, or rather, this belief became a new motive for them to preserve their individuality, for had not Ephraim from the very earliest times refused to submit to Judah? In the mean time the Jews were far in advance of them in religious and intellectual development, so that the Samaritans involuntarily became their disciples, and, excepting the deviations which resulted from the nature of the case, followed the track in which the Jews had preceded them. When the five books of Moses had undergone their final redaction—when and how this occurred, will appear hereafter—they were also adopted by the Samaritans; these books merely required an alteration here and there to serve them as holy records and as a canon.* Also the interpretation and extension of the Law, which took place among the Jews, found favour among the Samaritans. From time to time we shall find an opportunity of reverting to this subject—but even then we shall confine ourselves to a few remarks. A more special study either of the history or of the ideas of the Samaritans is not required for our purpose. It was merely necessary in connection with this subject to point to the important service which they, quite involuntarily in truth, have shown to Judaism. Had not Samaria stood open to the discontented Jews, perhaps the field would not have been cleared and the resistance to the new tendency quelled so speedily. Now that a refuge had been opened to them in the immediate neighbourhood, they could the sooner resolve to give up the struggle—from which they could scarcely hope to come out as conquerors.

If the foregoing conception of Judaism be not altogether wrong, the narrative of its institution should end in a review of the Mosaic legislation as now introduced. This will form the natural conclusion of the present chapter of our history. Hence-

---

* Comp. here Note I. at the end of chapter IX.

forward the Pentateuch is the basis of the religious, moral and political life of the Jews. Acquaintance with this canon for faith and conduct alone can enable us to form an exact conception of the further development of the religion.*

The common end which the prophets of Jahveh and the authors of the various collections of laws pursue, is *the formation of a holy people*—a people dedicated to Jahveh. Perhaps they would not all have expressed that end in these words, but none of them would have refused to subscribe to them. But each one's peculiarities, and thus also the difference between these advocates of Jahvism, would soon have come to light in the interpretation and application of the requirement of "holiness."

None of them would have approved of the formula employed here more than the authors of the priestly legislation. It is not only in their spirit, but it also agrees with their way of speaking. "Be holy, for I, Jahveh, thy god, am holy,"—even in the older portions of the priestly law this idea is constantly expressed,† and in the younger laws it is repeated time after time. "I Jahveh am thy god; ye shall therefore sanctify yourselves and be holy, for I am holy . . . For it is I, Jahveh, that brought you up out of the land of Egypt, that I might be a god unto you, and that ye might be holy, for I am holy :" so runs the conclusion of the ordinance concerning clean and unclean beasts.‡ And elsewhere it says, "Ye shall keep my sabbaths; for this is a sign between me and you throughout your generations, that men may know that I, Jahveh, sanctify you."§

It is already evident from these few texts that holiness is an attribute of Israel, but one which proceeds from or is based upon an act of Jahveh. Jahveh is holy himself and makes Israel holy, *i.e.*, "separates Israel from the nations,"‖ and dedicates her to his service. This making holy begins with the

---

* Comp. with some points of this review Note II. at the end of this chapter.
† Lev. xix. 2; xx. 7, 26, comp. 24; xxi. 8, 15, 23; xxii. 9, 16, 32.
‡ Lev. xi. 44, 45. § Exod. xxxi. 13. ‖ Lev. xx. 24, 26.

deliverance of the people from the Egyptian bondage.* From that time Jahveh is the god of Israel and Israel is Jahveh's people. So, as we saw before,† thought also the prophets and the older lawgivers. It is peculiar to the priestly law to conceive and represent *the establishment of Jahveh in the midst of Israel* as the manifestation of this relation. Of the altar for the tent of assembly it is said : "There I (Jahveh) will come to the sons of Israel, that they may be sanctified by my glory. And I will sanctify the tabernacle of the congregation, and the altar, and Aaron and his sons will I sanctify, that they may serve me as priests. So shall they know that I, Jahveh, am their god, that brought them forth out of the land of Egypt, that I might dwell in their midst. I Jahveh am their god."‡

But it is not necessary to dwell any longer upon this point. The reader will remember from the previous chapter§ how the priestly lawgiver, in his description of the Mosaic Israel, represents this dwelling of Jahveh in the midst of his people; he will therefore also comprehend how the sanctification of the tabernacle, the altar and the priesthood, is connected with the setting apart of all Israel to the service of Jahveh. We must now examine how the people, for their part, respond to Jahveh's favour, or, in other words, how the life of Israel and of the individual Israelite assumes a definite character under the influence of Jahveh's act. In doing so, we will bear in mind that the priestly lawgiver neither could nor would create a new state of affairs, but closely annexed himself to what he found in existence. Since the introduction of the Deuteronomic law, the temple at Jerusalem had been regarded as the only place of sacrifice, and the tribe of Levi as exclusively qualified for the priestly office; the sacrifices and feasts to Jahveh were of much older date; the difference between "clean" and "unclean" had long been part of the national consciousness, and together with it belief in the purifying and expiatory power of

---

* Comp. Lev. xi. 45, quoted above, and also Lev. xix. 36, &c.
† Vol. I. p. 39, and elsewhere. ‡ Exod. xxix. 43-46. § Above, pp. 166, sq.

the sacrifices. All this could remain in existence, and merely required to be regulated, enlarged and systematized.

Let us first fix our attention upon the priestly regulation of *public worship.* To this belong both sacrifices and feasts. With regard to *sacrifices,* the priestly law gives minute directions, which are based upon the distinction between four principal kinds—burnt-, thank-, sin- and trespass-offerings. Its ordinances relate to the quantity and quality of the offering, which vary according to persons and circumstances; to the manner in which the sacrifice must be offered; to the choice between the various sorts of offerings.* To most bloody offerings there belongs a meat-offering, of which again the ingredients and the proportions are minutely prescribed.† We shall return to all this shortly.

The feasts, as was to be expected, are regulated at great length. First of all the three yearly feasts, with which we are already acquainted,‡ are retained, although with a few alterations. Thus the observance of the paschal meal, to which the Deuteronomist had merely alluded,§ is described in detail;‖ the first day of the feast of unleavened bread is made a day of rest;¶ and an eighth day is added to the seven days of the feast of ingathering or tabernacles.** Besides this, the priestly lawgiver orders the religious celebration of the new moon or the first day of the month,†† and especially in the seventh month of the year.‡‡ And finally, with evident partiality, he gives copious directions concerning the day of atonement, to be kept on the tenth day of the seventh month:§§ its meaning will be shown hereafter. It is also noteworthy, that it is expressly prescribed how many and what sacrifices must be offered on each of these feast days. It had always been the

---

* Lev. i.-vii.   † Num. xv. 1-16.   ‡ Above, pp. 27, sq.   § pp 29, 31, comp. 92, sq.
‖ Exod. xii. 1-14.   ¶ Exod. xii. 16; Lev. xxiii. 7; Num. xxviii. 18.
** Lev. xxiii. 36; Num. xxix. 35.   †† Num. xxviii. 11-15.
‡‡ Lev. xxiii. 23-25; Num. xxix. 1-6.
§§ Lev. xvi. comp. xxiii. 26-32; Num. xxix. 7-11.

custom "not to appear before Jahveh empty"* on the festivals. But the priestly law describes minutely how many and what sort of offerings shall be slaughtered on each occasion in the name of the whole community. It thus regulates the daily morning and evening sacrifice;† the sacrifice on the Sabbath‡ and the new moons;§ and finally also the sacrifices on the feasts.‖ It even has its special demands for each day of the feast of tabernacles, which form together an artistically descending series.¶

In this priestly festival-legislation the *method* followed by the priests of Jahveh comes clearly to light. It cannot therefore be deemed inopportune, if we fix our attention upon it here. We have already pointed out, that in the course of centuries Jahvism was enriched with ideas and practices which had originally belonged to the service of other gods.** With the worship of those deities, they had gained admittance either into the whole of Israel or into single Israelitish tribes—and so had gradually been absorbed into the national life. It was no easy problem for the spiritual leaders of the people, what attitude they should assume towards these foreign elements. Nor was there any unanimity among them in this respect. *The prophets*, who were in general tolerably indifferent to the form of worship, especially condemned the heathen ceremonies without reserve. From their point of view they were right in so doing. But their strictness with regard to these externals was naturally an additional obstacle to the conversion of the nation to the Jahvism which they preached. The great multitude could not give up without some equivalent the customs which time had rendered precious and sacred to them. This the *Jahveh-priests* perceived. Or rather—for it would be incorrect to

---

* Exod. xxiii. 15; xxxiv. 20; Deut. xvi. 16, 17.
† Exod. xxix. 38-42; Num. xxviii. 3-8.
‡ Num. xxviii. 9, 10.   § Num. xxviii. 11-15; xxix. 1-6.
‖ See the remaining verses of Num. xxviii. xxix. and further Lev. xxiii. 12-13; 18-20.   ¶ Num. xxix. 12-38.   ** Vol. I. pp. 230, 241, sq.

ascribe to them intentional adaptation—the Jahvism of the priests stood nearer to that of the people, and therefore adopted the popular ideas and customs more easily, and, enriched by them, became the more acceptable to the multitude. The position thus assigned to the priests was to mediate between the prophets and the people. They undoubtedly took this task upon them and attempted to insure the sympathy of the people for Jahvism, especially by their regulations for the public worship in the temple at Jerusalem. Positive information as to their efforts in this matter is wanting. But the priestly legislation alone could prove that we are justified in forming this opinion of their labours. It shows unmistakably this tendency to increase the splendour and richness of ceremony in the service of Jahveh by including the originally foreign elements, and by so doing to bring it into harmony with the wants and customs of the people. I may content myself here with simply referring to what has already been said about *the new moon* and *the paschal meal*.* The originally heathen custom of celebrating the appearance of the Moon-deity with sacrifices has become in the priestly law an element of Jahvism, and thus at the same time harmless and innocent. The manner in which the paschal lamb was killed, prepared and eaten, was connected with the older conception of Jahveh's being and was undoubtedly derived from the time in which he was still thought of and worshipped as a nature-god. Instead of condemning and opposing this celebration, the priestly law adopts it and elevates it into one of the sacraments of Jahvism. In a previous chapter I called the Mosaic law "a compromise between the popular religion and the Jahvism of the prophets."† I can now add to this that it was *the priests* who made this compromise. A part of the scheme projected by them is already raised to a law in *Deuteronomy*; the priestly portions of the Pentateuch give us the final result of their exertions in this matter.

* Vol. I. pp. 242, 244, 266, sq.; above, pp. 30, sq., 93, sq. † Vol. I. p 230.

We return to the ordinances of the priestly law with regard to public worship. We need scarcely remind our readers that this remained confined to the one sanctuary. The lawgiver had no new regulations to draw up as to the arrangement of that sanctuary; it was evident that the best course to pursue here was to retain things as they were. The few alterations, which he brings forward in the form of a description of the Mosaic tabernacle,* tend to make the sanctuary completely correspond with the idea that Jahveh dwells in the holy of holies, and may be approached only with the utmost awe, by those who are properly qualified. In connection with this, the ark "of the covenant," or "of the testimony," with the cherubim attached to its lid, is described as Jahveh's throne, but then it further is ordered to be withdrawn from all eyes with the greatest care. The thick curtain which divides the holy of holies from the holy place,† had probably been already introduced by the priesthood at the building of the temple under Zerubbabel, and now also obtained a place in the law, with the tendency of which such a division agrees much better than the one which was used in the temple of Solomon. It is further decreed that the most holy place may only be entered once a year, by the high-priest. The right of entry to the holy place, where the altar of incense and the table of shewbread stand, belongs to the priests alone. The Levites and the laity stay outside in the court, where are the great altar of burnt offerings and the brazen laver. Thus the lines of demarcation between the divisions of the one sanctuary are sharply drawn, and no less sharply the corresponding lines of separation between those who approach Jahveh in the proper sense of the word, the priests, and the subordinate servants of the sanctuary with the laity.

The lawgiver could also build upon the existing state of affairs with regard to the revenues of the temple and the temple-servants, although he found himself constrained to

---

* See above, pp. 167. † Exod. xxvi. 31, seq. and elsewhere.

make more than one new regulation. It will be remembered how, almost 200 years before the time of Ezra and Nehemiah, the Deuteronomist had been mindful of the interests of the priestly tribe of Levi.* The matter could not remain as he had arranged it. Circumstances had changed in more than one respect. The king had ceased to exist, the priesthood had become the first power in the state. Also, after Josiah's reformation, the distinction between priests, "sons of Aaron," and Levites had arisen, which the authors of the priestly law not only recognize but also expressly maintain.† These things easily account for the fact that other ordinances, more favourable to the staff of the temple, occur in the new legislation in addition to those in the former. In the first place, the priests' share in the sacrifices is increased. They receive the skin of the burnt-offering,‡ all the flesh of sin and trespass-offerings,§ and part of the meat-offering.|| How far these precepts diverged from the actual practice, we cannot trace; the probability is that they entirely agreed with it. But with regard to the thank-offerings, a greater portion was now demanded than before: in Deuteronomy the shoulder, the two cheeks and the maw,¶ in Leviticus and Numbers the breast and the right shoulder.** In the second place, the gifts which the Israelite formerly dedicated *to Jahveh*, but ate with his family at sacred meals, are now assigned *to the temple-servants*. The tithes, not only of corn, must and oil, but also of cattle, fall to the Levites,†† who in their turn have to relinquish a tenth part to the priests.‡‡ The first-born of man and beast become priestly property; those of oxen and sheep are offered up, and, with the exception of the small portion burnt upon the altar, are eaten by the priests;§§ the others, the first-born of

---

* Above, p. 26. † Above, pp. 168, seq. ‡ Lev. vii. 8.
§ Lev. vi. 24-26, 29 ; vii. 6, 7 ; Num. xviii. 9, 10.
|| Lev. vi. 16-18 ; vii. 9, 10, 14. ¶ Deut. xviii. 3.
** Lev. vii. 28-34 ; Num. xviii. 18.
†† Num. xviii. 20-24, comp. Lev. xxvii. 30-33. See, on the other hand, Deut. xiv. 22-29 ; xv. 19-23, and above, p. 26, n. ||. ‡‡ Num. xviii. 25-32.
§§ Num. xviii. 17, 18 ; comp. Lev. xxvii. 26.

men and of unclean beasts, have to be bought off from the priest.* And further their right to the first-fruits, already recognized by the Deuteronomist,† is maintained,‡ and they are assigned all that which is banned (the *cherem*)§ and, in general, all heave-offerings (*therumah*) which the Israelites voluntarily give up to Jahveh.‖ It can hardly be said that the priests and Levites, *if these things really fell to their share*, were in bad circumstances. But the lawgiver has not been blind to the fact that it was easier to write out such imposts than to enforce them, and precisely for this reason has pitched his demands higher than would otherwise have been proper. Here and there in the priestly law itself evident traces occur of the ordinances upon this subject having been remoulded and amplified; after Ezra's time, too, alterations seem to have been introduced, for the purpose of making the Law answer practical wants.¶ This does not surprise us: the staff of the temple had not always the same numerical strength, and the readiness to contribute to its support was not always equally great. Still less are we astonished at the command of the priestly law, that 48 cities, with pasture for cattle, shall be ceded by the twelve tribes to the priests and Levites.** For many various reasons the realization of this demand was not even to be thought of. It has been included in the Law partly to guarantee to the temple-servants the landed property which in the course of time they had acquired,†† and partly as a wish for the future, which perhaps might one day, under quite altered circumstances, become a reality.

The characteristics of the priestly lawgiver come to light in the precepts concerning participation in public worship, admission to Jahveh's presence, even more than in the regulations for public worship itself and in the care for its continuance. The requisite qualifications vary for the laity, the priests

---

* Num. xviii. 15, 16; comp. Lev. xxvii. 27. † Deut. xviii. 4.
‡ Num. xviii. 12, 13. § Num. xviii. 14. ‖ Num. xviii. 11, 19.
¶ Comp. below, Chap. IX. and the Note I. belonging to it.
** Above, p. 171, seq. †† Comp. Deut. xviii. 8.

and the high-priest. *Cleanness* is required in all of them. But this conception differs in extent, according as it is applied either to the ordinary Israelite or to the priest. In defining it, the priestly lawgiver goes to work with great diffuseness. Most of his regulations he undoubtedly borrowed from practice. But before his time they had always been delivered orally by the priests, and thus lacked precision and completeness. Upon being written down, they were perfected and trimmed into a system, and at the same time became available for all, whereas formerly only those who asked the priest for instruction ("thorah") had become acquainted with them. Therefore they now acquired greater significance than they had before: the ordinary Israelite constantly came in contact with the precepts concerning "clean" and "unclean," and necessarily perceived from them above all that a new law had been introduced. Let us then note the demands of this law, and first of all those which it makes upon the laity.

The fact that *only Israelites* may take part in religious worship, stands in the foreground. The sign of their admission into the covenant with Jahveh is *circumcision*, upon which the priestly law emphatically insists.* Whatever may have been the orinal meaning of this act,† in the fifth century before our era it had become a purely conventional mark of the Israelite, and was looked upon as such by the priestly law. It is worthy of remark here that this law also requires the circumcision of the non-Israelitish slaves, of "him that is born in the house" as well as of "him that is bought for money."‡ This amounts to incorporating these strangers with the Israelitish community, and this incorporation is in general thought desirable and promoted by the priestly lawgiver. Thus he allows the stranger who is living in Israel—as distinguished from the itinerant day-labourer or temporary inhabitant§—to participate with his family in the paschal meal, if all who belong to the

---

* Gen. xvii. 9-14, 23-27 ; Lev. xii. 3. † Comp. Vol. I. p. 238, seq.
‡ Gen. xvii. 12, 13, 27. § Exod. xii. 45.

male sex consent to be circumcised.* "One law shall be to him that is homeborn, and unto the stranger that sojourneth among you," says the lawgiver upon this and other occasions.† On the one hand this precept bears witness to a certain inclination towards proselytism, which could easily arise when the voluntary accession of foreigners to the Israelish community occurred from time to time.‡ But on the other hand it proves that the original religious character of Jahveh's commandments was no longer upheld, and that they were now regarded much more than before as measures of policy, as rules of order. When the Deuteronomist, in agreement with the Book of the Covenant, permits the Israelite to sell to the stranger the flesh of a beast which has died a natural death and which therefore he may not eat himself,§ the religious character of the prohibition ("for thou art an holy people unto Jahveh thy God") remains untouched, whereas the priestly lawgiver relinquishes it or at all events weakens it, by extending this prohibition to the stranger as well.|| The accuracy of this remark will be confirmed more fully in the sequel of our review.

Having been admitted into the covenant with Jahveh, *the Israelite must guard against all pollution.* He must abstain from eating blood,¶ from the flesh of all clean animals which have died a natural death or have been torn by wild beasts,** and from the flesh of all unclean animals.†† He must also avoid contact with a dead body.‡‡

But it is already necessary to add "as much as possible" to this last precept. There are cases in which touching a dead body is obligatory, when, *e.g.*, a relative has died, or when the carcase cannot be allowed to remain, as in the case of an ox or a sheep falling down dead in the field or the stall. Then,

---

* Exod. xii. 44, (comp. Gen. xvii. 12, 13, 27); 48.

† Exod. xii. 49 ; comp. verse 19 ; Lev. xvi. 29 ; xvii. 8, 15 ; xxiv. 22 ; Num. ix. 14 ; xv. 29.   ‡ Isa. lvi. 3, 6, 7.

§ Deut. xiv. 21 ; comp. Exod. xxii. 31.

|| Lev. xvii. 15, 16; comp. above, p. 95, seq.

¶ Lev. xvii. 10-14 ; comp. iii. 17 ; vii. 26, 27 ; xix. 26 ; Gen. ix. 4.

** Lev. xvii. 15, 16 ; xi. 40.   †† Lev. xi.   ‡‡ Lev. xi. 39.

ESTABLISHMENT OF THE HIERARCHY.

therefore, pollution is unavoidable. But there are also diseases which make the Israelite unclean, first of all leprosy in its various forms, which according to the ideas of those days, attacked not only men, but houses also;* and then other diseases or natural functions of the human body.† Childbed also pollutes the mother, and this for forty days if she has borne a son, and for eighty days if a daughter.‡ The recognition of such involuntary and unavoidable pollutions as these imposes upon the priestly lawgiver the obligation of making all sorts of other rules respecting the degree and the duration of the uncleanness, and the way in which it may be removed. Preciseness is absolutely necessary here in the interest of the people and for the maintenance of the principle; and so we find that the ordinances of the priestly law do, in fact, descend to minute details.

If the uncleanness be the result of an illness, it lasts as long as the illness itself. Thus, *e.g.*, the leper must wait until he is cured and his cure has been certified by the priest, before he can return to society. The law describes minutely how the priest is to set about such an examination. If it has resulted satisfactorily the priest pronounces the cured patient to be clean. But before he is completely reinstated, an offering must be made as prescribed by the law—two lambs and a sheep one year old, the former for a trespass-offering and a sin-offering, and the latter for a burnt-offering; to these must be added a certain quantity of fine flour and oil.§ The healing of other diseases, *e.g.*, of running issues, need not be certified by the priest. Seven days after the malady has ceased the patient is clean; he then bathes in running water, and on the eighth day offers up two turtle doves or two young pigeons to Jahveh, as a trespass-offering and a burnt-offering.||

If the uncleanness arises from causes of a transitory nature,

---

* Lev. xiii, xiv.   † Lev. xv.   ‡ Lev. xii.
§ Comp. Lev. xiii. 1-46 (concerning leprosy itself, and the examination by the priest); xiv. 1-32 (concerning the purification of the healed leper).
|| Lev. xv. 2-15; 25-30.

whether it be from bodily defilement,* or from contact with a corpse or any unclean man or object, it only lasts a definite time, seven days or even a single day.† Purification is then effected by a bath and by washing the clothes. Sometimes an offering is required besides, *e. g.*, from a woman recovered from childbed,‡ or another expiation is prescribed, as in the case of those who have polluted themselves by touching a dead body.§

It was with a view to such numerous purification-sacrifices that I abstained just now (p. 253) from a more minute description and estimation of the offerings enjoined by the priestly law. This is the place to review the lawgiver's whole theory of sacrifices, and especially to bring to light the meaning of the expiatory sacrifice—*i. e.*, the sin- and the trespass-offerings.

The four classes of bloody sacrifices have already been mentioned. Their meaning is generally beyond doubt, and while it may have been defined somewhat more exactly by the priestly lawgiver, yet it cannot have been essentially altered by him: in this respect he was bound to the conception which had gradually gained acceptance among the people, under his predecessors in the priestly office. For our purposes a general characteristic of each sort of sacrifice is enough : we can leave the nicer distinctions to those who study this subject by itself, and not, as is the case here, as a subdivision of a larger whole. The *burnt-offering*,‖ then, is an act of homage to Jahveh, a public and solemn recognition of his supremacy and of the relation in which he stands to Israel; it is the most perfect and the most common, the principal sacrifice, in the true sense of the word, and therefore, *e. g.*, the daily morning and evening sacrifice, offered in the temple in the name of the whole community, belongs to this category. The *thank-offering*¶—as is also indicated by the Hebrew name—is connected with the welfare and the blessings which have issued or are expected from Jahveh. It is distinguished from the burnt-offering in this, among other

---

* Lev. xv. 16-24.
† See *e. g.* Lev. xv. 16-24 ; xi. 26-28, 31, 39, 40 ; Num. xix. 11-22.
‡ Lev. xii. 6-8.   § Num. xix.   ‖ Lev. i.   ¶ Lev. iii.

things, that only a small portion is laid on the altar and is consumed by the flame; the priest receives his share of what remains,* while the rest is eaten in a sacrificial meal. At sacrificial feasts, national as well as private, thank-offerings are therefore the main thing. The lawgiver also distinguishes between three sorts of thank-offerings: praise-offerings, voluntary offerings, and vow-offerings,† the last two of which are closely connected, and, at any rate in the younger ordinances of the priestly law, are regarded as less sacred than the first.‡ With respect to the *sin-offering* and the *trespass-offering*,§ it must first of all be observed that the expiatory power which they have is also attributed to the burnt-offering.‖ Perhaps this is to be explained by the fact that the burnt-offering is the oldest and original sacrifice, and thus was at first offered also in those cases which afterwards required the expiatory sacrifices proper. In the priestly law, however, the sin- and trespass-offerings are placed independently side by side with the burnt- and thank-offerings, nay, are even handled with evident partiality; in the spirit of the law, therefore, the expiatory power attributed to the burnt-offering, must be interpreted as a recommendation of this offering. The sin- and trespass-offerings have this in common, that a portion is burnt on the altar and the rest is given up to the priest, who must not eat it in his house, but in the holy place; the sin-offerings, however, which were offered for the whole people or for the anointed (*i. e.* the high) priest and the blood of which was sprinkled upon the altar of incense in the holy place and upon the curtain, might not be eaten, but had to be burnt.¶ And further, the priest makes atonement

---

* Above p. 257.

† Lev. vii. 12-15, 16-18. Praise-offerings are mentioned in Lev. xxiii. 19; Num. vi. 14.

‡ Lev. vii. 15, 16; xxii. 29, 30. In an older law, Lev. xix. 5-8, this distinction has not yet been made. Comp. above p. 84, a.

§ Lev. iv. 1—vi. 7 (Hebr. text, v. 26); vi. 24—vii. 7 (Hebr. text. vi. 17—vii. 7.)

‖ Lev. i. 3, 4.

¶ Lev. iv. 11, 12, 21; vi. 30, containing the exception: Lev. vi. 25-29; vii. 1-7 the rule.

with the blood, both of the sin-offering and of the trespass-offering, for the evil committed by the person who makes the offering, and the result is that he is forgiven.* On the other hand, points of difference between sin- and trespass-offerings are not wanting. First, the animals offered are not the same. A male animal, usually a ram, is always required as a trespass-offering; in the sin-offering the choice is much wider and it would even seem that female animals are used in preference.† But the question how the two sorts of expiatory offerings differ from each other *in meaning*, is of greater weight and at the same time much more intricate. Notwithstanding the pains which has now for many centuries been bestowed upon the solution of this question, that difference has not yet been clearly shown. Yet this labour has not all been in vain, for it enables us to assert with confidence that the problem is incapable of an entirely satisfactory solution, for obvious reasons. The laws as to expiatory sacrifices are based in part upon practice, which from its very nature is not strictly logical and easily admits slight divergences from the original distinction; moreover they are not from the same time, much less from one author. The most to which we can attain will therefore be to determine the original difference between sin- and trespass-offerings, paying attention to the most salient features, and further to explain how and why this difference is not everywhere adhered to. Now the ordinances respecting the trespass-offering‡ give us the impression that it is to serve to repair a wrong done to Jahveh or to one of the brethren; one might also say, to make good a violation of the right of property. Hence the trespass-offering is subject to the valuation of the priest,§ and compensation for the injury caused is

---

* Lev. iv. 20, 26, 31, 35 ; v. 6, 10, 13, 16, 18 ; vi. 7, where the formula adopted above is constantly employed for both sorts of sacrifices.

† Lev. iv. 3, 14, 23, 28 ; v. 6, 7-10 ; xii. 6, 8 ; xiv. 19, 22 ; xv. 29, 30, &c.

‡ Lev. v. 14-19 ; vi. 1-7 ; xix 20-22; Num. v. 5-8. The expression "trespass-offering" occurs besides in Lev. xiv. 12, seq. ; Num. vi. 12—to which passages, however, we do not allude above.   § Lev. v. 15, 18, &c.

often coupled with it.* The sin-offering is required after every involuntary transgression or act of negligence,† and therefore is much more common than the trespass-offering. This explains why it is that the priestly lawgiver prescribes a sin-offering after pollution.‡ If in two instances he requires a trespass-offering as well,§ this is not because precisely in these cases a trespass-offering was exacted or indicated, but because a second expiatory sacrifice seemed necessary and the first and most usual category was prescribed already.

We will now fix our attention upon the sacrificial ceremony itself. The person who presents the offering himself brings the beast which is to be sacrificed into the court, lays his hand upon its head and kills it. This precept applies to all the four sorts of sacrifices‖ and undergoes modification only when doves are offered: the laying on of the hand is then omitted and the priest kills the bird in a peculiar way which he has acquired by practice;¶ an exception such as this in fact confirms the rule. It follows at once from this rule, that the laying on of the hand cannot possibly indicate the transference of the guilt to the animal sacrificed; in that case surely it would only apply to sin- and trespass-offerings, and at all events would not have been prescribed for the thank-offering as well. Let it be rather considered that by this symbolic act the person presenting the offering makes himself known as him who is offering up the animal; he is there in the court not as a spectator, but as an actor; it is *his offering* which is soon to be placed upon the altar. Interpreted in this way, the laying on of the hand is as appropriate in burnt- and thank-offerings as in sin- and trespass-

---

* Lev. v. 16; vi. 4, 5. † Lev. iv. 1, seq.; Num. xv. 22-31.

‡ Lev. xii. 6, 8; xiv. 19, 22; xv. 14, sq. &c. It is always a sin-offering, and never a trespass-offering, that is offered in the name of the whole community, e. g. Lev. iv. 13-21; xvi. 9; Num. xxviii. 15, 22, 30, &c.

§ Lev. xiv. 12; Num. vi. 12.

‖ An example for each of the first three sorts: Lev. i. 4, 5; iii. 2; iv. 24. In the trespass-offering the laying on of the hand is not expressly required, but it is understood in the reference in Lev. vii. 7. ¶ Lev. i. 14, seq. and elsewhere.

offerings. The two last mentioned kinds possess peculiar characteristics of their own which distinguish them from the first. The chief difference lies in what is done with the blood of the victim. Part of this blood is always sprinkled on the altar by the priest, and the rest is poured out round about the altar,* but besides this the blood of the expiatory offerings is put upon the horns either of the altar of burnt-offerings or of the altar of incense; in the latter case the curtain is also sprinkled with the blood seven times.† After this—it goes on to say—" the priest shall make atonement for him who presents the offering, and it shall be forgiven him."‡ *How* this was done, is not said: the atonement was effected by the blood, so that it was complete as soon as the altar had been smeared with it; but it is not improbable that the priest now proclaimed that the object of the ceremony had been attained, whether by a verbal notification, or by sprinkling the person offering with the blood in his turn. However this may be, there always remains the question, why such an expiatory power was ascribed to the blood of the animal sacrificed. The priestly lawgiver replies: because *the soul* (the vital principle) is seated in the blood. " For the soul of the flesh (living being, man or beast) is in the blood; therefore have I, Jahveh, given it (the blood) to you upon the altar to make atonement for your souls; for the blood maketh atonement through the soul (therein contained)."§ In the meantime this explanation still leaves much unanswered. Is the conception this, that Jahveh accepts the soul of the animal sacrificed *instead of* that of the sacrificer? must this animal be therefore considered to have undergone death for him? or how else are we to conceive the connection between the offering of the blood and the atonement? The simpler the idea which we form of this, the nearer shall we undoubtedly be to the truth. Let it therefore be considered that according to the

---

* For single examples see as above, p. 265, n. ‖, Lev. i. 5; iii. 2; iv. 25; comp. for the trespass-offering Lev. v. 16, 18; vi. 7; viii. 7.

† Lev. iv. 6, 7; 17, 18; 25; 34, &c. ‡ See the passages, p. 264, n. *.

§ Lev. xvii. 11.

Israelite's notion, Jahveh in his clemency permits the soul of the animal sacrificed to take the place of that of the sacrificer. No *transfer of guilt* to the animal sacrificed takes place: the blood of the latter is clean and remains so, as is evident from the very fact that this blood is put upon the altar; it is a token of mercy on Jahveh's part, that he accepts it; " he has *given* it " —as we have heard—" to the Israelites to atone for their souls." Nor can it be asserted that the animal sacrificed *undergoes the punishment* in the place of the transgressor: this is said nowhere, and therefore, in any case, gives another, more sharply defined idea than that which the Israelite must have formed for himself; moreover it is irreconcilable with the rule that the indigent may bring the tenth part of an ephah of fine flour as a sin-offering.* " Shall I "—Micah makes one of his contemporaries say†—

" Shall I give my first-born for my transgression,
The fruit of my body for the sin of my soul?"

No, answers the priestly lawgiver: you need not do that; Jahveh allows you to manifest your consciousness of guilt in another way; he accepts your offering, and especially the blood of your beast, as reparation for the evil which you have done, and couples the forgiveness of your sin with the employment of this means of propitiation which he has ordained.

Now let it not be imagined that every sin can be atoned for by such an offering. It is only for *involuntary* transgressions that the Israelite obtains pardon by bringing sin- or trespass-offerings. " The soul that shall have done ought *with uplifted hand* (*i. e.* with premeditation, with evil intent), whether he be born in the land, or a stranger, the same reproacheth Jahveh: that soul shall be rooted out from among his people; for he hath despised Jahveh's word and broken his commandment; that soul shall surely be rooted out: his sin is upon him."‡

* Lev. v. 11-13.   † Mic. vi. 7b.   ‡ Numb. xv. 30, 31.

"The error,"* for which the expiatory sacrifice is prescribed, or rather, is allowed and accepted by Jahveh, is opposed to the "uplifted hand" mentioned here. If, however, we now examine in what cases a sin- or trespass-offering is required by the priestly lawgiver, it is evident at once that he places a very wide interpretation upon the notion of "error." He also places in this category sins committed out of heedlessness, weakness or fear;† nay, even transgressions done deliberately, if they are followed by repentance and due reparation be made.‡ This last class is strange enough to justify the enquiry whether the trespass-offering was not *originally* permitted after an ordinary, wilful violation of the right of property, so that the priestly law had also to call this an "error," because it wished to admit the expiatory sacrifice only for this kind of offence. Be that as it may, it is evident that the only case in which the lawgiver will hear of no offering is when the sin has been committed for the express purpose of insulting Jahveh, and thus bears witness to contempt for Jahveh's word. We by no means impute this clemency to him as a fault. It is the natural consequence of the severity of his punishments: for every transgression which does not fall within the notion of "error," "rooting out" is threatened.§ Still it cannot be denied that such a widening of that notion weakens the feeling of responsibility. How easily the transgressor could make himself and others believe that he had not sinned wilfully. How very likely it was that, with the expiatory sacrifice before his eyes, he would prove less strong in the hour of temptation than would otherwise have been the case.

On the other hand, this danger would have been in great measure averted, if the expiatory sacrifice had always remained a solemn and significant thing in the Israelite's estimation. But we can hardly suppose this to have been the case, when we observe how numerous the expiatory sacrifices were which were

---

* Lev. iv. 7, 22, 27; v. 15, 18; xxii. 14; Num. xv. 24-29.   † Lev. v. 1-4.
‡ Lev. vi. 1-5.   § We shall revert to this below (p. 275-277.)

demanded by the law. Irrespectively of the sin-offerings which were offered *in the name of the whole people* on the first day of the month, the paschal feast, the feast of weeks and on each day of the feast of tabernacles,* and of the offerings on the great day of atonement, of which more shortly; irrespectively also of the sin- and trespass-offerings which were offered in consequence of definite transgressions — the priestly law requires a sin-offering from the woman recovered from childbed;† a sin- and a trespass-offering from the leper upon his cure;‡ a sin-offering from the man or woman who has suffered from an unclean issue;§ a sin- and a trespass-offering from the Nazarite upon each involuntary pollution,‖ and a sin-offering at the end of his separation.¶ And finally, it also prescribes that anyone who has touched a corpse shall be unclean for seven days, and on the third and seventh days must cause himself to be sprinkled with a water of purification, which has been expressly prepared for this purpose and derives its purifying power from being mixed with the ashes of a red cow which has been killed as a sin-offering and then burnt.** All these precepts are based upon the supposition that every pollution, even though it be involuntary, excludes the Israelite from communion with holy Jahveh, and must be expiated by Jahveh's representative, the priest, before the former relation can be considered as restored. Taken together they are very well fitted to cultivate a deep awe for Jahveh, and it was undoubtedly with this object that they were promulgated. But it is obvious that the lawgiver has overshot his mark. A sin-offering offered without the consciousness of sin is an empty form. But how, in all the cases just mentioned, can he who presented the offering have been conscious of guilt? how therefore was the offering to be kept from degenerating into a mechanical, spiritless act? And, granting even that this was

* Num. xxviii. 15, 22, 30; xxix. 16, seq.   † Lev. xii. 6, 8.
‡ Lev. xiv. 19, seq.   § Lev. xv. 14, sq. 29, sq.   ‖ Num. vi. 9-12.
¶ Num. vi. 13, 14.   ** Num. xix.

possible, must not the expiatory sacrifice offered on account of this or that real transgression, committed consciously, have lost in great measure its awe-inspiring power by being placed upon a level with the offerings of which we are speaking here?

It may be remarked in general, that the priestly law threatens to weaken the fear of pollution by multiplying the cases in which uncleanness results. Men must gradually have become accustomed to that "unclean until the evening" which recurs so often. Nay, men can easily have come to accept the obligation and the subsequent washing of body and clothes which it imposed, if the gain or the enjoyment with which the pollution was connected, seemed to outweigh them. In other words, the temporary uncleanness could easily be regarded as a sort of penance, which one only had to undertake to be clear of everything. By eating the flesh of a clean animal that had died a natural death, the Israelite became unclean until the evening :* now, if he could afford to be unclean until the evening, there was no need for him to deny himself that food. Who does not perceive that by his minute precepts and distinctions, the lawgiver himself has considerably weakened the sublimity of the precept, "Be holy, for I, Jahveh, am holy?" It is true, a great deal depended upon the character of the Israelite. If he was scrupulously pious, he always continued to regard uncleanness as a real calamity or as a heavy punishment, and considered himself bound to avoid it as much as possible. But this gave rise to another danger. How could he then be free from uneasiness and petty, anxious precautions? Reflect that all sorts of clothes, household furniture and food were capable of becoming unclean,† and of polluting, in their turn, any one who touched them. What a life he must have led, who feared such pollution and yet could hardly escape it!

The lawgiver himself perceived that he must do something to remove this uneasiness. He had this in view, when he appointed the sin-offerings to which we have just referred, in

* Lev. xi. 39.   † Lev. xi. 31-40; xv. 4-12; 17; 20-24; 26, 27.

the name of the whole community, on the occasions of the new moons and the high festivals. But this purpose is chiefly served by the great *day of atonement*, the tenth of the seventh month, which can be truly regarded as the crown or the keystone of the whole priestly system of cleanness. The idea that the land in which the Israelites lived was made unclean by their transgressions, and therefore needed purifying, had long existed: the Deuteronomist had already prescribed such a cleansing for certain cases.* Ezekiel went further, when he ordered† that on the first and the seventh days of the first month a young bullock should be killed as a sin-offering, to cleanse the sanctuary "for him that erreth and for him that is heedless," *i.e.* to wipe out the taints which clung to the temple in consequence of the involuntary transgressions of the Israelites in the midst of whom it stood. This idea is adopted by the priestly lawgiver and worked out in a very exhaustive law,‡ which contains more than one detail at which we must pause for a moment. First of all we remark that from the point of view of the priestly law the day of atonement is pre-eminently the holy day, and that it was quite in conformity with the spirit of the law that the later Jews called it *Joma, the day*. "The humiliation of the soul," *i.e.* abstinence from food and drink, is prescribed exclusively for the day of atonement.§ On that day alone the high-priest enters the holy of holies.‖ The solemnities, also, which belong to the expiation, are peculiar and eminently adapted to make a deep impression. The offerings of the high-priest are a young bullock as a sin-offering, a ram as a burnt-offering; those of the people, two he-goats as a sin-offering, a ram as a burnt-offering. Lots are cast between the two he-goats; one is "for Jahveh," and the other "for Azazel." After the high-priest has now sacrificed first the young bullock

---

* Deut. xxi. 1-9; comp. also vers. 22, 23; Lev. xviii. 25.
† Chap. xlv. 18-20.   ‡ Lev. xvi.
§ Lev. xvi. 29, 31; xxiii. 27, 29, 32; Num. xxix. 7.
‖ Lev. xvi. 2, seq., 12, seq.

for himself and then the goat "for Jahveh" for the people as a sin-offering, and has sprinkled the blood of these animals in the holy of holies and the holy place, he takes the remaining goat "for Azazel," "lays his hands upon its head and confesses all the iniquities of the children of Israel and all their transgressions, according to all their sins, and lays them upon the head of the goat, and sends him out into the wilderness by the hand of a man who stands ready."* He then cleanses himself and offers the burnt-offerings.† Here, as is expressly stated, a transfer of sins takes place: the goat "for Azazel" takes them upon himself and carries them away into the wilderness. But this does not happen until the young bullock and the goat "for Jahveh" have been killed and their blood has been brought into Jahveh's presence; the sending away of the other goat, laden with the transgressions, is thus a symbol of what the real sin-offerings have already effected, and makes visible, as it were, the result and the fruit of the whole transaction. The contrast between the two goats renders it probable that *Azazel* is not a common noun, signifying "a sending away," or something of that sort, but a proper name, as well as Jahveh. Presumably it was used for a wicked spirit or unclean demon, which was believed to live in the wilderness, and to whom the scapegoat was yielded as his prey.‡ With regard, finally, to the extent of the atonement which was effected by the ceremony of that day, we have already learned that the lawgiver makes it include "*all* the iniquities of the children of Israel and *all* their sins;"§ he expresses himself elsewhere in terms as general.‖ We must not, however, be misled by this. He can mean nothing else than the *involuntary* sins,¶ but these he means without any exception, the moral errors, as well as the infractions of the laws of cleanness. From all these both the Israelites themselves and the sanctuary which was defiled by them, were

---

* Lev. xvi. 21. † Lev. xvi. 23-25. ‡ Comp. Isa. xiii. 21; xxxiv. 21.
§ In the passage quoted above, Lev. xvi. 21.   ‖ Lev. xvi. 22, 34.
¶ Above, pp. 267, seq.

cleansed on the day of atonement. So the lawgiver met the difficulties which oppressed the consciences of those who accepted his precepts in earnest. The abuse of the forgiveness offered so liberally was undoubtedly opposed to his intention, but—was it unnatural?

To complete our review of the ordinances relating to cleanness, we must now examine what was required of the priests and the high-priest. It is they who approach Jahveh, in the true sense of the word. We are not surprised, therefore, that they have to guard against uncleanness much more than the laity. Bodily imperfections render the descendant of Aaron unfit for the priesthood.* The ordinary priest may only marry a virgin or a widow;† the high-priest only a virgin.‡ The priest guards himself as much as possible from contact with a corpse; he may only show the last honours to his nearest relations;§ the high-priest even abstains from this: " he shall not defile himself for his father or for his mother;"|| so entirely must he devote himself to Jahveh, that he realizes in a literal sense what the poet had sung in praise of the tribe of Levi:

"Who saith of his father and his mother, 'I have not seen them,'
And his brothers he regardeth not,
And his sons he knoweth not."¶

The priest carefully avoids all unchastity: even in his daughter it is punished with unwonted severity.** For the obligation of purity lies also upon those who belong to the priest's family, in the same way that, conversely, they enjoy their share of the privileges connected with the priestly office. All the members of his household, including the slaves, those born in the house as well as those bought for money, may partake with him of the sacred flesh of the sacrifices††—always excepting the flesh of the sin- and trespass-offerings, which is eaten exclusively by the priests themselves;‡‡ it is only when

* Lev. xxi. 16-24. † Lev. xxi. 7, 8. ‡ Lev. xxi. 13-15.
§ Lev. xxi. 1-6. || Lev. xxi. 10-12. ¶ Deut. xxxiii. 9.
** Lev. xxi. 9. †† Lev. xxii. 10, 11. ‡‡ Lev. vi. 29; vii. 6.

his daughter has ceased to be a member of his household, by contracting a marriage, that this privilege is no longer allowed her; but she again shares in it, if she return childless to her father.* In conformity with all the rules already enumerated, the priest, by every pollution, becomes temporarily disqualified to perform his office, and also unfit to eat the sacred sacrificial food,† and he is unconditionally forbidden to eat of animals that have died a natural death or have been torn.‡ "Ye shall keep,"—so the lawgiver concludes his series of precepts concerning the priests—"Ye shall keep my commandments and do them: I am Jahveh. Ye shall not profane my holy name, that I may be hallowed among the children of Israel; I am Jahveh which hallow you, that brought you out of the land of Egypt, to be a god unto you: I am Jahveh."§

The close connection between these commandments and those respecting the laity is easily recognized. The climax is strictly preserved. Upon the highest step, the one nearest to Jahveh, stands the high-priest, the only man who, at least once a year, may enter the abode of his glory; from him, therefore, the strictest separation from all uncleanness is required. It is also worthy of remark, that he is somewhat restricted, it is true, in the choice of a wife and in the discharge of his duties as a son, by virtue of this intimate relation to Jahveh, but otherwise, like his brethren, he retains perfect liberty to marry. Asceticism —as the sequel of this history will teach us—found a few points of contact in the priestly law, but nothing more than that; that law did not prescribe or exact it.

All that we have said thus far of the priestly law, has been directly connected with public worship. And yet this has brought us almost to the end of our review of its precepts. The older laws concerning the civil and domestic life underwent no change, when the ritual precepts were annexed to them. The

---

* Lev. xxii. 12, 13.   † Lev. xxii. 1-7.   ‡ Lev. xxii. 8.
§ Lev. xxii. 31-33.

priestly lawgiver could easily rest content with those earlier regulations. Upon one subject alone, not directly connected with public worship, did he express himself somewhat more fully, viz. lawful and unlawful marriages.* His precepts in this respect, which are also allied in form to those of Ezekiel, appear to be a development and extension of what had already been laid down in Deuteronomy.† We refrain from a special discussion of their contents. The link between them and the ordinances relating to cleanness is obvious without farther demonstration. But besides this the priestly lawgiver gives a few detached rules upon other subjects, by which he either amplifies or alters those of his predecessors in legislation. In most cases it is at once apparent, why he expressly regulates just these subjects, and, in doing so, he never disowns his peculiar priestly standpoint. It is but reasonable that we should make ourselves acquainted with these ordinances as well. We do this the more willingly, because at the same time we shall obtain an opportunity of treating at greater length a few particulars upon which hitherto we have only touched.

We find in the priestly law one ordinance relating to *penal enactments*, which is peculiar both in contents and in garb.‡ It is presented in the freely-chosen form of a decision of Jahveh upon a question submitted to him by Moses. The son of an Egyptian man and an Israelitish woman had blasphemed Jahveh's name in a dispute in the camp. Moses wishes to know what must be done with him. The answer says that the blasphemer, whether he belongs to those born in the land or to the strangers settled in Israel, must be punished with death.§ Upon the same

---

* Lev. xviii. and xx. Upon the mutual relation of these two chapters see Graf, *die gesch. Bücher des A. T.* pp. 76, sq.

† Comp. Deut. xxiii. 1 ; xxvii. 20 with Lev. xviii. 8 ; xx. 11 ; Deut. xxvii. 22 with Lev. xviii. 9 ; xx. 17 ; Deut. xxvii. 23 with Lev. xviii. 17 ; xx. 14 ; Deut. xxii. 20 with Lev. xviii. 20 ; xx. 10 ; Deut. xviii. 10 with Lev. xviii. 21 ; xx. 2-5 ; Deut. xxvii. 21 with Lev. xviii. 23 ; xx. 15, 16. ‡ Lev. xxiv. 10-23.

§ Lev. xxiv. 14-16. Subsequently verse 16 was interpreted differently, as a prohibition to *utter* the name Jahveh, for which reason the Jews, to this day, in reading the Old Testament, substitute "God" or "Adonai" for it.

occasion—and from this it is evident that the historical circumstance with which the enquiry is connected, is fictitious—Jahveh declares that murder must be punished with death, and maintains the older laws of retaliation :* these decrees are also pronounced to be applicable to the stranger as well as the Israelite,† and, it would seem, are repeated by the priestly lawgiver for this very purpose.‡ The only new thing here, therefore, is the punishment of blasphemy with death. We can hardly venture to call it severe, when we see the number and the nature of the faults which, according to the same lawgiver, result in "the rooting out of the soul" that commits them "from his people." I will not enumerate them all here; let the reader consult the texts himself.§ It is evident at once, that this punishment is threatened not only for idolatry and for sacrificing beyond the one sanctuary, but for incest, neglect of circumcision, infraction of the laws concerning the sabbath and the high festivals, disregard of the precepts as to cleanness, &c. By far the most of the ordinances of the priestly law, including those of a purely ceremonial nature, are followed by the threat of this punishment—so that at first they even give one the impression of draconic severity and bloodthirstiness. Or have men, perchance, been mistaken in making "rooting out" synonymous with death, or at all events believed without reason that the lawgiver would have that punishment to be carried out by the authorities, whereas his meaning is rather that Jahveh will take upon himself the enforcement of his commandments and visit the offender with an extraordinary chastisement? Both these questions have been answered in the affirmative in former and recent times, but the lawgiver's words are absolutely

---

* Lev. xxiv. 17-21. Comp. Exod. xxi. 23-25.
† Lev. xxiv. 22.   ‡ Comp. above, pp. 259, seq.
§ Gen. xvii. 14; Exod. xii. 15, 19 (comp. Num. ix. 13); xxx. 33, 38; xxxi. 14 (c. Num. xv. 32-36); Lev. vii. 20, 21, 25, 27 (c. xvii. 10, 14); xvii. 4, 9; xviii. 6 20 (c. xx. 10. 14, 17-21); 21. 29 (c. xx. 2-5); 23, 29 (c. xx. 15, 16); xix. 8; xx. 6; xxii. 3; xxiii. 29; Num. xv. 30, 31; xix. 13, 20.

opposed to such a mitigated interpretation of his meaning. On the other hand it is absurd to suppose that immediately after the introduction of the priestly law, the authorities considered it their duty to inflict capital punishment on account of all the offences which it pointed out, and made arrangements to that effect. Nor does it escape our notice that it nowhere says *how and by whom* the "rooting out" is to be done, while no one can affirm that the manner and the agents were so well known that they did not need to be mentioned? This last observation brings us to a satisfactory solution of the difficulty which here presents itself. The penal ordinances of the priestly law are *threats*. They express, in a concrete and visible form, the conviction that the violation of the precepts of the law renders the Israelite *guilty of death*. The lawgiver *could* not go further; even supposing that he had been willing, he had not the power to execute all those sentences of death. But he cherished the hope that the commandment inculcated with such great emphasis would not be broken, and that thus the infliction of the penalty would not be necessary. In this he had been preceded by the Deuteronomist,* from whom really he only differs in this, that his ideal is more sacerdotal than ethic-religious, and therefore the penal enactment often seems to us entirely disproportionate to the evil against which it is directed. But the lawgiver himself was so very much in earnest in the realization of his ideal, that he did not hesitate to brand every wilful departure from it as culpable in the highest degree.

With regard to the *places of refuge*, the priestly law contains an ordinance which agrees, it is true, in the main with the older regulations, but though very near to them, can in no way be regarded as superfluous.† In the first place, it contains some rules, according to which unintentional manslaughter is to be distinguished from wilful murder, and thus tries to prevent the

---

* Above, pp. 25, 37, seq.
† Num. xxxv. 9-34, to be compared with Deut. xix. 1-13; iv. 41-43; Exod. xxi. 13, 14.

murderer from abusing a privilege which is meant only for the unintentional slayer. The motive which governs the lawgiver in this is clearly stated: "blood defileth the land, and the land cannot be cleansed of the blood that is shed therein, but by the blood of him that shed it;"* this rule may be departed from, when the bloodshed has been accidental, but then alone; in any other case the law must take its course, for the sake of the cleanness of the land. This law also enacts that the slayer must stay in the place of refuge "until the death of the high-priest, which was anointed with the holy oil;"† if he ventures beyond the walls of the city before that time, the avenger of blood may kill him with impunity; after that time the avenger would himself become guilty of murder by executing his vengeance. The placing of such a limit is a mitigation of the older law, the necessity of which had no doubt been brought to light by experience. Moreover the origin and the age of the law is marked by the fact that the limit is taken from the high-priest, who evidently appears here as the highest authority, which indeed he was—after the Babylonish exile.

The ordinances with regard to *the law of war*, also, are of true priestly origin. The romantic account of the expedition againt Midian, Numbers xxxi., serves no other purpose than to make visible the effects and the blessed fruits of keeping these laws. Twelve thousand Israelites kill all the fighting men of the Midianites, burn all their cities, carry away incalculable plunder, then, at Moses' command, murder in cold blood the Midianitish women and the children of the male sex, who at first had been spared, and are all the while protected so conspicuously by Jahveh that not a man of them is lost.‡ There are two subjects which the lawgiver wishes to regulate by means of this historical picture. In the first place, he defines which of the enemy's possessions the Israelite may appropriate and how he should cleanse himself from the uncleanness which, according to his notions, is occasioned by killing the foe and by touching

---

* Num. xxxv. 33.   † Num. xxxv. 25, 28, 32.   ‡ Num. xxxi. 49.

the slain.* In the second place, he gives rules for dividing the spoil. The gold, the silver and the valuables may be kept by whoever seizes them,† although it is a praiseworthy action to give up a portion of them voluntarily to Jahveh.‡ The spoil of men and beasts is allotted, half to those who went out to battle, and half to the whole congregation; of the former half $\frac{1}{500}$ is to be given up to the priests, and $\frac{1}{50}$ of the latter half to the Levites.§ It cannot be said that these demands in favour of the priests and Levites are inordinately large. We cannot accuse the lawgiver of avarice on account of this regulation. Yet it is impossible to deny that he shows himself here in a very unfavourable light. The cold-bloodedness with which the murder of many thousands of defenceless persons is painted as a religious duty, coupled with the scrupulous anxiety for cleanness and the minute calculation of each one's share in the spoil, is truly repulsive. Fortunately this terrible bloodshed is only committed on paper.

Equally remarkable are the priestly ordinances concerning the *ownership of land*. The place which it occupies in the lawgiver's system will be more apparent to us, if we first fill in a small gap in our previous researches. In speaking of public worship, I have only mentioned *the sabbath* in passing. It was scarcely necessary to say that the priestly law retained it. Now, however, I must point out that it clearly attaches great value to it and especially maintains the sabbath-*rest* most strictly. There are no less than four ordinances on this subject, and several points which we find there deserve our special attention.‖ First of all the vindication of the commandment of the sabbath-rest by referring to the example of Jahveh, who " in six days made heaven and earth and on the seventh day rested and took breath."¶ This motive was also adopted by the priestly lawgiver in the " ten words," at all events in the redaction which

---

* Verses 14-24. † Verse 53. ‡ Verses 48-52, 54. § Verses 25-47.
‖ Exod. xxxi. 12-17; xxxv. 1-3; Num. xv. 32-36; Exod. xvi. 22-30.
¶ Exod. xxxi. 17.

occurs in Exodus.* In fact, as we saw before,† the idea that
the creation of heaven and earth took place in six days and was
followed by a day of rest, is younger than the sabbath and resulted
from the already acknowledged holiness of the latter: both in
working and in resting, Jahveh was imagined to be after the
likeness of Israel. We are further struck by the fact that the
breaking of the sabbath-rest is expressly menaced in these laws
—for the first time—with death: "Every one that defileth the
sabbath shall surely be put to death; for whosoever doeth any
work therein, that soul shall be rooted out from among his
people."‡ In spite of this decree, Nehemiah, as we have already
seen,§ had to use force against trading on the sabbath: does
not this contain a proof that we were not mistaken just now in
our interpretation of the penal threats of the priestly law?—And
finally it is noteworthy, that, when these precepts were drawn
up, it was already a question which occupations were to be
considered as lawful or unlawful. *Absolute* idleness of course
was impossible. But they tried to get as near to it as possible.
Thus, *e.g.*, it is forbidden to kindle a fire; ‖ care for the ordinary
sustenance of life is confined to the barest necessaries; ¶ the
gathering of sticks is to be punished with stoning.** Under
such laws as these, the religious idea upon which the sabbath is
based—the hallowing of one day in the week to Jahveh—was
almost entirely lost; scarcely more heed was paid to the humane
tendency of the day of rest, which former lawgivers had placed
in the foreground;†† on the contrary, the subtle casuistry into
which the later scribes plunged, was more than prepared.‡‡

But however unattractive the further development of the
sabbath-commandment by the priestly lawgiver may seem to us,
it undoubtedly shows that he attached much importance to it,

---

* Exod. xx. 11. † Comp. Vol. I. pp. 262, seq. ‡ Exod. xxxi. 14.
§ p. 235. ‖ Exod. xxxv. 3. ¶ Exod. xvi. 22-30.
** Num. xv. 32-36. †† Exod. xxiii. 12; Deut. v. 14, 15.
‡‡ I. a. by the distinction between *work* and *servile work*, with which we meet in
Lev. xxiii. 7, 8, &c., and vers. 28, 30, 31.

and regarded it with great partiality. We are not astonished, therefore, that he maintains the idea of the sabbath in its closer application as well, and even carries it out more fully. In proof of this we must cite his ordinance respecting *the sabbath-year*,* which is distinguished from the older law† in this, that it prescribes that the land shall lie fallow every 7th year, whereas the former lawgiver had decreed that the produce of that year should be left for the poor. Here, therefore, we have the same high estimation of rest as such, which pervades the priestly sabbath-commandments. And further, we must notice here the very exhaustive law respecting the *year of jubilee*, which, on the one hand, must be regarded as the highest development of the sabbath-idea, and, on the other, displays the priestly notions upon the ownership of land.† After every 7 × 7 years, or seven weeks of years, a year of jubilee must be kept,§ in the following manner. On the 10th day of the 7th month, the great day of atonement, the sound of the trumpet (*jobel;* thence the name "jubilee") shall announce the commencement of that year, shall proclaim "liberty" (*deror*). It is a year of rest for the land,|| in the first place, as well as the preceding 49th year. Moreover, "every man returns" in that year "to his possessions and to his family."¶ The Israelite who is obliged from poverty to sell his land, does so with the prospect that in the 50th year he will again become its owner; thus he really sells not the ground, but its produce during the years which have yet to elapse before the year of jubilee.** In the same way, the Israelite who has sold himself as a slave gets back his freedom in the 50th year: thus he does not become the bondman, but the hired servant of his brother,†† or of the stranger settled in Israel, whoso service he has been compelled by want to enter.‡‡ There are other regulations which are connected with these. Every Israelite who has alienated

---

* Lev. xxv. 1-7.   † Exod. xxiii. 10, 11.   ‡ Lev. xxv. 8-55.   § Vers. 8-10.
|| Lev. xxv. 11, 12.   ¶ Verses 10, 13, seq.   ** Verses 13-16.
†† Verses 39, seq.   ‡‡ Verses 47, seq.

his land, retains the right of redemption: either he himself or his nearest relation, the *goel*, can resume possession at once, upon paying a part, proportionate to the time meanwhile elapsed, of the sum at which it was sold.* If he has sold his house in a walled city, he retains the right of redemption for one year; if he does not avail himself of this right, the house remains the permanent property of the buyer.† Houses in villages stand upon the same footing as fields.‡ The Levites who have sold their houses can redeem them at any moment, and they receive them back in the year of jubilee if they have been unable to make use of this privilege; their fields, situated in the space marked out round their towns, they may not part with at all.§ And finally, the Israelite who has sold himself to a stranger as a slave, can also be set at liberty at any time, on his ransom being paid by a kinsman, or out of the means which he has himself amassed; the compensation to the stranger for the loss which he suffers, is to be in proportion to the amount of the purchase money and the number of years which have yet to elapse before the year of jubilee.‖

Before we examine and criticise these precepts more closely, let us fix our attention upon the other ordinances which are intimately related to them. In the form of an account of an historical detail of the Mosaic time, based perhaps upon an old tradition, the priestly lawgiver expresses his conviction that when there are no sons, the landed property of the father should go to the daughters.¶ One condition, however, is attached to this law of inheritance: the daughters who inherit must marry men of the tribe to which they themselves belong, in order that the inheritance of that tribe may not be diminished.** If a man die childless, his property goes to his relations in a prescribed order.††

All that relates to the year of jubilee and the liberation of

---

* Verses 24-28. † Verses 29, 30. ‡ Verse 31. § Verses 32-34.
‖ Lev. xxv. 48-53. ¶ Num. xxvii. 1-11. ** Num. xxxvi.
†† Num. xxvii. 9-11.

Israelitish slaves, was intended to supersede an old ordinance which was included in the Book of the Covenant* and repeated by the Deuteronomist,† and according to which the Hebrew slave, if he chose, could get back his freedom after six years of service. The priestly lawgiver's chief object, however, was the maintenance of the hereditary ownership of land. With this in view, he thinks he must confine within very narrow bounds the right of the individual to dispose freely of his property. Or rather, he does not allow the individual any property, in the strict sense of the word. "The land is mine" —he makes Jahveh say‡—"for ye are strangers and sojourners with me." By virtue of this right of possession, Jahveh decides that the sale of real property—except houses in cities— may not take place, and that after fifty years each family shall receive back intact the inheritance allotted to it. Thus the lawgiver makes the religious idea—"Jahveh the owner, the Israelite the usufructuary of the ground"—of service in order to promote the greatest possible stability. But it does not escape our attention, that in laying down and developing this requirement he troubles himself but little or not at all about the reality. His ordinance sounds very well in theory, but practically it is impossible. Experience has pronounced judgment here. The sabbath-year, which was not observed before the exile,§ was kept regularly after it. But the year of jubilee never came into practice, and this in spite of the predilection of the priesthood for it, to which Ezekiel‖ and the fulness of the priestly law upon this subject bear witness. It is clearly evident, in truth, that we have to do here with a postulate, when we hear the lawgiver lay down separate rules for the Levites' cities, which, we know,¶ they never possessed but on paper. Nevertheless this law, with its two supplements, remains most remarkable, both because it throws light upon the

---

* Exod. xxi. 2-11.   † Deut. xv. 12-18.   ‡ Lev. xxv. 23.
§ Lev. xxvi. 34, 35, 43.   ‖ Chap. xlvi. 17. Comp. above, p. 191.
¶ Above, p. 171, 258.

theoretical and abstract character of the legislation to which it belongs, and because it shows most plainly the conservative spirit of the priesthood.

There is still one more group of priestly ordinances for us to handle. It is those relating to *vows*. A separate law is devoted to the vow of the Nazarite;* another law treats of vows in general,† and is further amplified by regulations as to the vows of women and young girls.‡ All these precepts are indeed most remarkable. A vow from its very nature is something voluntary, a natural product of religious belief in a certain stage of development. The Israelite is induced by gratitude to promise something which he values to Jahveh, who has loaded him with benefits. Or he connects a vow of this sort with the accomplishment of a desire upon which his heart is very much set. The terms of his vow vary according to circumstances. He can dedicate himself to Jahveh as a *nazir*;§ he can give up to him part of his means; "banning" (*cherem*), also, can take place in consequence of a previous vow to Jahveh.‖ Now what does the priestly lawgiver do with this natural product? He prunes and regulates and assesses it until it is in danger of losing its significance and worth. The Nazarites, in fact, did not fit rightly into the priestly ideal of the Israelitish state, and could even become dangerous to the priestly power. Yet it would not do to forbid them to appear. Therefore the lawgiver adopts an intermediate course, and only recognizes the *temporary* Nazarite vow, with regard to which he gives very detailed instructions.¶ His law respecting vows in general is based upon the understanding that the Israelites promised or dedicated to Jahveh not only their real or personal property, but individuals of various ages. The latter always had to be redeemed, according to a fixed rate of prices, which, *e.g.*, places the value of a man between twenty and sixty years at sixty shekels, and that of a woman of the same age at

---

* Num. vi. 1-21.   † Lev. xxvii.   ‡ Num. xxx.
§ Comp Vol. 1. p. 316.   ‖ Comp. *e.g.* Num. xxi. 2, 3.   ¶ Num. vi. 1-21.

thirty shekels of silver.* With regard to clean and unclean animals, to fields, houses, and other possessions given up by vow to Jahveh, he likewise has his precepts, which regulate, among other things, the application of the law of the year of jubilee, and further display an evident tendency to advance the interests of the sanctuary and the priesthood.† This last is also true of the ordinances relating to the vows of wives and daughters. In Israel too the woman had not the free disposal of her property; it was necessary, therefore, that the general rule should be that a vow made by her did not bind her husband, or, if she were unmarried, her father. The lawgiver does, in fact, allow this rule to continue in force, but he prescribes that the man's silence must be taken as consent— obviously in the interest of the temple and the priests, who by this means lost what was intended for them, only when the husband or father at once annulled his wife's or daughter's vow.‡

If the necessity for regulating this subject by law be acknowledged, but little objection can be made to these ordinances, or at all events they are as good as others which might be put in their places. But it cannot be denied that by laws of this kind the free utterance of the religious sentiment is fettered, and the real character of the religious action is in great part lost. The same observation has forced itself upon us more than once while considering the priestly ordinances. It is not unnatural, therefore, that with them we should take leave of the priestly lawgiver. If now, at the end of our survey, we recall to mind once more the contents of the whole, we cannot but own that they were grand and beautiful designs which the lawgiver had in view. He formed broadly the idea of a holy people dedicated to Jahveh, and tried to realize it on a large scale. He embodied it, as it were, in his institutions, and at the same time—no slight merit in truth—preserved it from destruction. But in conformity with the character of the

---

* Lev. xxvii. 3, 4.   † Verse 9, seq.   ‡ Num. xxx.

order to which he belonged; in the spirit of the age in which he lived, and—for we must not overlook this either—by virtue of his own individuality, he came of himself, as it were, to circumscribe and regulate everything, down to the very details. A *free* dedication of Israel to Jahveh he could not imagine; the nation's holiness, in his opinion, was bound up with the observance of the traditional practices, and of the new ordinances with which he thought it his duty to supplement and perfect them. The natural consequences of this tendency were not long in coming. Liberty never is, and was not in this case, restricted with impunity. Without himself desiring it, the lawgiver, by his endless and minute enactments, reduces his ideas to smaller proportions, and produces a mere outward conception of duties towards Jahveh and an empty formalism.

The soil was ready for the seed thus strewn; how it then sprang up, the sequel of this history will tell.

NOTES.

I.—*See pp.* 224 *n.* *; 228 *n.* *

My interpretation of Ezra's work, and especially of his exertions to introduce the Mosaic laws, is based in great part upon Neh. viii.-x. Objections, however, are made to the absolute credibility of these chapters, and I am the less able to shut my eyes to these objections, because I myself, now nine years ago, have acknowledged their weight. Comp. my *Hist. krit. Onderzoek*, vol. i. 347-52. It now seems to me that some of the difficulties put forward there can be cleared away, and that consequently the final verdict upon the whole pericope must be more favourable.

All the evidence advanced there for the proposition—1st, that Neh. viii.-x. is *not* from Nehemiah's hand, and 2nd, that these chapters were written by the redactor of the books of Ezra and Nehemiah (*i. e.* by the Chronicler)—retain their full weight. The same opinion is now upheld by Bertheau, *Ezra, Neh. u. Est. erklärt*, p. 11, and elsewhere, and by Schrader in de Wette's *Einl.* i. 389.

With respect, also, to the mutual relation of Ezra ii. 68—iii. 1, and Neh. vii. 70-73, I must maintain the belief expressed l. c. pp. 348, sq. Thus the narrative of the reading out of the Law by Ezra begins with the words: "And when the seventh month was come, &c." I was also right in observing there (p. 349) that Ezra iii. 1, seq. and Neh. vii. 73 b, seq. are from the same author, the Chronicler, and that this explains the great resemblance between these two narratives. But this remark can now be supplemented by what Schrader has put forward in *Stud. u. Krit.* of 1867, pp. 482, sqq. and de Wette's *Einl.* i. 390. According to him Neh. vii. 73 b, seq. has been *adopted* by the Chronicler from the source upon which Neh. viii.-x. is based, and the same source is *followed* by him in Ezra iii. 1, seq. This latter narrative is, in the strictest sense of the word, *the Chronicler's own work*. This also accounts for the conflict between Neh. viii. 16, and Ezra iii. 4. Here again the former passage is *borrowed* from the written original, while the latter is from the Chronicler's own hand; therefore nothing can be more natural than that in Neh. viii. 16, the feast of tabernacles which Zerubbabel kept according to the Law, should not be noticed at all; the *original author* was totally ignorant of it; it is even probable that the Chronicler was the first who mentioned it, and that *such* a feast of tabernacles did *not* take place immediately after the arrival of the exiles.

The foregoing remarks have already indicated where the difference between my former and my present view of Neh. viii.-x. lies. I did not deny, in my *Hist. krit. Onderzoek*, that the Chronicler, in writing these chapters, consulted and followed an older and purely historical account, but I was inclined to assume that he made a *very free* use of such an account (pp. 350, 351, sq.). By this freedom I explained the departures from history, the improbabilities and the exaggeration which I believed I observed in Neh. viii.-x. Now, on the contrary, I am of opinion that those departures, &c. are overrated, and that, conversely, I did not formerly give prominence enough to the phenomena which plead for the writer's dependence on his sources. It is these two points which must now be indicated more fully.

1. The reading out of the Law described in Neh. viii.-x. *cannot* be regarded as a single episode of Ezra's labours; much rather is it represented to us as the *real work* performed by Ezra: as the execution of the design which he had formed in Babylonia. But if this be so, why did that reading out not take place till after the arrival of Nehemiah? Formerly I was unable to find a satisfactory answer to this question (p. 350). Now I consider that the difficulty which it involves is entirely solved by the observations advanced above, pp. 223, sq., and 232, sqq.

Formerly (l. c. p. 351) I believed that it did not appear how Neh. viii.-x. is to be reconciled both with Ezra ix. x. and with Neh. xiii. But this difficulty also disappears at once, if we (1) reflect that after his arrival at Jerusalem Ezra was prevented from proceeding with his reforms, and (2) consider that the *subscribing* of the covenant is quite a different thing from the *faithful observance* of it: under the impression made by the assembly at Jerusalem, the heads of the people readily allowed themselves to be persuaded to enter into the engagement proposed to them; but when the first zeal had cooled down, the execution of the covenant left much to be desired; this would be the more natural, if they were really *new* laws which Ezra and Nehemiah introduced: it was only in the course of time that the national life could adapt itself to them.

The statement that a feast of tabernacles such as that of Ezra had not been celebrated since the days of Joshua the son of Nun (Neh. viii. 16), formerly appeared to me to be exaggerated, in connection also with Ezra iii. 4 (l. c., p. 351). That notion was wrong. Neh. viii. 16 is fully trustworthy: the feast of tabernacles was really celebrated then *for the first time* in accordance with the precepts of Lev. xxiii. 39-43. Ezra iii. 4 must be rejected for so far as it contains anything else. Comp. above p. 227.

My objections to the form of Neh. x. (l. c., p. 351) are not without foundation. But they plead rather against the skill of the Chronicler, who wrote the narrative as it now stands, than against the authenticity of the record itself. It is especially the joining of the act of the covenant to the prayer of the Levites (chap. ix. 6-37) which is open to objection. But if, as is very probable, the Chronicler composed, or at all events worked up and extended, that prayer, then he is responsible for that combination as well.

In chap. viii.-x. Nehemiah plays a subordinate part and Ezra is the principal personage. This may be strictly historical: Nehemiah, a friend of Ezra, may, upon an occasion such as this, have kept in the background and have left the place of honour for Ezra, in the latter's own domain. Should Nehemiah's passive behaviour, however, having regard to his character, be deemed less probable, no one would be justified on that account in denying the fact upon which everything depends, the making of the covenant. One would then merely have to assume that the historian, being himself highly prejudiced in favour of Ezra and his task, placed him too much in the foreground. There is indeed something to be said in favour of this hypothesis. Neh. viii.-x. are separated from Ezra vii.-x. by Neh. i.-vii., which were taken in their entirety and unaltered from the memoirs of Nehemiah himself. Thus the author of Ezra x.—again the Chronicler, who in that chapter gives excerpts from Ezra's memoirs—really takes up his pen again in Neh. viii. Now it is certain—especially on the strength of Ezra vii. 9, 10, 12-26—that that author was very fond of Ezra. Therefore it is far from strange that, the moment he begins to relate again himself, he not only brings that priest and scribe upon the stage, but also displays him in all his glory.

If the principal arguments against the authenticity of Neh. viii.-x. have been refuted, so much the more weight may

ii. be attributed to the passages which bear witness to the faithful use of the older documents by the author of those chapters. The principal ones are:

a. Neh. viii. 16, of which we have already spoken above. The Chronicler himself, writing *suo Marte*, would never have expressed himself in this way.

b. Neh. viii. 4. The authenticity of this list is very ably defended by Bertheau, l. c., p. 211. In other places the Chronicler does not hesitate to invent such statements. In this instance this is evidently not the case, but then he must have drawn upon contemporaneous information.

c. Neh. x. 2-8, respecting which compare Bertheau, pp. 228-30. I do not hesitate to regard this list of 21 divisions of priests as strong evidence in favour of the authenticity of the record to which it belongs. It must be taken in connection with Neh. xii. 1-7, 12-21 (the enumerations of the divisions of priests under the high-priests Joshua and Joiakim). If it entirely agreed with them, it would prove nothing for or against the document in Neh. x. But the agreement is only partial, and there is even comparatively a very great difference between them. This is not unnatural, since some years elapsed between the high-priesthood of Joiakim and Ezra's reformation, and after the exile the divisions of the priests constantly underwent great changes (so that, *e. g.*, the names which are given in 1 Chr. xxiv. 7-18 for David's time, differ considerably from those in Neh. xii. 1-7, 12-21). If now we had had a free composition before us in Neh. x., the author would most probably have held to one of the lists with which he was acquainted.

d. Neh. x. 29-39, the text of the covenant. A more searching study of this document has gradually strengthened me in my conviction of its genuineness. Here and there its form presents difficulties, or at any rate shows peculiarities for which we cannot fully account (*Hk. O.* i. 351). But on the other hand there is the fact that its contents are so peculiar and, upon a close examination, agree so little with the prepossessions of the Chronicler, that it becomes almost absurd to ascribe to him either the composition or even the rewriting of the record. With respect to verse 32 (the tax of the third part of a shekel for the temple) and to verse 37 (the tithes of the *land*) I will refer to Chapter IX. and Note I. at the end of that chapter. Besides this let attention be paid to the last words of verse 31 (which are difficult to explain, but which at any rate agree with Lev. xxv. 1-7 much less than would be the case, if the Chronicler had edited them; comp. Bertheau, pp. 232, sq.; Graf, *die gesch. Bücher*, p. 79); to verse 34 (an explanation of the origin of an institution which remained in existence among the Jews and subsequently by degrees assumed the character of a festival; comp. again Bertheau, pp. 234, sq.); to verse 39 (where "the porters and the singers" are mentioned separately and are apparently distinct from "the sons of Levi;" this is in harmony with the language of the older post-exilic documents and with the organization of the staff of the temple at that time; it is opposed to the ideas of the Chronicler. Comp. above, p. 204, and below, Chapter X.)

II.—*See p.* 251, *n.* *.

I have already explained the object of this note above, pp. 183, 192. As in Note III. to Chapter VII. (pp. 192-201), the relation between the priestly and the prophetic *narratives* is more clearly shown, so we must speak here of the priestly *legislation* in relation to Deuteronomy and the Book of the Covenant.

In the meantime this subject has been handled so fully and minutely by K. H. Graf (*Die gesch. Bücher des A. T.*, pp. 34-94), that with regard to by far the most of the points I can simply refer the reader to him. It is true, his treatise has here and there drawn down contradiction, but the latter, in my opinion, does not hit its mark. First of all I will attempt to prove this. Then I will handle a few groups of priestly laws, and will endeavour to vindicate the placing of them in the post-exile times.

I. In the *Studien und Kritiken* of 1868, pp. 350-79, E. Riehm published a critique of Graf's treatise which is well worth reading. Very many of his remarks seem to me to be irrefragable. Thus on pp. 356, sqq. he maintains the ordinary opinion that Gen. xvii. and the priestly laws sprang from a common origin, and were contemporaneous. He also points out (pp. 367, sq.) that several historical portions of the Pentateuch pre-suppose the priestly legislation, or at any rate cannot be separated from it. In the meantime, nothing more follows from this than that Graf has stopped half way, and has simply adopted the tradition as to the higher antiquity of the historical elements of the "Grundschrift" (the Book of Origins), without taking into account the conflict between that tradition and the results which he has obtained. He has since seen this himself, and has broken with tradition upon this point as well (comp. above, p. 193). He then at the same time admitted the justice of Riehm's objection (pp. 353, sq.) that he had been wrong in regarding the Jahvist as the "Ergänzer" of the "Grundschrift." Another of Riehm's difficulties is likewise beyond our main subject: I am no more able than he is (pp. 370, sqq.) to share Graf's opinion as to *the author* of Lev. xviii. seq., xxvi.; but in spite of this difference it seems to me that the exilic origin of those chapters must be acknowledged, and no less the correctness of Graf's opinion as to the relation in which they stand to the rest of the priestly laws (comp. above pp. 182-192). More weight would have to be attached to Riehm's assertion that the Deuteronomist was acquainted with the priestly laws (pp. 358, sqq.), if the evidence upon which it is based contained any proof of this. But that is not the case. We have already shown that Lev. xi. cannot possibly be older than Deut. xiv. 3-21 (pp. 94-97). Deut. xxiv. 8, is an exhortation to submit to the *thorah* of the Levitical priests; it does not appear that the latter had been committed to writing when the author wrote; much less that he had precisely Lev. xii.-xv. before his eyes. Riehm here takes as proved that which had still to be shown. He does the same thing when he borrows objections to Graf's opinion (p. 361) from Deut. xii. 15, sq., 20-22, compared with Lev. xvii. 3, seq.; (p. 362) from Deut. xvi. compared with the priestly laws concerning feasts, and (p. 363) from Deut. x. 1, 3, 5, 8, and x. 9; xii. 12; xiv. 27, 29; xviii. 1, 2, compared with the priestly ordinances respecting the ark and the descendents of Aaron and the Levites. His objections prove to my mind that *as yet* he is unable to detach himself from the traditional arrangement of the elements of the Pentateuch, which was also maintained by his master, Hupfeld. They are not at all conclusive; and this the less, because he admits at the end (pp. 369, sq., 372, sqq.) that the ritual laws were not carried out before the exile: they were included in the "Grundschrift," it is true, but they were not valid in practice, because the kings had proved indisposed to promote their observance and to make them laws of the land. Such a temporary abeyance of the ritual legislation is not inconceivable, but it cannot be admitted unless the much more simple and natural hypothesis which Graf gives us is proved to be absolutely untenable. In other words, it must be shown that the priestly laws *were in existence*, before we can proceed to search for the causes of their latent condition. Riehm does not furnish this conclusive proof.

No more does Nöldeke (*Untersuchungen*, &c., pp. 126, sqq.), whose sketch of the character of the "Grundschrift," masterly as it is in many respects, seems to me rather to confirm Graf's hypothesis as to the age of this work. It has already been observed (p. 193) that he is right in upholding the unity of the "Grundschrift," and thus in referring the historical documents to the same period as the legislative portions. But he does not succeed in making it clear why the whole "Grundschrift" may not be referred to the exilic and post-exilic period. When he denies all productiveness to those periods, and makes them a "Restaurationszeit," he certainly conforms to tradition, but—he is opposed to history. Our full consent must be given to that which de Goeje, *Gids.*, 1869, II., has written upon this subject. Nöldeke evidently attaches but little value to all the rest that he adduces against Graf. His concession (p. 142), *e. g.*, that no indisputable quotations from the "Grundschrift" exist in the prophets who wrote before the exile, is remarkable. He asserts that the Deuteronomist was acquainted with the "Grundschrift," but he does not prove it.

Schrader (de Wette's *Einl.* I. 8ᵉ Ausgabe) can still less be considered to have refuted Graf's chronological arrangement. He agrees with Riehm and Nöldeke in acknowledging the unbroken connection between the laws and the narratives of the "Grundschrift," or, as he expresses himself, "des annalistischen Erzählers." But when (pp. 316-18) he tries to fix the time in which that writer lived, he pays attention exclusively to a few historical allusions of very doubtful evidentiary value, and leaves out of consideration altogether both the contents of the laws and the character of the narratives—which are so obviously unhistorical. A few pages before this (pp. 297-99), he defines the relation of Deuteronomy to the priestly laws, without answering or even mentioning Graf's arguments against the opinions which he there defends. It is evident to my mind that

Schrader, convinced on good grounds of the unity of the "Grundschrift," has considered himself entitled to avoid a minute consideration of Graf's hypothesis, which in its original form denied that unity.

II. Without laying the least claim to completeness, I now wish to make a few observations upon the priestly laws, their relation to the other collections of laws and their age, preferring those remarks which seem to me calculated to lead to the settlement of the point in dispute.

A. It is universally admitted that the laws relating to feasts in Exod. xxiii. 14-18 (comp. xxxiv. 18-25) are the oldest of all: Knobel's opinion to the contrary, refuted in *Hk. O.* i. 142, sqq., has deservedly met with no acceptance. The law relating to mazzôth in Exod. xiii. 3-10 may be about contemporaneous with those feast-regulations. If now we compare both Deut. xvi. 1-17 and the priestly ordinances with these oldest documents, it becomes obvious at once that the Deuteronomist follows the Book of the Covenant, and not the priestly laws: even those who think that he was acquainted with them must admit this, and can find in his writings—as will be more evident directly—but few allusions to those laws. Even of itself this phenomenon leads us to the presumption that the Deuteronomist precedes the priestly writer: what could have induced him to pass over the much more exhaustive priestly laws and go back to the Book of the Covenant? No one answers this question satisfactorily. On the other hand, everything is in order, if the author of Deuteronomy was acquainted with nothing more than Exod. xxiii. 14-18; xiii. 3-10.

This provisional conclusion is confirmed by the points of difference between Deuteronomy and the priestly law. We have already noticed one of these above, pp. 84, sq. Besides this,

a. according to Deut. xvi. 7, 8, only the seventh, and not the first, day of *mazzôth* is a feast-day, upon which the people assembled in the sanctuary; express permission is even given to return home on the first day, after the paschal meal has been kept on the previous evening. This agrees with Exod. xiii. 7. But in the priestly laws we read (Exod. xii. 16; Lev. xxiii. 7; Num. xxviii. 18) that also on the first day of *mazzôth* there is to be a "holy convocation," and work must be put aside.—Which is most probable: that an addition was made to the feasts and days of rest, or that the Deuteronomist abolished a feast and a day of rest?

b. According to Deut. xvi. 13, 15, the feast of tabernacles lasts *seven* days; according to Lev. xxiii. 36, 39; Num. xxix. 35, an eighth day, likewise a feast and a day of rest, must be added to these seven. Here, too, it seems not difficult to decide who has the priority: it is almost inconceivable that the Deuteronomist should have fixed seven days, if the ritual law with which he was acquainted prescribed eight days. But in this particular case there is no need for us to rest content with probabilities. The later origin of the priestly regulation is evident from the testimony of Ezekiel, who (chap. xlv. 25) expressly mentions seven days. But there is something more. Let the reader remember that the feast of tabernacles is celebrated, according to Deuteronomy, from the 15th up to and including the 21st, and according to the priestly laws from the 15th up to and including the 22nd of the seventh month, and let him now compare together the two following accounts of a feast of tabernacles kept under Solomon, the first written before Ezra's time, the second from the third century B.C.:—

1 Kings viii. 65, 66.	2 Chron. vii. 8, 9, 10.
And at that time Solomon held *the feast*, and all Israel with him, a great congregation from Hamath unto the river of Egypt, before Jahveh our god, for seven days [and seven days, even for fourteen days]. On the eighth day he	And at that time Solomon kept *the feast* seven days, and all Israel with him, a very great congregation, from Hamath unto the river of Egypt. And on the eighth day they made a solemn assembly, for they kept the dedication of

sent the people away, and they blessed the king, &c.	the altar seven days and the feast seven days. And on the three and twentieth day of the seventh month he sent the people away into their tents, &c.

It is evident at once that the words of 1 Kings viii. 65, which I have placed in [ ], must be omitted; they have all the appearance of a gloss, and moreover are contradicted by the beginning of verse 66, where the fifteenth (and not the eighth) should have been named, if fourteen days (and not seven) had been mentioned just before. Thus Solomon lets the people go home *on the eighth day, i.e.* on the twenty-second of the seventh month. In other words, the author of this account knows nothing of the priestly regulation which makes the eighth day a feast and a day of rest; he only knows of the Deuteronomic law, with which his account entirely agrees. With the younger Chronicler it is otherwise. He *improves* the older account (1) by expressly mentioning the eighth day, and (2) by fixing the departure of the Israelites (not on the twenty-second, but) on the twenty-third day of the seventh month. Is it not as clear as daylight that the priestly law must have been made and promulgated *after* the author of Kings had written, and *before* the lifetime of the Chronicler? And, finally, let there be added to this the evidence in Neh. viii. 14-17, which we have already pointed out (pp. 226, sq., 289). To me the coincidence of all these indications is an incontestable proof of the accuracy of our chronological arrangement of the various collections of laws.

I will pass over other, subordinate points of difference between the laws concerning feasts. Now what have the advocates of the priority of the priestly legislation to advance against this? Really nothing more than the assertion that a few expressions in Deut. xvi. 1-17 betray acquaintance with the priestly laws. But nothing prevents us from assuming that, conversely, the priestly lawgiver here and there followed the Deuteronomist.

The name "feast of tabernacles," Deut. xvi. 13, 16, is certainly younger than "feast of ingathering" (Exod. xxiii. 16; xxxiv. 22), but it occurs also in Lev. xxiii. 34; the ordinance in Lev. xxiii. 39-44 is not the foundation of that designation, but, conversely, regulates more minutely the custom which is indicated by that designation. The proposition that the Deuteronomist combines the *mazzôth* and the passover, which formerly were distinct, and makes one feast of them (Riehm, l. c., p. 362), is true only if he is older than the priestly legislation: for do we not find this combination in the latter as well, Exod. xii. 1-14, 15-20; Lev. xxiii. 5, 6; Num. xxviii. 16, 17? The assertion that according to the priestly laws the paschal lamb is killed and eaten by the Israelites (not at Jerusalem, but) in their own cities, has already been refuted above, pp. 87, sq. To my mind, the conclusion is absolutely beyond doubt. We can now pass on to

B. the ordinances respecting the incomes of the priests and Levites (above, pp. 256, sq.). The difference between the deuteronomic and the priestly precepts need not be pointed out afresh (comp. *Hk. O.* i. 52, sq.). The only question can be, to which of the two must we ascribe the priority? When I was still fully convinced of the higher antiquity of the priestly law, I already thought it probable that its regulations *upon this subject* were younger than those of the Deuteronomist (l. c., pp. 147, sq., 154, sq.). It is indeed almost absurd to suppose that the demands in favour of the staff of the temple were not increased in the course of time, but moderated; that *e.g.*, *first* the tithes were allotted *to the Levites*, and it was *afterwards* decided that they were to be dedicated *to Jahveh* and thus to be consumed at sacrificial meals. It can by no means be granted to Riehm (l. c., pp. 364, sq.) that the priestly laws relating to the tithes do not presuppose Deut.: the younger lawgiver could hardly *quote* the regulations of his predecessor at the same moment that he modified them and increased their burden. He presupposes them in so far as he builds upon the idea that the tithes belong to Jahveh. But see further Chapter

IX. and Note I at the end of it, where I must revert to this subject. Upon the whole, the question as to the mutual relation of the two legislations can be reduced to another question, namely, which dates first, the religious thought or its introduction into practice to the interest of the priesthood? We can have the less hesitation in giving our answer, because it is quite certain that among the Israelites too the priesthood strove to extend its power and increase its revenues. With regard to this last, compare also Exod. xiii. 13 (xxxiv. 20)—which according to the general opinion are *very old* ordinances—with the priestly precepts in Num. xviii. 15, 16 ; Lev. xxvii. 27. The requirements of the religious idea have been satisfied when the firstborn colt of an ass has been killed; the priestly interests are not satisfied by this, and therefore *subsequently* the redemption from the priests is demanded. Comp. *Hk. O.* i. 34, sq., 159, n. 33.

C. What we have said on pp. 273, sq., about the rights and duties of the priests and the high-priest, leads us to speak of the legal regulations concerning *the difference between the servants of the temple in rank and competency.* They concern, as is well known, in part the distinction between priests and Levites, and in part the distance between the priests and the high-priest.

a. With regard to the first point compare Vol. I. pp. 337, sq. and above, pp. 26, sq., 116, sq., 168, sq. The main arguments for the later origin of the priestly laws concerning this subject have already been touched upon there, so that here I need merely bring them together and fill them in. Let us first of all observe that a reconciliation of Deuteronomy with Exodus—Numbers is not to be thought of. That the Deuteronomist considers *all* Levites without distinction qualified to fill the priestly office, is evident not only from the designations " the Levitical priests," " the priests, sons of Levi," of which he makes use, but also and especially from Deut. x. 8, 9 ; xviii. 1-8, where he expresses himself quite unambiguously. It is equally certain that the difference in competency between "the sons of Aaron" and the Levites in the three central books of the Pentateuch is consistently and strictly maintained—so much so even that it may be said to be altogether superfluous to quote passages to prove it. The only question can be, to whom must the priority be allowed, to the Deuteronomist or the priestly lawgiver? With respect to this question let it be observed,

1st. That a subsequent *limitation* of the capacity to become a priest is of itself much more probable than the *extension* of that capacity to persons who had not possessed it before;

2nd. That *omnium consensu* the priestly precepts triumphed in the end and ruled in practice: how is this possible, if the Deuteronomic legislation, which makes no distinction between priests and Levites, is the youngest? We can imagine that Deuteronomy *remained* a part of the Thorah, even after some of its regulations had become obsolete and new precepts had been added. But how can Deuteronomy have been *admitted* into the Law while at the same time one of its principal rules had been disregarded? Let it be reflected that the Deuteronomist, if he must be considered to have been acquainted with the laws in Exodus—Numbers, directly contradicts them upon this point and expressly allows (Deut. xviii. 6, 7) that which according to the priestly lawgiver (Num. xviii. 3) is punished with death. Again, we can conceive that regulations such as those of the Deuteronomist, because they had once been law and were regarded as holy, were *allowed to stand;* but how they can have been *added* to the priestly law already extant and known, without, however, being put into execution, is a mystery which we cannot solve;

3rd. That there is not a single trace in the prophetic writings of the distinction between priests and Levites. Jer. xxxiii. 18, 21, 22, and Isa. lxvi. 21 agree, even in language, with Deuteronomy; Zech. xii. 13 mentions "the family of the house of Levi," and nothing more; even Malachi (chap. ii. 1-9; iii. 3), the contemporary of Ezra and Nehemiah, still follows the time-honoured words of Deuteronomy. It has been not incorrectly observed that these prophetic instances are few in number. It is true, the prophets trouble themselves little or not at all about public worship in general and the qualifications for the priestly office in particular. But still the few allusions which we meet with in their writings do not betray the slightest acquaintance with the demands of the priestly law, and—what removes all doubt—the only prophet who speaks expressly on this subject, Ezekiel, shows clearly that he *is* acquainted with Deuteronomy and is *not* acquainted with the priestly laws. See this demonstrated above pp. 116, sq.

4th. That the older historical books (Judges, Samuel, Kings) do not know of the exclusive fitness of the "sons of Aaron," but again agree with the Deuteronomic laws. It is evident from Judges xvii. 7-13, that *the Levites* were deemed qualified (not exclusively, it is true, but yet) above others to perform priestly duties. The most probable interpretation of Judges xix. 18 is this, that the Levite referred to here is going to "the house of Jahveh" in order to become a priest there (comp. Deut. xviii. 6, 7). With respect to 1 Sam. ii. 27-36, comp. *Theol. Tijdschrift*, iii. 475, seq. In 1 Kings viii. 4, the priests, it is true, are distinguished from the Levites, but this is merely in consequence of a clerical error (?), which can be corrected by means of 2 Chron. v. 5 : it originally stood, "And the *Levitical priests* brought it (the ark) up;" comp. verses 3, 6, 10, where, in conformity with this reading, the priests alone are mentioned. 1 Kings xii. 31 is also very remarkable. The conclusion which may be drawn from this passage with regard to Jeroboam's time, has been pointed out in Vol. I. p. 338, n. §. We have now to give our attention to the historian's views. Judged by the priestly law, he is guilty of gross heresy. Had Jeroboam appointed priests "of the sons of Levi," he would, according to the historian, have acted legally. This is indeed the case—according to Deuteronomy. But this is not the case according to the priestly ordinances, which shut out the Levites *in genere*, and only acknowledge "the sons of Aaron." For the sake of completeness I will add, that 1 Sam. vi. 15; 2 Sam. xv. 24, also mention Levites. The first of these passages has most probably been interpolated (comp. Vatke, *Bibl. Theol.* i. 273, n. 4), but neither of the two can be cited in favour of the antiquity of the laws in Exodus—Numbers.

So much the more numerous—I fully admit—are the passages in the books of the Chronicles which bear testimony to the existence and the validity of the priestly laws in the preexilic times. But it is highly contrary to true criticism to side with the Chronicler in the conflict between these writings and the older historical books. I will abstain from dilating further on this point, referring the reader both to the remarks already made in Vol. I. upon the historical value of the Chronicler's statements and to the sketch of his principles and method in Chapter X. of this work.

Unless I be altogether mistaken, the time cannot be far off when the priestly law on this subject will be acknowledged as the final result of the whole historical development. Unless it be so, the fortunes of the tribe of Levi are inexplicable. It is not the place here to set forth my ideas about them in full; I shall only touch upon the main points of my interpretation. Levi was one of the twelve tribes from the very first. At the time of the conquest of Canaan it was one of the smallest, probably the smallest, and consequently does not succeed in conquering a territory for itself: the sons of Levi are dispersed throughout Canaan. Moses and Aaron were Levites; Aaron's family discharges the priestly office at the common sanctuary, the depository of the ark of Jahveh; the idea arises that the fellow-tribesmen of the lawgiver and conductor of the national sacrifices are peculiarly qualified for the priesthood; the Levites for their part willingly offer themselves, in order the better to provide for their maintenance (Judges xvii. xviii.). Priests of the tribe of Levi minister in the temple of

Solomon and at most of the "high places:" it gradually becomes an established conviction that they alone are fit to do so. "The blessing of Moses," Deut. xxxiii. (Vol. I. pp. 380, sq.). The Deuteronomic laws recognize that exclusive fitness of the Levites (above, pp. 26, sq.). Their regulations concerning the equalization of all the Levites are not carried out (2 Kings xxiii. 9; above, pp. 116, sq., 168, sq.); the distinction between priests and priest-servants arises, is justified and maintained by Ezekiel, remains in existence during the exile, and is finally made a genealogical distinction and established for good by the priestly law. At a later date all the officers of the temple, even the singers and the porters, are included in the tribe of Levi (above, p. 204, and below, Chapter X.).

Into this sketch fits admirably one of the priestly narratives of the Pentateuch to which I have not yet referred: the account of the rebellion of Korah, which, linked and partly fused with an older narrative about Dathan and Abiram (comp. Deut. xi. 6), lies before us in Num. xvi., xvii., and serves as an introduction to the ordinances relating to the priests, the Levites and their revenues in Num. xviii. Of late years much care and acumen has been spent upon the critical analysis of Num. xvi., xvii., by Knobel, Graf (l. c., pp. 89, sq.), Land and Oort (*Godg. Bijdragen* of 1865, pp. 997, seq.; 1866, pp. 205, seq., 416, seq.). The result of their investigations seems to me to be this, that the narrative of Dathan and Abiram has been worked up *twice*, first for the purpose of upholding the rights of the Levites against the rest of the tribes, and secondly to show the exclusive fitness of the "sons of Aaron." I will not work out this opinion further here; on this point I agree almost entirely with Oort. It is obvious at once that it is in perfect harmony with the course of the historical development which has just been sketched.

b. In investigating the degrees in rank of the priests themselves, and especially the difference between the priests and the high-priest, we must again start from the evidence of the older historical books, and leave the Chronicler out of consideration for the present. That older evidence is meagre, incidental and fragmentary; therefore we are not surprised that it is found to be insufficient to give us an idea of the development of the offices connected with the temple. On the other hand, it leads us to an incontrovertible *negative* result: prior to the Babylonish exile the ordinances of the priestly law were *not* observed, and there existed amongst the priests at Jerusalem degrees of rank which lie quite outside the regulations of that law. The principal passages are: 2 Sam. viii. 17, 18; xx. 25, 26; 1 Kings iv. 6; ii. 24, seq. (comp. *Theol. Tijdschrift*, iii. 472-74);—2 Kings xii. 11; xxii. 4, 8; xxiii. 4, and xxv. 18=Jer. lii. 24 (from which passages it appears that one of the priests, who bore the title of *Kohén hagadôl* ["the high-priest"] or *Kohén rôsch* ["the head-priest"], at any rate from the days of Jehoash, stood at the head of the Jerusalem priests);—2 Kings xxiii. 4; xxv. 18=Jer. lii. 24 (from which we gather that this high-priest had a *deputy*, of which office the priestly law is altogether ignorant);—2 Kings xii. 10; xxii. 4; xxiii. 4; xxv. 18=Jer. lii. 24 (where the door-keepers, three in number, are mentioned; their post was evidently held in high honour, and, according to 2 Kings xii. 10, was one of trust); Jer. xx. 1, comp. 1 Chr. ix. 11 (=Neh. xi. 11); 2 Chr. xxviii. 7; xxxi. 13; xxxv. 8 (which passages teach us that one of the priests superintended the temple, or, in other words, kept order there, in which duty he was of course assisted by others; it follows from 2 Kings xi. 18; xii. 12; Jer. xxix. 26, that this post was instituted by Jehoiada, the contemporary of king Jehoash);—2 Kings xix. 2 (where "the elders of the priests" occur, as in 2 Chr. xxxvi. 14 "the chief of the priests," and in 1 Chr. xxiv. 5; Isa. xliii. 28 "the chief of the sanctuary").

With respect to the divergent accounts of the Chronicler comp. *Theol. Tijdschrift*, iii. 469-72.

There is a wide difference between the actual state of affairs to which the passages quoted bear testimony, and the precepts of the priestly legislation. Upon reading and weighing these precepts in their mutual connection, one receives an impression that the high-priest is much more than the temporal head of the officiating priests. He has a distinct dress (Exod. xxviii. 1-39; xxxix. 1-27, 30, 31) and is thereby exclusively qualified to consult Jahveh by means of the urim and thummim (comp. Vol. I. p. 96, sq.); on this account Lev. xxi. 10; Num. xxvii. 21 attach great value to that dress. He alone is anointed with the sacred anointing-oil; " the crown of the anointing-oil of his god is upon his head;" comp. Lev. xxi. 10, 12; iv. 3, 5, 16; vi. 13, 15; viii. 12; xvi. 32; Exod. xxix. 7; Num. xxxv. 25. It is true that, according to the priestly laws and accounts, Aaron's sons are also anointed (Exod. xxx. 30; xl. 13, 15; Lev. vii. 36; x. 7; Num. iii. 3), but not in the same manner as their father and his successors in the high-priestly office; it was in harmony with the lawgiver's intention that the Jewish tradition confined the anointing to the high-priest (comp. Kalisch, *Hist. and crit. Commentary on the O. T., Leviticus, Part* I. 574, sq.). He has moreover, as we were reminded above, pp. 273, sq., his own rights and duties. In a word, the high-priest of the ritual legislation occupies a special place in the theocracy; he is its head and representative; as he is the mediator between Jahveh and the people, so his sin reacts upon the people and the people bear the guilt of it (Lev. iv. 3). If these notions had existed before the exile, would not some trace of them occur here or there? Do they not, moreover, carry with them, in their exaggeration, the proof of their later origin? Is not Ezekiel's silence as to the high-priest an insoluble riddle, if in his days that dignity was already looked upon in the light in which it is now described in the priestly law? It is asserted (comp. p. 293) that that law existed before the exile, but was not put into execution; therefore we must also assume this with regard to its ordinances on this head. But how comes it, then, that the priest Ezekiel entirely ignores them? Can

admissible reason be given for this silence on his part oth
than—the later origin of the priestly regulations?

D. Let the following remarks serve to elucidate what h
been said, pp. 281, sq., about *the sabbath-year* and *the year
jubilee*.

The Book of the Covenant decrees (1.) the liberation of t
Hebrew slaves after six years' service, Exod. xxi. 2-11; (:
the giving up of the produce of every seventh year to the po
and to the beasts of the field, Exod. xxiii. 10, 11 (comp. 1
O. i. 143).

There are two ordinances in Deuteronomy which correspo
to these two laws, namely (1.) chap. xv. 12-18, a repetition
an abridged form of Exod. xxi. 2-11, with the addition of
exhortation to give liberal presents to the slave who receiv
back his freedom, (verses 13-15); (2.) chap. xv. 1-11 (con
xxxi. 10), an ordinance concerning the release (Hbr. *sjemitte*
in every seventh year: in that year the debtor is not to be co
pelled to discharge his debt, but must be left in peace; t
Israelite must not be deterred by the prospect of this y
from lending to the needy. It is clear that this law corr
ponds to Exod. xxiii. 10, 11. It relates to the seventh or sabba
year; besides this, the word "release" is borrowed from Ex
xxiii. 11. But the contents of the two ordinances are not
same: the Deuteronomist does not speak of the giving up
the produce of the land; for this he substitutes—because it l
been found that the people would not observe it?—a l
which could be more easily carried out and was equally to
interest of the needy.

The priestly law also contains two corresponding regulatic
namely, (1.) Lev. xxv. 1-7, relating to the rest of the land
every seventh year; and (2) Lev. xxv. 8-55, relating to the y
of jubilee (comp. pp. 281, sq., upon the contents of this ordinanc
In the latter law the decree respecting the Israelitish slave
verses 39-43 is parallel with Exod. xxi. 2, seq.; Deut. xv.
seq., but at the same time is quite irreconcilable with it:

release, which according to the Book of the Covenant and Deuteronomy is to take place after six years' service, is here placed in the year of jubilee (comp. *Hk. O.* i. 35).

Now it is very evident that these three groups of laws follow each other chronologically in the same order in which they are enumerated here. It will not do to insert Lev. xxv. between the Book of the Covenant and Deut. How could the Deuteronomist, if he had known that law, have (1.) omitted to mention the rest in the seventh year, and (2.) retained the release after six years' service? Selfishness was strongly opposed to the execution of the precept to that effect. Thus we are not surprised to learn from the prophet Jeremiah (chap. xxxiv. 8, seq.) that hitherto it had been *altogether* disregarded, and that it was not till Zedekiah's reign that *the first* steps were taken to carry out the release. Yet—according to the hypothesis which I contest—the Deuteronomist left that law unaltered, and this notwithstanding that an ordinance already existed, Lev. xxv. 39-43, which was much easier to carry out, since it followed from it that by far the majority of the Israelitish slaves died before the year of their liberation arrived! In addition to this there are the arguments taken from the form and the contents of Lev. xxv. : the prolixity, the theoretical and abstract character of the precepts given here, the reference to the law concerning the day of atonement (verse 9) and to the precepts relating to the cities of the Levites (verses 32-34).

Upon Ezek. xlvi. 17, see above, p. 191, seq.

END OF VOL. II.

www.ingramcontent.com/pod-product-compliance
Lightning Source LLC
Chambersburg PA
CBHW030811230426
43667CB00008B/1157